Dressing to Win

Dressing to Win

HOW TO HAVE MORE MONEY, ROMANCE, AND POWER IN YOUR LIFE!

Robert Panté

PHOTOGRAPHED BY SUZANNE ESTEL
ILLUSTRATED BY LELAND NEFF

1984
DOUBLEDAY & COMPANY, INC.
GARDEN CITY, NEW YORK

Library of Congress Cataloging in Publication Data
Panté, Robert.
Dressing to win.
Includes index.
1. Clothing and dress.   2. Fashion.   I. Neff, Leland
II. Title.
TT507.P3   1984   646'.3   82-46016
ISBN: 0-385-18821-8

Acknowledgments

Dick Kleiner: Very special thanks and heartfelt gratitude to the man who took my ideas, thoughts, and philosophies and captured my essence so perfectly with the written word.

Maria Theresa Caen (my agent): Whose joyous love, persistence, and encouragement have been invaluable in the completion and publication of this book.

Donald Hazel (my business partner): Your intelligence, skills, and hours of support have made this book possible. Thank you.

Abra Edelman, Collette Hayes, Monib Khadami (my initial sponsors): Their love, faith, and friendship launched the Panté Presentation Salon/Seminars.

Beth Trier (Fashion Editor, San Francisco *Chronicle*): A very special thank you to a woman whose expertise and assistance brought added richness and depth to Chapters 12, 13, and 15.

Wilkes Bashford (retailer): To me he is the "Prince of Merchants." He intuitively and instinctively has mastered the art of merchandising. His brilliance at serving his customers and their needs has gained him international acclaim and has enriched the lives of thousands of my clients.

The People Who Contributed: Tom Luhnow, Robert Reed, Arnie Linsman, Dennis Forbes, Ken Nakamura, Bill Downs, Joske Thompson, Paul Glick, Chicki Kleiner, Carol Bolster, Vicki Keltner, and the staff of Wilkes Bashford.

VERY SPECIAL THANKS TO:

Louise Gault: Doubleday Editor, who was with me all the way from the beginning to the completion of this book.

Alex Gotfryd: Doubleday Art Director, whose artistic expertise and advice added so much to this book.

Foreword

I remember once reading a meaningful and inspiring quote by Stewart Emery that spoke about "mastery." He said,

> It is remarkable how much mediocrity we live with, surrounding ourselves with daily reminders that the average is acceptable. Our world suffers from terminal normality. Take a moment to assess all of the things around you that promote your being "average." These are the things that keep you powerless to go beyond a "limit" you arbitrarily set for yourself. The first step to *having what you really want* is the removal of everything in your environment that represents mediocrity, removing those things that are limiting. One way is to surround yourself with friends who ask more of you than you do. Didn't some of your best teachers, coaches, parents, etc.?

Stanley Marcus is another person we think of who has inspired us to go for the best. Knowing that there is so little of the very best, we must develop our senses and recognize "quality" craftsmanship and superior product. What we give our energies, love, and gratefulness to we will never be without in our lives.

Human beings have an inner drive always propelling them forward, always reaching for ultimate perfection.

Contents

PART I

You Deserve It All!

1

Are You Living in the Fast Lane?

Are you pleased and excited with your wardrobe?

Are you totally satisfied with the amount of money, romance, and power you have in your life?

If you are, then you are already in the fast lane. If you are not, then it's high time you switched over and began living life more. This book will help you make that switch, and even if you think your life is good as it is, this book can make it fuller. This book will excite you into action! You either run the money, sex, and power in your life or they run you.

Here's how you can tell for sure if you are in the fast lane:

Do you do exactly what you want to do, exactly when you want to do it, in exactly the manner and style you want to do it, at least 51 percent of the time?

If you can say, "Yes, I do," then you definitely have a footing in the fast lane.

The fast lane is for anyone who dares to aspire to it. Perhaps you have seen others enjoying a type of life you have only dreamed of—having the best, the most, the greatest, the grandest. You can have that life, too. It begins with the realization that such a life is real, that it does exist, and—most important—that it can be yours. To make it yours, all you have to do is take it.

How do you take it? How do you get to enjoy all the good, grand, and glorious things that life has to offer? You just have to release the brakes that are holding you back.

This book is the brake-releaser!

This book is designed to show you how to get more money, romance, and power by playing all out.

We all know that there's a better life than the one we have now. We have a feeling inside us that moves us, encourages us to dream, forces us to envision a life for ourselves that is constantly expanding and thrusting upward and outward. Our dreams, aspirations, and visions are possible—if we release our brakes and discover the "catalytic elements" that will catapult us into a life-style of greater appeal, affluence, and influence.

Every person is born with the potential to be powerful. Every person is born with the potential to increase their money. Every person is born with the potential to enjoy wonderful romantic experiences.

The amount of money you aren't making is your greatest expense.

The quality of romance you aren't enjoying is your greatest deprivation.

The power you aren't experiencing is your greatest discontentment.

The trick is to turn those potentials into realities. Most people are behaving like they are vanilla; for many this book will add the nuts, cherries, and spices. For others it will dramatically change the "flavor" of your life.

This book is designed to support your intentions to be where you want to be, when you want to be there, and to enjoy yourself in the manner and style you desire.

A young actress I know was working on the soap opera, "General Hospital," when Elizabeth Taylor played a role on that ABC show for a few episodes. The two ladies worked together and became friendly. My friend mentioned to Liz how well things were going for her at that time—she had a good, regular job, she had chances to do other parts on the side, she was making good money, her love life was happy.

"Things are really great for you now, aren't they?" Liz summed up.

"Oh, absolutely," said my friend. "Things are the best they've ever been for me."

"Well," said Elizabeth Taylor, fixing my friend with her lovely violet eyes, "let me tell you one thing, young lady. When things are going well—*want more!*"

That philosophy should be yours. When things are going well, *want more*. And, of course, it follows that when things are going badly, *want a lot more*.

Most people are not willing to let go of the good in their lives for the better.

You can always want more than you have. That isn't being greedy or selfish, it is merely being practical and sensible. It is your inheritance. There's not much point in living without a dream to dream, without something to look forward to, without a goal to aspire to and work for. This is the elixir of living.

Where you are may be O.K.—but where you *can be* is much, much better.

Want more!

That's how the people at the top think. There is always another plateau to reach.

"Whatever you can do, or dream you can, begin it," wrote Goethe. "Boldness has genius, power and magic in it."

Begin it. That's the key. Dreaming is pleasant and fantasizing is fun. But until you actually *begin it*, you stand no chance of making those dreams or fantasies happen.

To get what you want, you have to first make a start. You have to move, go after it, whatever it is, even if that means totally changing your way of life. You have to start somewhere, some time, if you want to move into life's fast lane.

When you discover who you really are it will blow your socks off.

Life is really a lot like a superhighway with a lot of lanes. I can count at least five. There is the first lane, the lane you start in. That's for puttering along, getting nowhere slowly. Then there is a lane I call the coasting lane. You're moving, but just coasting. The third lane is for those who are picking up speed, but it still takes them a long time to get anywhere. Move to the fourth lane for people with purpose. They are fairly speedy. But the fast lane is reserved for those who are all out to get ahead. That's for the super-speedy.

You could make a similar analogy with athletes. There is, first, the kid who plays on the street—just a beginner. Next, he moves to the playground where the competition is a little tougher. Then, if he has talent, he moves on to school teams, bigger and harder. College comes next, and that's for those who play the game seriously. Finally, he turns pro, which is the fast lane for athletes. The pro ranks are the place for the cream of the athletic crop. Winning takes total effort and involvement.

Whatever you do, you must advance the same way, by stages, with your goals always being the top—the fast lane.

You can stay in the slow lane—puttering—or in one of the middle lanes—coasting, picking up speed, going along fairly fast. But if you want to have it all, you must go for the fast lane.

The choice is yours. When we make our debut in this world, we all start out the same—we all yell with the same voice. We start out with equal hopes. But then something happens, and some of us make it and some of us just bog down. Some of us arrive at that fast lane, and some of us never get out of first gear.

If you aren't a super-hitter, you are denied many of the objectives you'd like to achieve. Money? Sex? Power? Forget them—those are goals beyond those in the slow lanes.

But you don't have to stay in those slow lanes. It is simply a question of risking, stepping up your pace, and moving over into the fast lane. And this book will show you how.

Humans are readily capable of moving from position to position with unbounded velocity—drop any adverse thought structures that may clutter your progress.

The Bible tells us we are created in God's image—and surely God is a winner, so we are winners, too. The Constitution says we are created equal, and thus are equal to the achievers in our country. And educators tell us that our greatest resource is the human resource and its quality is infinite and expandable. So everything—religion, our Constitution, education—is telling us that we are winners.

But the main thing is to look at the logical side of it. And the plain, unvarnished truth is that it is a lot more fun to be a winner, to be a fast-lane traveler, than it is to be unproductive in the slow lane. It is better to achieve than not. It is more satisfying to have everything rather than nothing. It makes more sense to be at the top than the bottom.

You may be saying, right about now, "Well, O.K., I'll agree with you, Robert, that winning beats losing. But easier said than done. Sure, I'd like to have more money, sex, and power, but I can't seem to make it. I'm trying my damndest, really I am, and nothing happens. I'm still only the third assistant to the night manager of the branch office, making a lousy $150 a week plus all the frustrations I can carry. Of course I'd like to make more money and afford to buy nicer clothes and have a better car and a bigger house and all that good stuff. I try hard, I work hard, I don't goof off. But here I am, in a very deep rut, and I don't see any way of improving my life."

Good—you are angry and bored. It is when we reach a point of anger or boredom that we begin to take action.

You have to understand that nobody said this would be easy. Certainly I would never say that. I know—a handful of years ago, I had sixty-three cents to my name. I was broke—but I was never poor. That's because I never, ever felt poor or thought poor or behaved poor.

I always knew the impossible was possible, and the possible was probable. If you want it, you can have it. And it was when I had that incredible sum of sixty-three cents that I resolved to make it to the fast lane. I'm there now. I was determined not to live a meager existence. And I am going to share with you the knowledge of how to live a fuller and richer life. Remember if you avoid risk you also avoid opportunity, because risk is the price you pay for opportunity. You can't hate risk and hope for freedom.

Here's a small secret: Moving from the slow lane to the fast lane isn't really so tough.

You just have to change your direction (if you don't, you will wind up where you are presently headed) and the speed at which you are moving.

Remember that money never smiles or cries. It's powerless to govern itself; it doesn't have volition of its own. Money gets its impulse from you based on the quality and passion of your thoughts and actions.

You already *have* prosperity—it is built into your bones—but you have to exercise it. It doesn't matter whether you have five dollars, five hundred dollars, or five million dollars, if you have that positive attitude coupled with enthusiasm and a passion for living. Somebody can spend five dollars with a positive attitude and it means more than somebody else who parts with a part of his five million dollars cheaply.

Moving into the fast lane is a process you, yourself must initiate. I like to think that there is a millionaire lying dormant within each one of us, wanting to come out. But your millionaire is a prisoner down there and can't emerge into the sunlight unless you let him or her be free. It's up to you—and I'm going to be here to help. Everybody deserves a chance to make it big. Being newly rich is a much better condition of living than being established poor.

One of my favorite sayings is this:

If you refuse to accept anything but the best, you'll get the best. Begin to live as you wish to live.

That is the very first step in the trick of switching lanes and zooming over to the fast lane.

One of my favorite questions is this:

"Are you willing to be independently wealthy in this lifetime?"

You have to realize that *you* deserve the best, and you can't settle for anything less. And you have to believe that you can do it in this lifetime, and not wait for some future time or future life. If not now, when?

Certainly you deserve the best. There's no reason why you should accept anything less. We all deserve the best.

We are all—every one of us—what I call a *Living Human Treasure*. We are all created equal, created in God's image, created to fulfill our destinies, created to have the finest of everything.

Where is it written that Mr. A can drive around in a Porsche, but Mr. B is doomed to drive forever in a used VW bug with a dent in the fender?

On what stone is it carved that Sally J. can have a mink coat (with her initials in the lining), but Mary Y. will never have anything but a cloth hand-me-down (complete with moth holes)?

Show me on what brass plate it is etched that Roger can have a fat bankroll, but Jerry must go into hock to afford a one-room walk-up flat.

You won't find those restrictions anywhere, of course. All of us have the same golden opportunities.

We are all born to be *Living Human Treasures*.

I believe that the first step in reaching a goal is to set it. Tell yourself exactly what you want. Maybe it's money. Or power. Or sex—more, better, juicier. Perhaps it's a particular thing—a special car, a certain man or woman, a house you'd like to own, a more rewarding job.

Whatever it is, place it firmly in your mind. Etch it there in vivid colors. Forget negative thinking. Don't say, "Wow, how I would love that car! But, of course, it's totally impossible." That's loser talk. Instead, say, "Wow, how I would love that car! And I'm going to get it!" That's winner talk. That's how it is in the fast lane—first you set a goal, then you go out and achieve it.

The fact and evidence that something is really yours always precedes the desire to have it. (Like a steak, new auto, banana and yes, oxygen, you only desire what is already there for you to make obvious in your life. Desire is God speaking from within you.

Goals are attainable if it is your intention to bring them to fruition. You have to define and clearly make known to yourself and others what it is you are demanding of yourself, and attain it. Expand your power. Power is your perceived capacity—it's how you're perceived by yourself and others.

The way to start attaining your goals, objectives, and desires is by "knowing" them. You may have been giving your best, but this hasn't been quite enough to truly actualize what you really desire. Expand your best. You always have more than you think you have. Develop a standard for excellence. Without distinction there is extinction.

So you must begin by turning your own image from that of someone who never quite got there to someone who always gets there.

Your every act and every look can express a quiet, rich assurance of success. Every spark you radiate, every message you transmit to the world around you will enroll others in your game. You want to look successful, think successful, act successful—and you will be successful.

The minute you have established that sort of positive posture for yourself, you are well on your way to success in whatever you choose to do.

People tell you to be reasonable in your dreams. Nonsense! The top jobs in every field and the top honors and glories are reserved for the unreasonable. Your greatest dreams and ideals are actually closer to you than your smaller dreams and ideals.

What one needs to advance from a so-so life to a socko life is to forget the reasonable and be unreasonable in your thrust to the top. Being unreasonable is the hallmark of the great achievers and influencers of our time. Samuel Johnson wrote, "Nothing will ever be attempted if all possible objections must be first overcome." Today we would say, "You'll never make it if you don't take a few chances."

Naturally, you can't expect to leap from the bottom to the top in one fell swoop. There will be some necessary intermediate steps. Each of those intermediate steps will be a way station on your route to the very top. There is a preponderance of power in everyone.

"If one advances confidently in the direction of his dreams," wrote Henry David Thoreau, "and endeavors to live the life which he has imagined, he will meet with a success unexpected in common hours."

But understand this: *You* must do the advancing. *You* must move constantly toward your dream. It is *your* vitality, *your* velocity, *your* fervor that will make things happen. The good life isn't going to come and fetch you and that dream of yours. *You* have to work for it. The ball is in *your* court, and merely dreaming or wishing or hoping isn't enough. *You* have to take positive, affirmative actions. Why not accelerate?

Consider this:

To most people you meet, you are a stranger. Your friends and your relatives know you, and they know what a sterling character you are, how brilliant and charming and lovable. But ninety-nine and nine-tenths of the world doesn't know you from Adam. Or Eve.

When you meet someone for the first time—someone who has the key to that dream, a person you want to sell something to, or get a job from, or induce to hop into the sack with you—you are meeting a total stranger. It is therefore up to you to make a terrific impression right from the word go. *You can't impress somebody if that somebody thinks you look terrible.*

So when you meet someone for that very vital first time, *you must change yourself from a total stranger to an intimate friend in the twinkling of an eye.*

My goal in this book is to see that you are looked at, not through.

I want you to be seen, not just part of the scenery.

I want you to be noticed, not given notice.

Think of your own reaction when you meet someone for the first time. What is the first thing you are aware of?

Is it the face? The figure? The clothing? The look in the eyes? The way the hair is combed? The jewelry? The shine on the shoes?

Probably it is not any one single thing, but the total combined effect of all of them. All those elements work together to create one overall picture. What we all notice is the *total* appearance, the sum of all the parts. Of course, in extreme cases, one facet of that total appearance stands out. Obviously, if somebody weighs three hundred pounds, you will first notice that fat fact and your brain will get a terse message from your eyes, "Oh, boy, look at that lardo!" Or, if the stranger has a diamond the size of an egg on the finger, that will be the thing that commands your eye and your attention. Or if the suit is full of wrinkles and stains, you will immediately notice that sorry condition.

In most cases, the stranger will at first glance appear to be an Average Joe or Normal Nancy, and so your eye will message your brain something bland such as, "Stranger ahead, let's wait and see on this one, Boss."

Suppose you are the stranger. Wouldn't you rather have that message be more positive? Wouldn't you like every eye that catches sight of you to message every brain, "Here comes someone who looks special!" When your body shape, presence, and allure are contagious, people immediately want to be with you.

That's the response I am going to have you create before you finish the last page in this book.

The impression you project, which is so vital in establishing a relationship, should first be one of consistency. Everything about you should work toward one goal—pleasing and encouraging friendship. Your face. Your hair. Your figure. Your clothing. Your attitude. It should all be a whole. Don't, for example, let your clothing speak louder than you.

We must be consistent in the image we project.

Next, consider your attitude. You must understand that it is not merely your clothing and your hair and your face that broadcast the message of who and what you are—it is also the *attitude* you have inside that clothing and behind that face. It is "how you wear" that clothing and the expression on your face that helps to create your attitude and, thus, helps to create the *real you*.

And so it follows, as the night the day, that the better our exterior looks, the more confident our interior becomes. The confidence that a handsome exterior breeds within us extends all the way down, into our most sub-subconscious. Beauty is more than skin deep: It is in the very marrow of our bones. Beauty is soul deep. Beauty is not an illusion; it is power.

You have undoubtedly heard the nutritionist's pet cliché, "You are what you eat." I would like to paraphrase that—"You achieve as you dress."

I know a successful politician who says that when he addresses a group, he thinks his audience responds to what he says about 10 percent of the time, to his mannerisms another 30 percent, and to how he looks 60 percent. Needless to say, he pays very close attention to how he looks and how he dresses.

If you present yourself to the world as a refugee from some charity's thrift shop, the people you meet will automatically and immediately categorize you as poor. They accept the fact that you look poor at face value. Why not? Why should they have any reason to doubt it? It may not be the real you, but they don't know that. If you dress like a failure, they will assume you are a failure.

But, on the other (and happier) hand, if you dress like a success, they will assume you are a success. Maybe you're not there yet, but, to them, you have already arrived. So merely by dressing like a success, you have taken the first big step toward becoming a success.

My experience has shown me very clearly that *those people who start presenting themselves as having already arrived are well on their way to being there. It pays to dress beyond your current job and life-style.*

The attitude you project eventually becomes something you don't have to think about. It becomes second nature. It is the sum of all your attributes.

What are those attributes?

Think of what the eye sees when it first catches sight of a stranger. Ordinarily, it sees only a small fraction of the actual person—just the face and hands are bare and uncovered and visible to the eye. And that face and those hands (and sometimes legs too) may amount to perhaps 10 percent of the total individual. The balance—the other 90 percent—is covered by clothing. So it follows that the garments you wear, and how you wear them, are absolutely vital to your total appearance, to the attitude you are projecting.

Another attribute, of course, is the physical you—your figure, your face, your hair, all that.

Those are the attributes that combine to create the image you project to the world. Let's go over them again: Your face. Your clothing. How you wear that clothing. And the broad outlines of your body—whether you are fat, thin, tall, short, or just about average.

The eye sees. The eye sends messages to the brain. The brain then registers those impressions and banks them for future reference.

In his book, *You Are What You Wear: The Key to Business Success,* William Thourlby talks about first impressions and why they are so vital in everyone's relationships.

He says that people jump to ten decisions *at once* when they meet someone for the first time. Maybe they make more than those ten, he says, but they will certainly make those ten assumptions in the wink of an eye. And they are:

1. Your economic level
2. Your educational level
3. Your trustworthiness
4. Your social position
5. Your level of sophistication
6. Your economic heritage
7. Your social heritage
8. Your educational heritage
9. Your success
10. Your moral character

I want to add one more of my own:

11. Your future

So even before you have opened your mouth, that stranger has formed those eleven assumptions about you. Then, once you begin to talk to that stranger, more impressions are fed to his or her brain via the other sensory organs that come into play—ears, nose, hands. You *hear* how the stranger sounds, what he or she has to say, and how he or she says it. You *smell* strong perfume and / or an unpleasant body odor. You *feel* the way the stranger's hands feel when you shake hands. The mind now has more data on which to make its initial opinion— now you can consider not only how the stranger looks, but also how he or she sounds, smells, and feels.

All that information goes into the file in the brain, the file that is beginning to take shape and is labeled: Stranger's Impact.

The importance of the first impression has been stated beautifully by Professor Ellen Berscheid, a psychologist at the University of Minnesota, and the co-author of *Close Relationships*, in an interview in *U.S. News & World Report*.

> The importance of first impressions and one-time interactions between people is increasing because of urbanization, greater geographic mobility, frequent job changes and a rising divorce rate. Since we more frequently interact with strangers, we more often judge others—and are judged ourselves—on the basis of first impressions that never get a chance to be corrected. Once the impressions are made, they are very difficult to overcome. Even if interaction continues, *initial impressions set the course for what happens later*.
>
> So first impressions probably have become more important as our society has become increasingly fragmented. [Italics mine.]

Of all the initial impressions we emit or receive, I believe the strongest is how we are dressed. That is logical because clothing constitutes the largest percentage of what we see in that first glimpse. If the stranger is dressed sloppily, that first impression—"A slob!"—will be very difficult for any later transformation to overcome. If the stranger is dressed well, that first impression—"Looks pretty good!"—will last a long time, too.

That's why I place so much importance on dressing well. What we wear is paramount in how we are judged by the people we meet. Yet it is not simply a question of dressing well. Perhaps even more important is the need for us to dress *appropriately*. The delicate skill of picking out the proper dress, or proper suit, is just as tricky as the delicate skill of shopping for the finest clothes. You will discover how to refine your "natural knowingness" about clothing.

It begins, of course, with your purchasing habits and your buying procedures. How you spend your money on clothing can greatly change the way you ultimately live and the way you can attract what you want in life. Your method of spending either increases your returns, or it doesn't. We will have much more to say about shopping in later chapters.

But at this point I simply want to start you thinking about the importance of shopping in creating the appealing you we plan to build. It is not only what you buy, but how appropriately you wear the garment when you get it home.

If you have on a magnificent cocktail dress, when everyone else is in casual attire, you will look and feel foolish no matter how lovely the dress is. And feeling foolish won't help you to create a positive, winning attitude. So you must not only assemble a great wardrobe, but know when to wear what, and how.

If you dress *well* and also dress *appropriately,* then you are on your way.

It goes without saying that you must have an attractive body on which to display those appealing and appropriate outfits. You must be believable, and you can't be believable if your body is a mess.

Have you ever considered the fact that quite possibly the reason you are not winning—the reason why you are traveling in one of the slower lanes—is because you are dressing like a loser? As Confucius should have said, "He who dresses to lose achieves his goal."

There is a widespread lie being circulated nowadays. It goes: "It doesn't really matter how you dress or how you look—that stuff is for show-offs and clothes horses—as long as you have the right stuff in your soul." Of course you have to have the right stuff in your soul. Invariably it is true: As is the inner, so always and inevitably will be the outer. The quality of your presentation to the world should be equal to the quality of your life.

Suppose you are applying for a job, along with a dozen other applicants, and you go into the employment office to meet the personnel officer doing the hiring. Your soul and your heart may be marvelous—pure and shining—and you may be the perfect person for the job, but if you look like something the cat threw out, the hiring person will never get to become acquainted with the Marvelous You hidden deep inside that unattractive exterior.

Give yourself a chance! An attractive presentation is your passport, the way you get a chance to let people come to know the real you.

That big lie—"It doesn't really matter how you look"—is something circulated by unsuccessful and frustrated people. And the world is full of unsuccessful, frustrated people. You will never catch a genuine success saying that it doesn't matter how you look. *Successful people know that you must look good to win big. Winners have a knack for looking good.*

Present yourself as a winner and you will be treated like a winner. That's basic human nature, and you might as well capitalize on it.

Of course talent counts. And ability. And proficiency. All those wonderful things. You have to have the right stuff, and be able to deliver when your opportunity comes. Ability is the quality that finally and ultimately determines who wins and who loses—but first you have to be given the opportunity to show that you have the ability. In baseball, unless you get a chance to bat you can't hit a home run. In life, the same principle applies.

So give yourself a chance to come up to the plate. The best way to insure that you have that chance is to dress as if you have already arrived. More people see you and evaluate you by your clothing than by anything else—your home, your car, your job, your family, anything. Strangers see you and make a snap judgment on how you are dressed. People are introduced to you and a judgment leaps immediately into their minds, based largely on what you are wearing. Much of the business world and the social world conduct their affairs based on snap judgments, such first impressions. And those snap judgments and first impressions are almost totally a product of *how you look and what attitude and mannerisms you project*.

Right this very instant, take a look at yourself in the nearest mirror. You can level with yourself. What do you see? That image looking at you is all that strangers have to go on when they first meet you, so put yourself in their place. Are you giving off a winning look? Or are you a never-made-it dressed to go nowhere? What you project is what you seem (to others) to want out of life. Present yourself as a loser, and you'll be given a lot of chances to lose. Present yourself as a winner, however, and golden opportunities will come knocking at your door.

You can't dress in-between. There is no neutral way of picking out and wearing clothes. *You always make some kind of statement with the way you dress—powerful or inept.* And, unfortunately, it is my conclusion, after many years of watching my fellow man and woman, that *the majority of human beings dress for failure.*

Clothing has the awesome power of evoking an emotional response on the part of others. That emotional response can be positive or negative, and it is tremendously difficult to change. It is up to you to determine what that response will be.

I will help you in this book. But don't expect specific dogma about what *you*, particularly, should wear—I cannot know the particular, unique needs of each of my readers. What I will be giving you, however, are many insightful suggestions you can apply to your own situation. Keep your eyes open to the photographs, and keep your mind open to the words. Then do your own thinking and sorting and selecting—*for yourself*. This way you have choice and freedom.

This is not a checklist fashion book, an A-B-C-D, step-by-step mandatory "how-to." But you will definitely learn how to "market and position" the powerful and captivating *you*. For quick appraisal and acceptance—that's high-octane fuel for moving into the fast lane. Your "standards of living"—possessions, quarters, food, and conditions of work and play—will explode! You will acquire dressing panache.

Even in my Presentation Salon/Seminars, when I meet people face to face and contribute to the enrichment of their lives, I don't attempt to tell them what is "right" for them to wear in every situation. Rather, I show them how to distinguish the appropriate from the inappropriate. I tell people how certain things work and how certain things don't work, and thus try to aim them in the right direction. Crutches don't create savvy dressers!

You cannot teach good taste. That's something that can only be recognized by a gut reaction. "That's it," you will say, when you spot something great. We can all recognize the tasteful, we can all spot success, and we all know when we feel that we are really on the beam. And so I won't tell you—either in my Presentation Salon / Seminars or in this book—exclusively what to wear and what not to wear. I can expose you, however, so you will recognize what really works, and what doesn't work for *you.*

This isn't a by-the-numbers book. It is a guidebook. *It is a catalyst for million-dollar heroes.* It generates directional signals so you can switch over from the slow lanes and zip off into the fast lane.

I know it's hard for some people to accept new ideas, new ways of living, new systems of looking at themselves and the way they should function in the world around them. But if your goal is to cruise along gracefully in the fast lane, you are going to have to know the options that work, and do them. You may have to change a great many things. You will develop a standard for quality and good taste.

Life in the fast lane, compared to how things are in the slow lanes, is considerably different. When you move from the one to the other, you are subjecting yourself to an advanced case of "option shock." It will bring the blessings of an incredible range of choices.

You have to be prepared for it. The simple act of making up your mind, of taking that first step and saying that you are going to make the move, is the first step in that preparation. You will be shaking up your life, so you'd better get ready for a lot of new adventures and experiences.

What is holding you back?

It could be your appearance, the way you look—but it is probably that plus many other things. It is your entire outlook and attitude. Perhaps there are some simple, mechanical things—such as your grooming, the way you cut your hair or apply your makeup—that are easy to change once you recognize them. Very often, too, it is your figure—or lack of one. That's a challenge to change, but certainly possible. And most of the time it is the narrow, limited concept and image you have of yourself as reflected by the choice of clothing you have "settled" for.

These are inhibitors that can be turned into positives virtually overnight.

When you change the restrictive things about yourself, you will be shaking your life up. That change happens automatically. A trimmer figure creates a more optimistic attitude. Better clothes give you more confidence. A more attractive hair style forges a surer personality. It's the same old you, but with a new and more positive outlook—you have made that grand and glorious move from the slow lanes to the fast lane. And you'll find that it is wonderful!

There is an old saying that is applicable here:

"If I give you a fish, you'll eat for one day. But if I teach you to fish, you will always eat."

This book isn't giving you a fish, or even a school of fish, but it is going to teach you how to land the *big* fish. It will teach you the importance of quality and the styles of clothing that are appropriate and how to recognize them for yourself and shop for them for yourself.

But none of this will matter if you are unresponsive, negative, or refuse to listen. You *must* open your mind and your heart to new ideas and new philosophies. You *must* tell yourself that if you are to get what you want—whatever it is that appeals to you about fast-lane living—then you must necessarily give your life a shake-up. You *must* tell yourself to listen to what I have to say because you and I have the keys to your new life. Together we will develop your staying power.

The distinguished architect Frank Lloyd Wright once said:

"We all know the feeling we have when we are well dressed and we enjoy the consciousness that results from it. It affects our conduct. I have always believed in being careful about my clothes, getting supremely well-dressed, because I could then forget about them."

He's right, of course. He was successful, obviously. He certainly moved in the fast lane (he practically designed the fast lane). Successful people mostly travel in the fast lane.

People who are unattractive and poorly groomed are putting themselves in financial and social jeopardy. But if you are attractive, well-groomed, and dressed in outstanding clothing, then you are presenting your best possible face to the world around you. And, by presenting that best possible face, you are conveying a greater sense of presence, of authority, of believability, of likability, of sophistication.

I treasure an advertisement I once saw in *The Wall Street Journal,* placed there as a public service by the United Technologies Corporation, of Hartford, Connecticut (see following page).

In my private work, my Presentation Salon / Seminars, at which I teach and demonstrate how to look great and dress appropriately, I work personally with thousands of men and women, from all walks of life, representing all age and ethnic groups, and people of as wide a spectrum of personalities as you can possibly find. And I almost always effect a marvelous change in their life-styles, moving them into the fast

**Aim So High You'll
Never Be Bored**

The
greatest waste
of our
natural resources
is the
number of
people
who never
achieve their
potential.
Get out
of that
slow lane.
Shift
into that
fast lane.
If you think
you can't,
you won't.
If you think
you can,
there's a
good chance
you will.
Even making
the effort
will make
you feel
like a new
person.
Reputations
are made
by searching
for things that
can't be done
and doing them.
Aim low:
boring.
Aim high:
soaring.

lane, enabling them to increase their earnings, expand their social lives, and change their standards of living for the better.

That makes it sound as though I have taken them and totally rearranged their molecules and made new people out of them. No, I don't do anything quite that dramatic.

They have simply made themselves realize the potential that had always been there. I am not about creating an exact image for them; I am about confirming the one they have not given themselves permission to reveal.

It is my contention—no, my conviction—that we are all living human treasures. We are all unique. We are all authentic. We are all ourselves.

We all, however, can pursue the dream and work at reaching the fast lane. You want a "statistical edge" over your yesterdays.

Life stands still for you—until *you* move on.

PART II

Identifying Your Individual Look

2

Four Different Types of Ladies

CHIC, ELEGANT, GLAMOROUS, AND SPICY

It is my distinct pleasure to introduce you to four very different ladies. Each one, in her own way, is a gem, a marvel, truly a work of feminine art. Each one has her own particular fascination. Each one has her own style, has her own preference in clothing, likes to do her hair her own way, has her own special makeup preferences. Each one, in short, is a very separate and distinct personality.

And one of those ladies is you.

It is vitally important for you to know the *type* of woman you are, because nothing confuses people as much as when they come across a woman who is one type and yet dresses or behaves in a way that is totally contradictory to that type. They may not consciously be aware of what disturbs them, but that is it—they realize the lady is acting against type.

In this chapter, I will introduce you to these four different ladies, and let you get to know them immediately. In that way, you will be able to recognize yourself as one of those four, because, through years of working with women, I have observed that there are these four supertypes—no more. Of course, it is very possible for a woman to be primarily of one type and yet embody one, two, or three of the others. Still, it is to one type that she owes her primary devotion.

The four types are these:

CHIC

ELEGANT

GLAMOROUS

SPICY

There are women who appear to be other types like exotic, sporty, academic and country. They do dress and act this way; however this is a way of being "sometime" which can fit into the broader four types.

It is curious how people are born with certain traits, distinct and powerful from infancy. Gilbert and Sullivan put it best when they have Private Willis, the Grenadier Guard sentry, sing his soliloquy about that peculiarity in *Iolanthe:*

> *I often think it's comical*
> *How Nature always does contrive*
> *That every boy and every gal,*
> *That's born into the world alive,*
> *Is either a little Liberal,*
> *Or else a little Conservative!*

In this case, every girl is born either a little Chic, a little Elegant, a little Glamorous, or a little Spicy. Women have their type imprinted in their personalities from the crib on. Of course, men have their types, too, and we'll deal with them in the following chapter.

For women, there is a certain look that is the tip-off on which type they are. That look is extended to everything they do and wear— clothes, hair, makeup, the works. And that type is a combination of all the factors that contribute to the total woman—appearance, personality, taste, aura.

Let's meet these four types, one by one, and analyze them carefully so you can determine which of the four is you.

1. CHIC

She is perfection personified. She says, confidently, "Here I am!" She is almost always in total control of her world and her surroundings. She is usually a city person—urban and urbane. She appreciates the city and uses it as a backdrop for her style. She always insists that her grooming be impeccable, yet never forced, always precise. She shops for her clothing with total self-confidence, and she prefers things that are timeless in terms of style. Even when she wears something three or four years old, she has a knack of making it look new and up-to-the-minute. She demands the best. She knows what she wants, can quickly weed out the genuine from the phony. She has a great flair for mixing styles, for combining colors—gray with green, white with beige, blue with purple, brown with yellow—and so she is never predictable. She has a first-rate fashion sense. She is eclectic.

If the Chic woman were an automobile, she would be a Jaguar. If she were a fruit, she would be a perfect red apple. If she were music, she would be a Mozart symphony. If she were a dog, she would be a Great Dane. If she were a season she would be spring.

Among the exclusive Chic women's society are such recognizable figures as Louise Nevelson, Marina Schiano, Audrey Hepburn, Barbra Streisand, Lee Radziwill, Nan Kempner, Empress Farah of Iran, and Nastassia Kinski.

I see the Chic woman on the deck of a sleek new yacht, cruising the sparkling Caribbean, wearing a crisp white summer blouse, pale blue slacks, a red bandana whipping around her neck and trailing off with the warm tropic breeze.

I see the Chic woman striding purposefully down Fifth Avenue or Rodeo Drive or Bond Street, in a light tweed topcoat over a classically simple gray suit, or a side-buttoned boat-neck dress in wool or silk.

Wherever I see her, everything is perfect, everything is always just so. She would be aware of even the smallest crease in what she was wearing. If she found a speck of dust on a table or if even one fringe outlining her oriental rug on the living room floor was out of step with its neighbors, she would know it. She is a woman of infinite detail.

I have noticed two types of Chic women: the "Bon Chic" woman who wants strongly to impress and the "Slick Chic" woman who underplays and is quietly Chic.

Are you a Chic woman? If you think that is your type, then shop for your clothing accordingly. You are the kind of person whose taste is so precise that you can mix creations by different designers easily. You can experiment with odd but striking color combinations. You will always look marvelous, because you are *chic*. Being Chic is adding "direction" to elegance.

2. ELEGANT

The Chic woman is the one who says, "Here I am!" The Elegant woman doesn't have to say anything. Her presence is so strong, so pervasive, that she just has to stand there and she will be noticed. It is inevitable. There is about her, as we observe her making her entrance, an air of importance that commands attention. The Elegant woman can sweep into a bank and nobody would ever think to question her signature or ask her for identification. She is the lady who is always waited on quickly and efficiently in any store. Head waiters will always find her a table, even if they have to boot out a few bank presidents to do so. Elegance implies top quality, of course, but not garishness. In fact, the Elegant lady is generally on the restrained side, although there is always about her an aura of luxuriousness. Fabrics: luxurious. She carries the finest leathers, sometimes trimmed in real gold or silver. Jewelry: luxurious. Diamonds, pearls, rubies (or clever imitations, but she only wears the imitations when she is out shopping during the day). In fact, fine jewelry is often the signature of the Elegant lady. Despite her hauteur, there is often about her a demureness that may border on the modest—you will never see her wearing anything that is split up too high or sliced down too low. Nor will she ever wear extremes in anything—no spiked heels or platform shoes, no garish colors, no fashion/fad gimmickry. Not that an Elegant woman can't be sexy; she just does it in a more subtle way. A large percentage of the jet set—or whatever they are calling that group in today's vernacular—are Elegant, and they are the kind who know the designers personally, call them by their first names, swap stories about them. You don't have to be a jet-setter to be Elegant, of course, but it improves your Elegance if you, too, know the work of the various designers and understand which one is the most suitable for you. And by the way, quite simply, get yourself a mink! Sable! Stone marten!

If the Elegant woman were an automobile, she would be a Rolls-Royce. If she were a fruit, she would be a kiwi. If she were music, she would be a grand opera, preferably one by Wagner. If she were a dog, she would be a standard poodle or an Afghan. If she were a season, she would be winter, stark, black, leafless branches against an all-white background.

You will know some Elegant woman of your own acquaintance, but among celebrities they number such figures as Nancy Reagan, the late Princess Grace, Ann Getty, Pat Buckley, Dina Merrill, Diana Vreeland, and Jacqueline de Ribes.

I see the Elegant woman at a Monte Carlo gala, in something basic and black, with only a single strand of perfect pearls around her long, graceful neck.

I see the Elegant woman presiding over a meeting of the board of directors of her late husband's corporation, wearing a handsome navy blue suit, adorned with a diamond-and-ruby clip, diamond earrings, and a diamond-and-ruby ring.

I see the Elegant woman as the gracious hostess of a lavish dinner party, the table set with the finest in crystal and china, and she herself set in a pale pink gown with gold jewelry, handmade for her by the artisans of Venice, working from her own design.

She may have come up from poverty through her own hard work and talent, but you would never guess her origins by looking at her. She gives the impression of having been born to the purple, or at least the violet. She has that air of great breeding, of having sprung from wealth and opulence. No apparent *nouveau riche*, here. Her makeup is understated, soft and muted, and blends in with her face perfectly. Her coiffure is as elegant as the rest of her, simple yet stylish. She generally prefers either an antique setting for herself, or else one that is starkly modern.

She is the epitome of my theory that we are all *Living Human Treasures*. Certainly, the Elegant woman is a treasure (although I am only guessing here, since I have no way of knowing positively). I would imagine her underthings are elegant, all satin and silk and lace.

Are you an Elegant woman? I envy you your great taste, and I suggest you shop accordingly. You probably wear mostly the basics—blacks, whites, blues, an occasional startling red in the right place at the right time. Your jewelry is your biggest extravagance, because it is your trademark. Even if you are not in the diamonds or rubies bracket financially, you can satisfy your urge with some of the costume jewelry that is so expertly and artistically made today. And, if you are unable to afford designer originals, look in the fashion magazines, find the ones you like and shop around for copies or near-copies, which will do until your financial ship comes in.

3. GLAMOROUS

The Chic woman said, "Here I am!" The Elegant woman passively stood there and was duly noticed. Ah, but the Glamorous woman is like sirens and fireworks going off! She stands there and attention comes her way from her eager subjects. Eyes turn to her, pulled by her power and fascination. Generally, the women who are born with total beauty fall into this category—the ones who are physical perfection, or close to it. The top models are Glamorous women. Most of the movie and television stars are Glamorous women. The Glamorous woman knows the power of her beauty to win friends and influence men. Her hair is often loose, flying provocatively in the wind. Her lips are full and either very red or else left totally untouched. Her perfume is stronger than most other women would dare to wear. She is the woman men whistle at, toot their horns at, dream about. The same head waiter who quickly made room for the Elegant woman would just as quickly make a pass at the Glamorous woman. She is alive, vital, fresh. You'll find her on the beach, playing volleyball, or at the football game—leading the cheering. In men's better-quality fantasies, she is there—perhaps sitting at the end of the bar, with a cigarette, a bourbon, and a come-hither look: perhaps alone on a sunny, sandy, South Pacific beach, in a little white bikini; perhaps driving by in her racy, perky red convertible, with her long red hair (or blonde or brunette) flowing behind her. Of all my four types of women, she can be the most daring, and usually is—she can show more skin, wear tighter jeans, dazzle with bare-midriff and off-the-shoulder styles. She can adopt every trendy fashion gimmick that comes along, and on her, it can't help but look good. She is the one with the wildest boots, the brightest colors, the flashiest, zaniest, nuttiest costume jewelry. She is also the one with the reddest red hair, the blondest blond hair, the blackest brunette hair. She is alluring, mysterious, gorgeous, elusive, enticing, contagious. She is very confident of her own ability to enchant—and with good reason—a miracle indeed!

To quote Jacqueline de Ribes, an internationally acclaimed woman of elegance and beauty, "First of all you must know that glamour is a totally American invention. It's an American word. Glamour is a worldly style, lots of allure, a touch of flamboyance, a deep know-how, all wrapped up in natural seduction. Glamour has often been connected with the glitter of money, which is not always true. Successful people really ought to wish to be glamorous. Glamorous people bring something to others. They are seductive, attractive, and it has nothing to do with frivolity. Glamour sticks to people" (*Interview Magazine*, Reinaldo Herrera).

If the Glamorous woman were an automobile, she would be a bright red Ferrari. If she were a fruit, she would be something tropical, probably a mango. If she were music, she would be loud and raucous rock. If she were a dog, she would be an Irish setter. If she were a season, she would be summer.

There are, as you would expect, many celebrities who qualify as Glamorous women—Sophia Loren, Catherine Deneuve, Cheryl Tiegs, Ann-Margret, Zsa Zsa Gabor, Diana Ross, Farrah Fawcett, Christie Brinkley, Cicely Tyson, Karen Black, Raquel Welch, and most of the great ravishing beauties of our time.

I see the Glamorous woman on the patio of a Malibu home, the ocean sparkling behind her, with a pair of oversized sunglasses and an undersized orange bikini, presiding over a party in which all the guests are Hollywood stars.

I see the Glamorous woman getting out of her convertible at the airport, waving to the mechanics, then jumping into her silver Lear jet and zooming off for Acapulco, clad in a skin-tight jump suit (lavender and silver, to match the plane) and goggles (white, for contrast).

I see the Glamorous woman leading a safari in Kenya in her designer African explorer's safari suit (white, accented by a blood-red sash and scarf), her blond hair thrusting out from beneath her red-and-white pith helmet.

Wherever she is, the Glamorous woman is the object of attention. But she is, of course, used to that. She was the most popular girl in her class, even in kindergarten, and grew up sweeping all those titles (Most Beautiful Preteen, Most Popular Senior, First to Get Kissed, Miss Southwest Wyoming) and being so popular that she eventually had to leave the phone off the hook. She will always be popular, and she thoroughly enjoys being the center of attention.

Are you a Glamorous woman? If you think that's your type, settle back and enjoy it, and take advantage of it. Your clothing can be wilder than the other types because the spotlight embraces the extraordinary. Things that the Chic woman and the Elegant woman would not touch are made to order for you. The only danger to be careful of is that you can go overboard. Develop a keen eye for finery that flatters.

4. SPICY

The Spicy lady doesn't have to say, "Here I am!" like Miss Chic, nor does she just stand there, waiting for attention like Miss Elegant, nor does she bowl everybody over, like Miss Glamorous. That's because the Spicy lady doesn't really give a damn whether she's noticed or not. She just goes her way, having a good time, and if people notice her, fine and dandy, and if they don't, that's their problem, not hers. But they generally do notice her because she is usually a bit on the outrageous side. If there is an avant-garde style, our Spicy woman will find it, use it, and adapt it to her own special needs. She therefore often creates her own styles as she goes along, adding something to her outfits, or subtracting something from them, thereby forging something that is uniquely her own. The Spicy lady tends to be short, for reasons known only to whoever or whatever it is that invents people. She's short and vivacious and bouncy and very, very alive. Wherever she is, tempests tend to follow—her highs are monumental, her lows cataclysmic. She will have strange hairdos—wild, curly perms or waist-length tresses— and splash on makeup that can be every color of the rainbow. She looks good in dresses pulled from the Thrift Shop racks, often worn with hiking boots or sneakers. But the Spicy lady, if she puts her mind to it, can be as Chic, Elegant, or Glamorous as anybody—because she generally has the imagination to out-chic Miss Chic, out-elegant Miss Elegant, or out-glamour Miss Glamorous. If that head waiter who made room for the Elegant lady and made a pass at the Glamorous lady confronted the Spicy lady, he'd probably offer her a job as a cocktail waitress. Or else he'd propose to her. The Spicy lady is bright and funny, probably was a tomboy as a kid, loves to cook but hates to clean up afterward. She can get away with a lot, in her clothing—she looks great in high-fashion designer creations, but feels more comfortable in jeans and a T shirt and, with her style, she can turn that outfit into something zesty. She's electric! She's saucy! She's earthy!

If the Spicy lady were an automobile, she would be a VW convertible, a Datsun 280 ZX, or a Jeep. If she were a fruit, she would be a fat, juicy peach. If she were music, she would be hot jazz by Chuck Mangione. If she were a dog, she would probably be a dachshund. If she were a season, obviously she would be autumn—she is full of bright colors and spicy promise.

You'll find Spicy ladies all over the place. Some you may know are Dolly Parton, Eartha Kitt, Gina Lollobrigida, Cher, Bette Midler, Margaret Trudeau, Bianca Jagger, Charo, Cheryl Ladd, and Shirley Mac-Laine.

I see the Spicy lady riding her bike along a dirt road high in the mountains, a backpack strapped behind her, wearing blue jeans with stars appliquéd on them and a yellow T shirt with a message that reads, "Just Passing Through."

I see the Spicy lady attending a symphony concert, in a rich blue gown with swirls of silver, her hair done up in a blue-and-silver ribbon, and carrying a single, snow-white rose. And wearing earrings the size, color, and shape of Ping-Pong balls. As a matter of fact, they *are* Ping-Pong balls!

I see the Spicy lady at a PTA meeting, leading the fight for more paprika on the kids' luncheon goulash, dressed in a neat gray suit with a scarlet silk shirt and carrying a gray-and-scarlet wool cape. On her head, I see a little gray hat with an enormous red feather sticking straight up. (Her scarlet red is as lush as a ripe tomato. She is electric. Her image is sharply seen; she is alive!)

Because of her aliveness, in every situation she is the one who catches the eye—and often the ear—first. She is the rum in the rum baba of life. If anybody starts a fight, look for her to be in the thick of it. As a kid, she always got in trouble because she always said what she thought—and she still does. She feels more, loves more, laughs more, cries more, hurts more. She will never be ignored.

Are you a Spicy woman? If that's your style, count your blessings. Your life will have its ups and downs, but it will never be boring. You'll still be going strong at eighty, still sassy and feisty. And you should let your imagination go, when it comes to what you wear. With your personality, it really doesn't matter if things match or they don't, if the fabrics are right or wrong, if colors clash or not. You can, with the force of your vibrant personality, turn it all into one large mass of sultry, exotic pleasure, no matter how confusing it might look on others. You will only be uncomfortable if you try to squeeze too much into conformity. Be yourself.

At the beginning of this chapter, I said that most women are not totally one type or the other, not a one hundred percent Chic lady or an entirely Spicy woman. Nobody is all anything. Chances are when you read this chapter, you recognized yourself primarily in one of the four ladies, and yet feel that you have some tendencies toward the other types. That is probably true. You will be predominately one of the four, with perhaps a dash of one, two, or even three of the others. But concentrate on being the one that is most *you*. And the rest of *you* will take care of itself.

Be who you are; don't play for safety. It's the most dangerous thing in the world.

3

Three Different Types of Men

DISTINGUISHED AND ELEGANT, SHARP AND HUNKY, CASUAL AND DOWN HOME

Men, of course, will demand equal time and equal representation in these pages.

Try as I can, research as I can, I cannot come up with four different types of men, to match the four different types of women we met in Chapter 2. No, there are only three different, distinct masculine types. I imagine sociologists will have a field day with that bit of information; the fact that women come in a wider assortment than do men.

Just as with women, however, there is significance in what type of man you are. A man should be aware of his type, of the sort of image he projects, and key his wardrobe and his presentation to that type. And, just as with women, a man should be aware of the fact that while his main thrust may be one type, he probably has traces of other types in his personality, as well. But it is the one primary type that he can capitalize on most, which should be of chief importance to him, his own brand of charisma.

The three types of men are:

DISTINGUISHED AND ELEGANT

SHARP AND HUNKY

CASUAL AND DOWN HOME

And now let us examine each of the three, in brilliant close-up, one by one:

1. DISTINGUISHED AND ELEGANT

This is the masculine counterpart of the Elegant woman. The Distinguished and Elegant man is the diplomat, the banker, the corporate executive, the supreme court justice with his judicial robes off. He may have started in the ghetto or he may be the son of the yacht club commander, but he has made it on his own. He has arrived, and everything he wears emphasizes that fact. He has considerable flair and dash. He is definitely in the fast lane; in fact, he is driving the pace car. He enjoys the good life and feels not one guilty pang for doing so. He figures he's earned it. He dines well. He dresses well. He demands the best service—but in a quiet voice—and gets it. He is most often seen with a beautiful woman; she is either a Chic woman, an Elegant woman or, less frequently, a Glamorous woman. But no Spicy women—they would boggle him. To the Distinguished and Elegant man, clothing is a matter of great importance. He lives life in the grand tradition. He knows all the best shops, but has his favorites. He is a man of great loyalty, and so once he finds a shop he likes he would never think of changing unless they offended him grievously. He likes to buy certain things abroad—shirts from Bond Street in London, shoes from a little artisan in Rome—but still makes many purchases at the finest store in the nearest big city.

If the Distinguished and Elegant man were an automobile, he would be a Lincoln Continental, a Rolls-Royce, or a Bentley. If he were a tree, he would be a redwood. If he were a painting, he would be a Gilbert Stuart portrait of George Washington. If he were an animal, he would be a lion. If he were a time of day, he would be the promising hours of morning, crisp and clear and untroubled.

Distinguished and Elegant men are familiar to us all. I believe Fred Astaire to be the epitome of this elite group, but George Hamilton, Bill Blass, Douglas Fairbanks, Jr., Clement Stone, and the late David Niven belong, as do Sir Laurence Olivier, Marcello Mastroianni, Billy Dee Williams, and almost any one of your friendly neighborhood tycoons—all snappy and debonair.

I see the Distinguished and Elegant man arriving at the White House, stepping out of his limousine, acknowledging the salute of the guard, and looking like a million dollars in his power navy blue suit, white-on-white shirt, blue tie with the simple, narrow lighter blue-and-gray diagonal stripes.

I see the Distinguished and Elegant man in his tuxedo, pleated shirt, hand-tied bow tie, strolling along the porch of the country club, with an Elegant woman clinging to his arm, while a Chic woman eyes him covetously from a doorway and a Glamorous woman winks wantonly from behind the crystal punch bowl.

I see the Distinguished and Elegant man in his office, wearing a three-piece gray suit with a pale gray shirt and a maroon silk tie with a barely noticeable foulard print on it, dictating to his efficient secretary and, at the same time fingering swatches of fabric sent to him by his Savile Row tailor.

He cuts a dashing figure, doesn't he? And, of course, he is well aware of his dash. Having power, being a winner, as he is, is something that cannot be ignored, although he has come to take it for granted by now. At this time in his life, he hardly has to shop for himself, although sometimes he enjoys it. His measurements are on file in all the best stores and, since he is a regular exerciser, those measurements do not vary a centimeter from year to year. If you feel that you belong to this type, shop accordingly. Nothing overt, nothing flashy. Even when dressing for relaxation, the Distinguished and Elegant man is conservative—his tennis clothes are traditional whites, his knocking-about-the-estate duds are blue jeans or stylish trousers (pleats, gusseted pockets, or riding jodhpurs) topped with a casual shirt and a blazer, and even his swimming trunks are classic (no bikini bottoms for him). He simply insists on the best of everything and anything—it must be made from the finest fabrics (wools, silks, linens, cottons, leathers, suedes) and the tailoring must be nothing less than total perfection. He pays attention to the smallest detail—on his suits, he frets about the drape, the hang, the line, how the trousers crease when he sits and how the jacket folds when he stretches. With his ties, he even goes so far as to measure their width to make sure they are precisely what the proportions of the outfit demand—not a hair more or less. If you feel that you fit into the Distinguished and Elegant category, you, too, must be particular and careful. Excellence is your motto.

2. SHARP AND HUNKY

"Sharp" alone may not be the precise word for this group, but it's pretty close. Still, it needs something else, and that's why I added "hunky." Together, I think you get what I mean, can visualize the kind of man who is the second type of male. Women become more "womanly" and less of the "lady" when with him.

By Sharp and Hunky, this seductive combination, I mean a man who projects sex appeal and bravado, who is daring with his clothing, who is the first to try new styles, who is very active and outdoorsy and yet just as much at home being lazy and indoorsy. The Sharp and Hunky man is restless, moving and movable, comfortable in both bedroom and board room, a man who will take on all the jobs he can because he loves challenges and cannot stand idleness. He is the most physically fit of all my three types of men, was probably the one who was the best athlete when he was young, and still is an enthusiastic athlete—tennis or golf, jogging or swimming. He looks great in sports clothes and yet, because of his basic good looks (you seldom catch him without a tan) he also looks marvelous in his go-to-business suit and just as spectacular in a tuxedo (although he probably looks better in summer formal, with the white dinner jacket, than in winter formal, with the darker jacket). New styles look good on him, whereas Mr. Distinguished and Elegant might look awkward in something daring— even if he didn't look awkward, he would feel uncomfortable. Mr. Sharp and Hunky, however, thoroughly enjoys being somewhat experimental and even a touch outlandish. The Sharp and Hunky man looks fine in tight-fitting trousers, in super-short and ultratight swimming trunks, and he keeps his sports shirt unbuttoned a few buttons below what other men might do. Because of this, he is vitally concerned with the fit of his garments. He enjoys things like silk shirts and velvet jackets, and has probably a larger selection of shoes than any of the other types of men. The Sharp and Hunky man oozes self-confidence, and is a highly successful ladies' man—and they adore him for it. He is in tune with the times and is prepared to break with tradition when it is important to do so.

If the Sharp and Hunky man were an automobile, he would be a Maserati, a Lamborghini, or a Mercedes, one of the classic models. If he were a tree, he would be a mighty oak or a dogwood in bloom. If he were a painting, he would be something by Dali. If he were an animal, he would be a black panther. If he were a time of day, he would be high noon on a blazing summer's day.

Many of Hollywood's biggest names are Sharp and Hunky men— Warren Beatty, Tom Selleck, Burt Lancaster, John Travolta, Mel Gibson, Christopher Reeve, Richard Gere, and Ryan O'Neal, plus many of the top sports figures, too—from Joe Namath to Sugar Ray Leonard— belong to this elite group and give it some of its sparkle.

I see the Sharp and Hunky man in blue jeans and a pale green cotton pullover T shirt, barefoot and hatless sitting on a rock on one of the deserted beaches of Bora-Bora. But on the second look, the beach isn't deserted after all—there is that lovely, fawn-skinned Tahitian girl, with the white flower behind her ear, and nothing else.

I see the Sharp and Hunky man on the Twentieth Century-Fox lot in Hollywood, entering the commissary to meet a couple of big producers, and waving at Alan Alda and Mike Farrell as they stroll by. You can tell him not only by his clothing—white linen slacks and richly blended gray and black silk jacket, white cotton sports shirt open down to the third button—but also by his marvelous sense of freedom and his panache.

I see the Sharp and Hunky man paddling his canoe across a New Hampshire lake in a pair of light blue cotton wash pants topped by a flatteringly fitted royal blue shirt of a unique design. The woman in the bow of the canoe is of a unique design, too. She is most likely Spicy or Glamorous.

I suspect that men who want money and power envy the Distinguished and Elegant man, whereas men whose dreams are more of sexual conquests would envy the Sharp and Hunky man. But the Sharp and Hunky man does not confine his victories only to the bedroom. He is equally successful in business, or in whatever profession he designs to enter. So he dresses for success, but always with his own stamp, his own style. You won't ever catch the Sharp and Hunky man copying anybody else. One of his main objectives in planning his wardrobe is that it allows him room to move freely and comfortably. Always active, he can't stand anything that binds, ties, slows, or in any way inhibits his movements during business hours. His sense of taste is innately correct, and he has the knack and flair for combining things—trying something new, experimenting with different and unusual fabrics, cuts, designs, combinations. He is admired by other men. The Distinguished and Elegant man is respected, the Casual and Down Home man (whom we have yet to meet) is a buddy, but the Sharp and Hunky man is what all men want to feel they are when on the prowl—carving out their own turf.

If you are a Sharp and Hunky man, a man who is daring with both clothing and life, let yourself go in the clothing department. Your unique gift is awesome. Use it—appeal is power. Don your dynamic duds with confidence.

Be daring, but within taste. With your great physique, you make clothes look great. Just remember that you were given beauty to enjoy it and doors will open in your wake.

3. CASUAL AND DOWN HOME

Far and away the largest segment of the male population belongs to this group, the Casual and Down Home man. To him, clothing is a part of a total life-style which places the emphasis on the informal. The Casual and Down Home man treats his appearance casually, as he treats a lot of other things in his world casually. His clothes often times have a confident shabbiness—a cashmere sweater with alligator loafers—a somewhat grown-up preppy costume that has taken him from college campuses to bars, to parties, and picnics—it's the American boy out of puberty. He's the wizard of ease.

In my Presentation Salon / Seminars, I often play games with the men and women who attend. I ask them to choose, from among others, the man or the woman who best fits some label I give them. I ask the women to pick the man, of all the men in the room, they feel is the one their mothers would want them to marry. Almost always, they pick a guy-next-door type, a solid citizen sort of man who poses no threat, who doesn't seem as aloof as the Distinguished and Elegant man or as overtly sexy and intimidating as the Sharp and Hunky man. That is the Casual and Down Home man—everybody's big brother, everybody's pal, the cozy, comfortable, sit-by-the-fire, whittle-a-stick, easy-going person that most men, in truth are. You may fantasize about being Distinguished and Elegant or Sharp and Hunky, but nature has, instead, rewarded you with your role as a good, steady, Casual and Down Home man.

And there is nothing wrong with that; in fact, it's pretty good. The Casual and Down Home man is considered a good catch, so he often gets the best-looking women. After all, the Casual and Down Home man shares their dream of a home, a family, a good life. And, while the Casual and Down Home man has manners that are shy and boyish, and tastes that are simple, his dreams may be big and his accomplishments king-sized, and he often ends up rich and successful. You will find many Casual and Down Home men cruising along cheerfully in the fast lane. Still, they are able to relax and settle back and lead a very comfortable life.

The Casual and Down Home man started out in life as the all-American, freckle-faced kid—the Tom Sawyer and Huckleberry Finn sort. He grew up and matured into the good guy, everybody's idea of the perfect neighbor, cheerful and friendly and pretty much liked by everybody he comes in contact with. The Casual and Down Home man looks great in his carefully unstudied clothing. His taste is basically simple and, generally, conventional. If the tie isn't precisely right for the suit and shirt, well, it'll have to do. If the fit is a shade off, well, better luck next time. If the pants have a few wrinkles, does anybody really notice or care? The Casual and Down Home man would probably never buy a severely designed suit—first, he thinks that is an affectation and, second, he doubts he'd look good in it. However, he still manages to look great. He prefers a looser fit and, consequently, disdains all those overly tight garments. He is much more comfortable in sports clothing—a good old tweed jacket over a good old pair of wool slacks with a good old sports shirt. Even at work, given half a chance by his boss, he'll wear sports clothing rather than his dress-up clothes. Informality is his middle name. When he's not working, every Saturday and Sunday he'll be in the same outfit—his trusty polo shirt and comfortable old cotton wash slacks and his loafers—and then, on

Monday morning, he sends them to the laundry. He likes sweaters, too, and he probably looks better than the other two types in his sweaters. (Picture him in twill trousers, tasseled Gucci loafers without socks, Shetland sweater, button-down oxford shirt, and a fabric belt or simple leather belt.)

If the Casual and Down Home man were an automobile, he would be a Ford Mustang or a Porsche. If he were a painting, he would be anything, as long as it was by Norman Rockwell. If he were a tree, he would be a clump of white birch. If he were an animal, he would be a trained brown bear. If he were a time of day, he would be twilight.

There are a lot of Casual and Down Home men who have achieved success. Burt Reynolds is Casual and Down Home; so was Henry Fonda and are James Stewart, Dustin Hoffman, Richard Thomas, Alan Alda, Robert De Niro, Gary Collins, Kenny Rogers, and Jack Nicholson.

I see the Casual and Down Home man going to the movies on Saturday night, after having had a pizza and a beer. He's the one with the penny loafers, gray flannel slacks, blue blazer, and the blue-and-white striped shirt, open at the neck. His wife (or maybe it's just his girlfriend—it's hard to tell from this distance) is one of the Glamorous types, who, beneath all that glamour and glitter, really loves the casual life. They make a great-looking couple.

I see the Casual and Down Home man in the office, one of a dozen almost-identical-looking desks in a row. What sets this one apart is that he is better dressed than his colleagues. He has a very comfortable summer suit on, a good-looking camel color, coupled with a beige shirt and a tan tie with a slender yellow stripe. His boss looks at him with interest. Obviously, this Casual and Down Home man is going to be promoted; he has the option of being a Distinguished and Elegant man when we see him again.

I see the Casual and Down Home man on vacation, off in the mountains. He and his wife and the children have rented a mobile home, and it's parked in a glorious setting, with views of lofty mountains and splashing waterfalls. He's wearing jeans and a red-and-black-checked flannel shirt, boots, and a baseball cap with the insignia of the St. Louis Cardinals on it.

You can go through life as one type of Casual and Down Home man—the type that chooses his clothes more by a process of elimination than by any other method—or you can be one who chooses to be Casual and Down Home because he likes the look. To the latter group, being Casual and Down Home is as much an art as being Distinguished and Elegant is to that type of man, or being Sharp and Hunky is to that type.

The true Casual and Down Home man works hard to achieve the

proper look of comfortable informality. There is a continuity of the past in his clothing selections; understated fashion. Curiously, it is sometimes difficult for some men—particularly the Distinguished and Elegant man—to look as though they belong in casual, informal clothing. But the Casual and Down Home man fits into that costume easily and comfortably. It is a look that appears, on the surface, to be careless and indifferent, but often is acquired only through the most intentional of efforts.

The Casual and Down Home man appeals to all the various sorts of women because he is the marrying kind, whereas the Distinguished and Elegant man is either (a) already married, or (b) the type whose hobby is collecting mistresses, or (c) both of the above. And the Sharp and Hunky man is most likely to hold off making an alliance, marriage or otherwise. They have many oats to sow and many women to make happy.

If you are a Casual and Down Home man, you are a part of America's social majority. You look good, you look free! You feel good, too, and generally have a good life. After all, you probably have a lot of friends, a happy home life, and you feel good with yourself. Rejoice over who you are!

PART III

Taking an Honest Look at Yourself

4

The Self-Sabotagers

PEOPLE NOT IN TOUCH WITH THEIR BRILLIANCE!

We all start out in life pretty much the same. A few of us, the lucky ones, have a big head start, coming from wealth and power. Silver spoons and all that. A few of us, on the other side of the luck, have a terrible handicap, being born into grinding poverty. Cast-iron folks.

But most of us start out life somewhere in the middle, with virtually identical financial and social gifts—a normal body and mind, enough money to get by, and most importantly, the opportunity to improve, the chance to be somebody, the shot at the brass ring, the freedom to move into the fast lane if we want what it has to offer.

So why is it that only about 5 percent of us are actually moving in that happy, affluent place on the highway of life? Why are the other 95 percent of us dragging along, slowly and unsurely, almost making it— but not quite? Most of us settle for the ordinary when we have within us the power and opportunity to have the extraordinary.

I honestly don't know why it is, and I've given the matter serious consideration, but too many of us dress to lose, make ourselves up to lose, let our figures go to pot to lose. We seem to be trying to put our worst foot forward.

Too many of us are living just to get by.

Ninety-five percent of the people are sabotaging themselves. They may not know it and would probably hotly deny it, but it's true. They are doing everything humanly possible to ruin themselves, to cheat themselves out of the good things that life has to offer. They are committing social suicide.

Self-sabotage! It is the ruination of more lives than anything up to and including cholesterol.

And you are guilty of it when you deliberately choose to dress down and think small. You are dressing and thinking to lose. You are dressing for poverty, dressing to perpetuate that poverty.

How many clothing mistakes do you now have in your closet?

YOU SABOTAGE YOURSELF WITH YOUR CLOTHING IF YOU:
1. Buy cheap clothing.
2. Let yourself wear worn-out clothing.
3. Wear clothing made of fabrics that are unnatural and hence, tacky.

YOU SABOTAGE YOURSELF WITH YOUR CLOTHING IF YOU:
1. Look like a loser.
2. Look sloppy and / or slobby.
3. Project a one-dimensional image—sharp and cool, hick or hokey, preppy, whatever.
4. Dress too cutesy, too gadgety. Anything that is too anything.

YOU SABOTAGE YOURSELF WITH YOUR CLOTHING IF YOU:
1. Stress your bad physical features.
2. Minimize your good physical features.
3. Look your worst, instead of your best.

YOU SABOTAGE YOURSELF WITH YOUR CLOTHING IF YOU:
1. Send out a confusing message with the clothes you are wearing— your clothing must always have a positive, unified statement.
2. Improperly match and blend items in your wardrobe.
3. Wear inappropriate accessories, things that stand out garishly.
4. Dress without any flair, always dull and uninteresting, uninspired, always the same.
5. Wear cheap jewelry and cheap, cheap shoes.
6. Mix high-quality and low-quality pieces together. It makes the whole picture look low quality because those low-quality things necessarily stand out and overshadow all the rest.

YOU SABOTAGE YOURSELF WITH YOUR CLOTHING IF YOU:

1. Dress inappropriately—casual when you should be elegant, or vice versa.
2. Allow yourself to be escorted by, or to escort, someone who is dressed inappropriately.
3. Dress for the wrong age—if you are mature, don't tog yourself out like a youngster, and if you are youthful and fresh, don't dress like an old-timer.
4. Dress down, on purpose, so you think you are being very democratic, melting into the crowd, when on the contrary, you are simply demeaning yourself and everyone else.
5. Slavishly follow all the latest fashion trends, blindly and obediently and thoughtlessly. Some of them simply may not look good on you, and anyhow, if everybody looks the same, nobody looks.
6. Allow apparel clerks to sell you, rather than serve you.

Maybe there is something of the lemming in the human condition, the desire to commit mass suicide and so let's all go jump off a social cliff. But it saddens me when I see people who seem to be doing their level best to look their worst. And succeeding at it. What is a first-class person like you doing in a third-class outfit?

You won't find any other species, except man, who does that. I don't understand what makes us do it. In my Presentation Salon / Seminars, I ask people, "Why on earth would you wear a getup like that? A polyester jacket that looks like it was a leftover from a garage sale at a real garage, and pants that are two sizes too small and shoes that elephants would throw out."

Only the human animal tries to look bad. You never see a wave in Hawaii slowing down because it feels it is too overwhelming, or a lemon tree dropping its fruit because it feels it is too abundant, or a golden sunset in Tahiti dimming itself because it is too gorgeous. Only we humans have this odd tendency to negate our own brilliance.

In my Presentation Salon / Seminars, I speak very frankly to my clients. That may seem unduly harsh, but fully 95 percent of these people openly thank me later—because I got them to see themselves as the rest of the world sees them. I told them the truth about themselves and, often in this context, the truth is the only thing that works. And I never tell people what they are not ready to hear about the way they appear. They come to me to hear and see the truth, and I feel it is sometimes necessary to express that truth in plain, everyday language. We laugh a lot. In a later chapter, you will read how some of these people turn from looking like losers to impressive winners as a result of hearing others' reactions and doing something about it.

I ask them why they dress so badly, why they appear looking, it seems, as though they have gone out of their way to look unattractive. Is it some kind of self-denial, some desire to ruin themselves before they even get started? Is it a lack of taste? Or a lack of money? Or is it simply a lack of caring, a lack of interest in looking their best?`

I don't think there is any one specific answer, in most cases. With each individual, it is something different, or a combination of several different factors. And, of course, often they do not realize how badly they look.

It is that attitude of self-sabotage that you must get rid of first—right away!—if you want to move into the fast lane, and pursue some of the delicious objectives that are out there for the plucking.

You won't find winners hurting their own chances by sabotaging the way they look. *The word is out—sweet success is fun!*

People who don't dress to win—for whatever reason—are giving themselves no chance to ever win. They are sabotaging their lives as surely as if they punched their boss in the face or deliberately chewed a clove of garlic before kissing their date good night.

So, first of all, stop thinking cheap or poor or shoddy. Your wardrobe shouldn't be a disaster area. You shouldn't look as though you are auditioning to play first monster in a "Creature Feature."

POVERTY IS SELF-PERPETUATING. Look poor and you will be treated as poor. Act poor and you will stay poor. Maybe they'll give you a few food stamps, but that's hardly going to get you first-class treatment—caviar and champagne—at the best restaurants.

Poverty is self-perpetuating. And that is why I always suggest that people go out and buy one really great outfit instead of three outfits that are less-expensive compromises. You may spend the same amount of money for the one as for those three, but you will look *great* and, therefore, feel *great*, too. You will feel three times as great as you would had you bought those three tacky outfits.

You will shake the poverty monkey off your back, and it feels wonderful to walk about knowing you own the world—and looking every bit as good as you feel.

My position against poverty and what it does to the human spirit is not something I invented. It isn't a totally new philosophy. Back in ancient times, four hundred years before Christ was born, the great Greek historian, Thucydides, wrote:

"The real disgrace of poverty [is] not in owning to the fact but in declining to struggle against it."

I say don't struggle, follow your natural inclination to reach up and step out. The simple thought of wanting and then acting will move you into the fast lane. This is the first step in route to your ultimate triumph.

Never forget that others judge you on the basis of how you look. You can be as rich as a well-to-do Arabian sheik, but if you dress as though you were a $2.75-an-hour employee, you will be treated as though you were a $2.75-an-hour employee. Oh, I grant you there are a few exceptions, but very few—so why risk it, and why try to do it the hard way? Nobody knows how much money you have—or don't have—when they first meet you. Your bank balance doesn't flash on your forehead like a computer display.

So you can look like a soon-to-be millionaire, even without the income to match, and you will be treated like a millionaire. Or you can keep on sabotaging yourself and dress like a down-and-outer, and you will be treated like one. The choice is yours. It's really that simple.

What does it take to sabotage yourself?

It's very easy. Buy cheap clothing. Buy clothing made of unnatural fabrics—the artificials, the synthetics, the chemicals—and right away you radiate an aura of cheap and synthetic yourself. Unnatural fabrics do not drape properly or move gracefully with the body's natural flow. Unnatural fabrics do not take on nature's true colors well when they are dyed. Compare the colors of synthetics to the colors you get with cottons and wools and the other natural fabrics. The natural ones dye into colors that are true, vibrant, alive. In addition, unnatural fabrics do not feel good, they smell unpleasant when you perspire, and they don't allow fresh air to caress your body.

So the first way you can sabotage yourself is to buy garments made with synthetic fabrics. Right away, you are well on your way to killing off any chances of looking special.

Do you know that 100 percent polyester will not permit negative ions to enter the body, and they are vital to our survival? Do you know that in Kirlian photography, which is being extensively used in Russian research, an aura cannot be photographed through polyester fabrics? And—the following observation may not be for family consumption—people who wear polyester don't smell so good. In fact, the armpit of a polyester wearer smells rather like a sewer in summer.

Thomas E. Barnes, who is manager of men's-apparel marketing for Cotton, Inc., has written this, with which I fully concur:

"Synthetic fibers, slung out of an oil barrel, clamor for our attention in the marketplace with claims of naturalness; yet, cotton can be imitated but never duplicated. Mother Nature wasn't fooled for an instant."

A second way of self-sabotage is to buy clothing that doesn't fit properly. Again, such garments are almost always cheap because cheap is inclined to be ill-fitting. When something is billed as a bargain, it is almost always guaranteed to fit poorly.

Cheap will probably have imperfections, too. Perhaps those imperfections will be in some small thing, but it doesn't take much to sabotage yourself. Maybe you will be the only person aware of that imperfection, that slightly bad fit, that nearly invisible miss-stitch. It may all be miniscule, but miniscule is significant. Nobody else may notice but *you will know,* and you will therefore never feel absolutely comfortable and confident wearing that garment. You will always know that you are wearing something that is a little bit off—and self-confidence can banish with that realization. Doing what is right keeps your consciousness satisfied—this builds self-confidence.

Frequently, of course, the fit is bad enough so that everybody else—the whole world!—knows it, too. A jacket may be too tight, too confining—so not only do *you* feel awkward and uncomfortable wearing it, but everybody else is aware of creases and wrinkles and bulges whenever you turn or stand or sit or whatever.

Cheap garments are necessarily made cheaply. Buttons pop off—generally at inopportune or embarrassing moments. (Even when they are on, they look tacky, and often simply replacing cheap buttons with fine bone, horn, or leather buttons can work wonders with a cheap garment.) Hems loosen and sag, and for a lady, there is no better way to sabotage yourself than to walk into some important function—a heavy date, a job interview, an essential meeting—with the hem of your dress drooping sadly. The garment may also pop open at some location that is even more embarrassing.

When you buy cheap, you get cheap. Colors are off. Styles are tacky. Cheap shoes squeak and groan, besides generally feeling awful because they don't breathe and so your feet become hot and cry out for mercy. Heels snap off. Leather is poorly treated and processed. Garments come back from the dry cleaner or the laundry with their shape gone and their seams split. Often they are beyond redemption, and they are put back in your closet and you chalk it up as another mistake.

Wear things like that and everybody takes one look at you and *knows* you are not tuned in. Asleep. One of life's also-rans.

The best way to know what to wear at any occasion is to find out what the hosts will be wearing; where will the event be held; who are the people attending; and what is the purpose of the event.

Even if you buy fairly good clothing, you can still be sabotaging yourself in many ways. Taste is the killer. Bad taste has sabotaged more people than a sale at the local Army and Navy Surplus Store. By taste I mean you know precisely how to convey to others what you are about. The good Lord makes only a small percentage of fine athletes, artists, dancers, and scientists—what makes people think that He made everyone tasteful?

Note how many homes you have been in that you feel are not tastefully done. You know for certain, from your own feelings in those houses, the uncomfortableness of being in an environment that doesn't please. This is the same when looking at people who are tastelessly attired. You just know and feel it. It is no shame to be considered tasteless—we are not born with taste, we choose to develop a "tasteful" appreciation of things. And then we develop and fine hone it. By being around tasteful people, places, and the milieu of tastefulness, we learn to make it our own. It is your deliberate choice to be tasteful, your concentrated passion to know, that directs you to the current mode of what is tasteful now.

Every one hundred years a small percentage of men and women are born who determine what is tasteful. They design our automobiles, fabrics, fine homes, and office buildings.

One way to demonstrate taste is to avoid what I call "matchy-poo." It may look smart and "nice" to have everything match—tie, belt, handkerchief, scarf—but you wind up looking as though you're in some kind of uniform. Instead of having your belt and shoes match, try having them blend. For example, instead of having burgundy shoes, burgundy belt, and burgundy tie, wear a black belt to reduce the predictability. Predictability in clothing isn't bad, but it is boring—it's passé. Instead of having the tie and the pocket square made of the exact same material, try having them made out of materials with colors that complement each other. If the tie is burgundy with a small print, make the pocket handkerchief a plain burgundy or a silver-gray. Instead of having your scarf and jacket fabricated from the identical material, try having them in colors that form an interesting counterpoint, like highlighting a plum, burgundy, and brown-tweed jacket with a bright, canary-yellow scarf just peeking out. Matchy-poo is easily overdone.

You can sabotage yourself in ways that only you know, too. Suppose for example, you go out and buy a batch of bargain handkerchiefs. They are made, necessarily, from fabrics that are harsh and even though people around you are unaware of it, you know it. So you will use your cheap hankies and, every time you use one, you will feel their cheapness. And you will almost certainly be telling yourself, sneeze by sneeze and blow by blow, that you are settling for less because you are allowing yourself to use cheap things. The same type of self-sabotage is apparent when you buy yourself cheap underwear—itchy, crawly, loose threads that make you squirm. The world may not know how cheap you are—but you know, and that is bound to affect your psyche.

That's self-sabotage. And it can work against you in two ways—first, people who see you in cheap, shoddy, bargain-basement duds will leap to the conclusion that you, too, are a bargain-basement "personality"; and, equally important, you will feel second-rate when you wear second-rate clothing. You take a step backward—you shrink some. And, believe me, that shows. *Your clothing must be equal to the quality of your life.* The bargain is not what you pay; it is what you receive.

I realize that a great many people do most of their shopping by going to stores when there is a sale going on. Only in super-fine clothing stores are you snapping up a bargain. Buy ferociously if the merchandise warrants it.

Nine out of ten times, sales in department stores and other shops are held for one of these reasons:

1. To move merchandise that has arrived late and may go out of fashion if not worn right away.
2. To generate more merchandise flow and store activity (more people come in).
3. To get rid of unpopular clothing that hasn't moved for the last six months or so. (If no one has wanted the item for six months, there must be a reason. Why should you buy it?)
4. When they have an overstock of a quality item that sells well. (This is an ideal time to take advantage of a great buy.)
5. When the buyer misjudges how well the customers will accept an item.

I feel that sales, in anything but the best of shops, don't save you anything. I believe that the constant pursuit of sales diminishes your prosperity consciousness. Please remember that your time can be used much more profitably by multiplying the quality of your products or service, which will in turn greatly increase your finances.

When you buy something at the majority of sales, you really wind up buying something that is a flop and looks it (nobody wanted it, did they?), and chances are you will look like a flop in it. And, worse, in your heart of hearts, you know all that already. So all the sale has done is to sabotage you a little more than you already were.

Instead of asking what something costs, ask what you have gotten for your money.

Most bargain shoppers—most self-sabotagers—wind up with a wardrobe that is full of items that have no relationship to each other. And so it is virtually impossible for these people to put together a coordinated, balanced, consistent outfit. They end up with a confused appearance, and anybody who sees them picks up on that confusion. Perhaps the people who meet them cannot put their fingers on just what it is about them that looks odd and peculiar, but it is simply that basic fact—these unfortunate self-sabotagers have put together their outfits from a little of this and a little of that and have come up with a lot of nothing. When you add zero and zero together, you never get anywhere. Don't put "fillers" in your closet.

Your clothes always make a statement. That statement should speak in a forthright, coordinated way. It shouldn't be confused and mixed up.

Nor should that statement be negative. If it is, you will be telling the world, "I don't care about my clothes." And when you say that, by extension you are really saying, "I don't care what you think of me—I don't care what anybody thinks of me." People who meet you quickly catch that message. And if that is the message you are sending out, you can't expect to get immediate support, because winners obviously care about how others see them and think about them. *Men and women who are well-dressed are being tremendously generous of themselves.* Men and women who are not well-dressed are holding themselves down.

Remember, *you can't dress in a neutral way.* There is no way you can put on clothing and not be saying something about yourself with that clothing. Even if you wear gray from head to toe, you are saying something about yourself. Everything you put on your back makes a statement of some kind—good, bad, or indifferent. You want to make that statement a good one.

Whatever you wear on the outside is a signpost to what you are on the inside. And so if your clothing is giving the world a false impression of the true you, then you are not being fair and honest with yourself. You are not giving yourself a chance.

Self-sabotage!

Let's get down to specifics. There are many ways in which a human being sabotages himself (or herself) by the way in which he (or she) selects what to wear. I am going to point some of these out to you, one by one, and let you be the judge of whether or not you are guilty of these blunders. See if you recognize any of these in yourself because these are the things that can keep you mired in mediocrity and prevent you from moving forward toward that richer life.

1. CHEAPNESS

I said it before and I say it here, and I'll probably say it again—perhaps the most frequently committed error by those determined to sabotage themselves is to buy cheap clothing. If you settle for anything less than the very best, then you are buying cheap (some people call this being "thrifty"). I have found that even people who can afford to buy the best often settle for far less—people who can easily stand the cost of a $500 business suit or a $750 evening gown will, instead, think they are smart to buy two $250 suits or three $250 gowns. But when they do that they are out-smarting nobody but themselves. *If you can buy what you really want today, you will be spared the time and effort and cost of replacing it with something better tomorrow.*

Winners—and we'll look at the personality and buying habits of winners in a later chapter—don't do that. Winners know that something is inexpensive because it is *cheap*, and cheap means exactly what it says—it means it is made of cheap materials, fabricated in a cheap and shoddy manner. Cliché Number 694—"You get what you pay for"—it is trite but true. And when you buy cheap, you get cheap and you look cheap, and thus, you are sabotaging yourself in the extreme.

A corollary to that is what I call Wardrobe Frugality. Maybe you buy the best, but you don't buy enough of it, and you—many of you— are particularly stingy when it comes to accessories. The same old belt, day after day. The same shoes. Or hat. You may have a half-dozen really good outfits, but if you wear the same accessories repeatedly, you will begin to feel that way too.

Of course, accessories must and should do double duty and even triple duty, but don't force them to work every day. Accessories, I have found, are powerful. *A woman's jewelry is her signature; a man's tie is his signature.* But if a signature is signed too often, it tends to become illegible, and if you wear the same accessories too often, you become bored with them and you begin to look boring, too.

2. DRESSING INAPPROPRIATELY

You see it often. Good-looking people dressed in something totally inappropriate for the occasion. I cannot understand what goes on in their heads, to go to a fancy cocktail party or elegant dinner in sports clothes, or to go to a casual affair in something better suited to the evening. Why? It only says that (A) they don't know any better, or (B) they don't care. In either case, they are sabotaging themselves, ruining their chance at success at that party or affair and for anything that might come out of the associations they could make at those occasions.

3. BEING OVERDRESSED

The person who is "dressed to kill" frequently winds up killing. But he/she kills himself/herself and his/her chances. *Your clothes should not speak louder than you do.* If they do, you are overdressed. If you are overdressed, you are sabotaging yourself because being over-dressed is a type of dressing inappropriately.

Avoid going to a party or an affair or a business meeting or anywhere where you are liable to meet anyone while you are wearing clothing that is overpowering. Too much makeup for a woman is in that same class of looking overpowering. Too much jewelry. Too much fabric; too much flow in the clothing. Too much fashion. Overaccessorizing—accessories are very powerful and you should keep them to a minimum. For men, one of my pet overdressing peeves is the too-free use of the monogram—initials on shirt pockets, initials on suit jacket sleeves, initials on handkerchiefs, initials on initials. Can't these people remember their names? A little monogramming goes a long way; too much of it is overdressing, and overdressing makes you look a little on the ridiculous side. One tip if you are monogram mad: keep the monogram the same color as the shirt or blouse fabric. At least that way it is tasteful.

Another form of overdressing is to wear clothing that is predictable. For example, being a *clone* of everyone else—all lawyers look like all other lawyers. Clothing should be a reflection of you and your own particular taste, style, appropriateness, and ability to be your own person. Anything else is ordinary and predictable and, hence, another form of self-sabotage.

You have to consider what being overdressed does to the people you encounter. Just think of how you would look to a job interviewer if you came in to apply for a position and were hopelessly overdressed. The first thought that might flash into that interviewer's mind could be: "Hmmm. I wonder whether this person will fit in here?"

Avoid any look that can put those ideas in the minds of the people who you want to impress. No-nonsense dressing is what gets you employment votes. So, when in doubt—leave it out. One thing I *always* suggest that men leave out is the pocket handkerchief in their business outfits—unless you feel comfortable with it. I always suggest that women take particular care to select the just-right handbag—one that conveys the message that she is a woman of quality, class, and importance, that here is someone who is to be respected. It's a matter of letting your grooming and your clothing contribute to who you are, but not dominate you.

4. BEING UNDERDRESSED

This is just as bad, maybe even worse. Nothing makes a person feel as uncomfortable as showing up somewhere and finding that everybody else is dressed to the nines and you are only dressed to the sixes or sevens. Suppose you watched the President of the United States being inaugurated and he was wearing a tweed sports jacket and a turtleneck sweater. Definitely underdressed for the occasion, and in that very act of underdressing he would immediately arouse a sense of non-confidence. If you are underdressed, the people you meet will instantly feel uncomfortable around you.

The sixties left us with a legacy of being more informal as a nation than we had ever been before. Sometimes informality is marvelous, but there are times when it can be offensive. There are times and places for everything, and certainly informality has its time and place—but it also has its non-time and non-place. Be careful how and when you choose to be informal—the wrong time and place can spoil your chances.

Many people go out of their way to be informal at occasions where informality simply does not belong. The notion that informality can be universal is an idea whose time has passed. I've seen men at theater first nights wearing open shirts and casual pants and hiking boots. They look totally out of place. I've seen women at fashionable affairs in slacks and boots, and they look dreadful. Always add to any social situation you find yourself in by your appropriateness and watch the good feelings you engender in the people you meet. *Men and women who are committed to beauty are being tremendously generous of themselves.*

I've seen couples attempting to get a table at a fancy restaurant trying to look "hip" in denims and chambray. They look ridiculous. They also don't get a table for an hour or two. At other times and other places, they would have been perfectly attired. But they were underdressed for that particular time, that particular place.

If you are underdressed, you will almost always sense it, and you will feel incomplete and inadequate!

Did you know that you can be underdressed for the simple act of going out to shop? It's true. Many of life's non-savvies make that common, self-sabotaging mistake. If a man goes into a fine store to buy a fine suit and he's wearing an old sports shirt and faded, overworn slacks, he will look out of place, and consequently, the service he gets will be the bare minimum. If a woman goes out to buy an elegant evening gown and she's wearing flats and no makeup, nobody is really going to go all out to wait on her.

When you are underdressed, you are saying to the world, "I really don't know what I'm doing here. I'm confused about who I am and what I am." Or, perhaps, even worse, you are saying, "I'm too lazy to dress properly—and I really don't give a damn how I look to mere shopkeepers." You may have bought the lie that if you look good you have misplaced your life's priorities and values. But the absolute opposite is the truth—*ugliness is an illusion, and being beautiful is reality. Your kingdom is not so great that you don't have time enough to groom.*

5. BEING INCOMPLETELY DRESSED

Dressing incompletely is a variation on the underdressed theme. Dressing incompletely is omitting little things, things you have perhaps forgotten or consider unimportant or feel that nobody will notice anyhow. Collar stays left out. Necktie not quite tight enough. Worn-down heels. Dirty handkerchiefs. Shirts that need pressing.

But, believe me, the world does notice those little things. People pick up on the least detail, and if you are incompletely dressed, the others will notice.

I'm talking about things like a man not wearing a belt, even though his slacks have very visible belt loops (of course, some trousers—jeans, particularly—are designed to be beltless and that's fine), or a woman who is all spiffed out but arrives at an affair without the right perfume or without an outer wrap that enhances the total statement, or when a woman's coiffure does not reflect a professional stylist's attention. That woman looks older than she has to when her hair is not as alluring as it can be.

You are sabotaging yourself when you commit one of those omissions because you are advertising your total lack of caring. Or your lack of consciousness of making an impact. Or your lack of respect for the people you will be coming in contact with. Those people may not be consciously aware of it, but they will resent your carelessness and therefore resent you, and right away you will have a couple of strikes against you. Self-sabotage again.

6. MIXING FASHION STYLES

This is another way in which you can be sabotaging yourself. It's jarring to the people you meet—although, again, they may not be conscious of what it is you are doing that is jarring to them—and so they will view you with some discomfort.

Suppose you are wearing your best suit, a handsome Brioni creation, but on your feet are a pair of penny loafers. They don't belong together. The suit says one thing; the shoes say another.

It's like putting mustard on top of a banana split.

For the ladies, it could be showing up in a lush, flowing chiffon gown—and wearing a pair of stacked-heeled wedgies.

Now it's catsup on that banana split.

When you mix two distinct, opposing styles, the total effect is a letdown. You ruin yourself and your chances.

Self-sabotage, you see, is doing anything that second-rates you, harms you, makes those you meet think less of you, puts you out of the running.

7. OVERUSE OF COLOR

Here is another common type of self-sabotage. Color is a tricky thing to handle. It's like alcohol—one or two drinks make you feel good and, therefore, some people conclude that a dozen drinks will make them feel even better. It doesn't work that way, of course, and people who think that if a little color helps, then a lot of color will help even more, are a little off base. It doesn't. The point of diminishing returns sets in very quickly in the area of using color in personal attire. In that respect, color is something like perfume—never use too much.

You can sabotage yourself, too, by using too many different colors at one time. Or colors that are too bright. Or too much of one color. Or a color that doesn't flatter your complexion. So take it very easy with color—a little goes a long way.

8. MISUSE OF FABRICS

It is also true that fabrics have to be used carefully, as well. If you're out in the heart of summer in heavy wool, not only will you suffer by being too warm, but you will look foolish—and that's the height of self-sabotage.

Be careful about mixing fabrics that are texturally incompatible. Wool and linen don't enjoy each other's company, for example. A 100 percent wool item doesn't mix well with a 100 percent polyester piece either. There are certain fabrics that are winter fabrics, certain summer fabrics, certain daytime fabrics, certain evening fabrics, certain elegant-affair fabrics, certain casual-affair fabrics. Wearing the wrong one at the wrong time looks odd, and that's another way in which people frequently sabotage themselves. We'll discuss fabric choices in a later chapter.

9. WEARING THE WRONG SIZE

Don't let your ego get in the way of your good sense. Sure, it's nice to be able to tell the clerk that you're a size 10—when size 12 feels much better on you. And it makes your ego feel marvelous when you can squeeze into that size 10, or when you hold in your stomach to get on a size 32 slack, when you know size 34 would allow you to breathe. But consider how you *look* in that wrong size—terrible. There are wrinkles where there shouldn't be any, bulges where there shouldn't be, maybe even split seams where there shouldn't be.

In this same area there are self-sabotaging errors committed by people choosing patterns that are wrong for their construction. The obvious example is the overweight man or woman in big plaids, gigantic checks, or horizontal stripes. Or, just as obvious, the tall, skinny person overemphasizing his or her skinniness with vertical stripes or with clothing cut too short or too tight.

I would also caution musclemen and busty women against wearing too-tight clothing—short-sleeved shirts or grapeskin-tight pants, which emphasize each and every muscle and curve. It's wonderful to be proud of your body, but too much equipment showing may repel some, as well as attract others. Do what works!

So be very careful in your selection of garments that they complement your shape, size, and age, rather than emphasizing any weak point you have. *Proper fit and contour bring an advantage to your strongest physical features.*

10. ACCOMPANY AN IMPROPERLY ATTIRED ESCORT

Sometimes, of course, you cannot regulate what your escort will be wearing. But, in the case of husbands and wives, or live-in partners, it is possible for two people to consider how they look side by side. And, indeed, they should consider that. A very subtle form of self-sabotage can be committed by two people who are dressed in conspicuously mismatched styles.

I suppose the most common illustration of this horror is the chic wife clinging to the arm of her tackily dressed husband. There they are, at some fancy restaurant or intimate little dinner party, and she is dressed to the teeth while he is dressed to the feet. She is all elegance: he is in his double-knit leisure suit, scuffed loafers, and a shirt with a 4½-inch collar flapping out.

But I have also seen the reverse—the man, dressed neatly and elegantly, and his date or wife in her displaced person, artsy-craftsy outfit, complete with the scarf and long gypsy earrings.

Opposites may attract, but they look strange when seen together. Remember that your escort—be it mate or friend or whatever—is as much a fashion accessory as your belt. Maybe more. So try not to sabotage yourself by appearing with somebody who is dressed in such a contrasting style to your own that everybody does an amused double take. You may be the innocent victim of self-sabotage that way.

11. DRESSING TOO YOUNG

This applies primarily to people who are over forty years of age. Mature people should dress with their age in mind. I don't like to see middle-aged people cavorting around as though they were in their mid-twenties. It looks out of place. I'm not saying you should dampen your youthful vitality and exuberance. However, a man in his forties who still sports a Beatles-style pageboy bob and wears bright blue sneakers and stove-pipe jeans that are too tight for his bulgy middle, looks like a misfit. Even in a casual setting, he looks out of place. And, similarly, that matronly mama of three teenagers who goes strutting around in oversexy, too fashionable, ultrayouthful clothing isn't fooling anyone but herself. All that would not be so bad if the "old folks" were going to some '50s masquerade party, but for casual wear today it's self-sabotage in a textbook example. It makes them look foolish, and looking foolish is no way for anyone to build respect and esteem. *Don't apologize for who you are.*

12. RETRO-DRESSING

Retro-dressing is my expression for wearing something that is actually a period costume. Anything from an earlier era qualifies as a period costume—anything from a zoot suit to a bobby-sox getup of the '50s. You might not think anyone today would wear that sort of thing, except to a masquerade party, but it is amazing how many people have the idea that period costumes are smashingly fashionable. They're not. They attract attention all right, but that attention is almost always negative, not positive. People look at you with curiosity, but it's the "Gee, look at that creepo" kind of curiosity. And that is certainly self-sabotaging.

13. WEARING WORN-OUT CLOTHING

Loyalty is a wonderful quality in a human being, but don't become so attached to an article of clothing that you keep it beyond its normal life-span. Worn-out clothing disempowers you and, thus, sabotages you. (Obviously the same is true of wearing garments that are soiled and / or wrinkled; that goes without saying, so I shouldn't even bother to say it.) Old, scruffed, rundown shoes may be the most comfortable things God has ever put on earth, but they tell people that you are poverty stricken. Maybe you aren't poor, but old, beat-up shoes tell the world you are.

Remember, people you meet don't know anything about you, except from your appearance. Dress poor, even if you're not, and strangers will immediately stick you in the category labeled "Poor." So, even though it breaks your good and loyal heart to part with those old, familiar, and comfortable garments, part with them the minute they begin to look old and worn out, unless you use them for gardening, housecleaning, or relaxing at home.

14. WEARING THE WRONG ACCESSORIES

You are a total package as you stand there. And the accessories you wear are as important to the looks of that package as the main garment—just as the ribbon is as important to the looks of a Christmas package as is the paper. If the accessories you have on or are carrying are wrong for the garment, then the overall effect is jarring and wrong. And, hence, self-sabotaging.

Maybe it's a lady in her very casual clothes, wearing her formal jewelry. (Bang, Crash, Jarring.) Or the opposite, the lady in her finest evening gown with cheap glass beads and tin jewelry. (Smash, Boff, Jarring.)

A woman executive may have to carry various papers and documents, just like her male counterpart, but she looks wrong toting a boxy, male-style attaché case—she should get something feminine. That doesn't detract from her efficiency, it merely enhances her feminine power.

Or, putting the shoe on the other sex, consider the man in his best blue business suit, carrying his wife's orange-and-green-plaid umbrella on a rainy day. A total jar. Spend a few bucks and get a genuine man's umbrella.

Your accessories are as much a part of the total you as your suit or your dress. Choose them with similar care.

15. DRESSING TO PLEASE SOMEBODY ELSE

When you were a little boy, or a little girl, you would put on exactly what Mother told you to put on. And for some years after, when you would pick your own clothes out of the closet, you would put on what you felt your mother liked and approved of. Mother knew best.

But you're hitting the "high time" now so it's high time that you dressed to please yourself and not somebody else.

People in the winner's circle, people traveling in the fast lane, don't leave their clothing decisions to anybody else. Nor do they dress to please anybody else. They *know* what looks best on them, and consequently they dress to please their image in the mirror. They dress to please themselves and in so doing please others.

I have told you that I consider a man's signature to be his necktie. When he lets a woman, no matter how well-intentioned, pick out his necktie, he is abdicating his own rights. He is letting someone else sign his signature, and therefore that signature has become a counterfeit. I have also found that many women shoppers tend to look at men's neckties the way they look at their own scarves, and the only similarity they see between a tie and a scarf is that they are both worn around the neck. You are one of the blessed if your female counterpart has the knack of picking out that perfect tie for you every time.

Another way people sometimes dress to please somebody else—and lose in the process—is when they are given something as a gift. You probably wear it, like a nice person, no matter how bad it looks on you, rather than hurting the feelings of whoever it was who gave it to you. There are, however, times when you have to be smart and think of yourself first, and this is one of those times—dress to please yourself, because *you* are the one who will be hurt if you look bad.

16. BUYING CLOTHING LIKE YOU BUY FAST FOOD

If you're in a great hurry, maybe it doesn't hurt once in a while to gobble your lunch at a fast-food counter. Lunch is one thing, but clothing is something quite different. Clothing isn't a quick meal, and there are no anti-acid pills you can chew if the outfit you have bought in a rush gives you sartorial indigestion. Your clothing isn't just sustenance for a few hours, it is something you know will last you for some time.

But consider the chap who shops at a discount chain store, buying his clothing packaged in neat little sets—shirt, tie, socks, all done up in a dandy little cardboard-and-plastic box, or slacks, jacket (reversible) and sweater in one cozy set (three pieces you can wear nine ways!). The poor guy who gets his clothing as he buys his hamburger-fries-and-Coke lunch will pretty quickly realize that he has a case of wardrobe heartburn.

17. DRESSING POOR-CHIC

There are still some people among us who feel that in order to sympathize with the downtrodden, the poor, the hungry, the disadvantaged, it is necessary to dress shabbily.

Nonsense. Our heart goes out to the unfortunates of this world, and our checkbooks go out to them too. But we're not helping them one bit if we look as needy as they do. They may think that they can't help how they look; we know we can expand how we look. We can't afford to not look our best, and it would be total hypocrisy on our part to dress shabbily.

I know there are some millionaire eccentrics who love to walk around in clothing that bums would discard. But you have to be a genuine millionaire to get away with that. (More of them and their odd habits later.) But if you are still playing the game, still trying to get somewhere in this scrambling, challenging world, you had better look your best at all times. If you look your worst—even with the purest of motives—you will be treated the same as the poorest get treated. And that doesn't help anyone. So save your sympathy for where it will do some good, and that is by pitching in and donating, not by imitating how down-and-outers dress. Remember, the poor would probably prefer to look rich if they could afford to. You *can* afford to!

18. DON'T LET CLERKS DO ALL YOUR SHOPPING FOR YOU

There are great actresses and mediocre actresses, skilled doctors and unskilled doctors, talented cowboys and untalented cowboys—and there are informed clerks in clothing stores and uninformed clerks in clothing stores. It is an act of supreme self-sabotage if you let an uninformed clerk (especially in a tacky store) convince you what you should or should not buy. If you have total confidence in a salesclerk and are shopping in a genuinely top-of-the-line store, that's a different situation. But it is inviting disaster to place yourself completely in the hands of an unknowing or incompetent. (Later, in the chapter on shopping, I'll give you some hints on how to tell the competent clerks from the incompetents.)

Remember, in almost all cases, clerks in clothing stores operate on a commission basis. They get a 2 to 8 percent commission (generally) on whatever they sell. This doesn't mean they are solely interested in their "commission." I have observed hundreds of really interested and caring salesclerks who are as much interested in having you leave the store feeling great and looking topnotch as they are in earning their commission.

Again, let me stress that there are many clerks who have the intelligence to know that if you are happy, you'll come back some other time, so they place your interests paramount. However, we have all encountered the others, the shortsighted ones who are looking out exclusively for making today's fast dollar and couldn't care less about developing tomorrow's return customer.

These hard sells can do you a disservice. They can push you a little hard into buying something not totally complimentary. They can push you into buying merchandise that doesn't belong on you and seriously is contrary to the image you want to convey. They may push you into buying something they personally like even though it might be all wrong for you.

Even well-intentioned clerks are human, and they have their own taste. They can develop a sudden case of tunnel vision regarding their suggestions and brook no opposing viewpoint.

If you really have no confidence in your own taste, then take a friend with you, rather than hope that you'll run across a clerk with great taste. Or go to one of the great stores, which I will list for you in that upcoming chapter on shopping. There are a number of top stores where you can have total confidence in the sales people. But in the run-of-the-Main-Street store, beware. Trust a clerk in one of those places and you might as well cut your own social throat. If they really are comprehensive and have fine taste, those clerks would be working in one of the better-quality establishments.

Self-sabotage!

As you have seen, there are a myriad of ways you can be committing it; many ways in which you are going out of your way to look your worst.

The first thing to do, then, on your way to the fast lane, is to stop all those acts of self-sabotage. Cease and desist the act of hurting yourself. Start dressing attractively all the time. And begin it now. When people are committed to anything, providence steps in. Good luck and miracles start happening.

And the place to begin is in your closet.

5

Surveying Your Closet

GREEN-BAGGING ALL THOSE DISASTERS!

Just suppose the smoke alarm in your home or apartment went off right now as you are reading this book. For the sake of argument, let's say that you don't panic, but immediately run and check to make sure your family is safe and out of the building, and then you call the fire department. Now you have a few minutes to save your most precious belongings. You grab the photo album, the cat, the bundle of love letters and head for your closet.

Is there anything in there that is worth rescuing before the flames devour the whole place? Or is it all old and tired and useless stuff that you wear just to stay modest and keep out of the cold?

In this chapter, I am going to rummage through your closet with you, and see what there is that's worth saving. I'm going to be pretty ruthless—Panté the Warrior—because to me the foundation of the whole idea of moving into the fast lane is you *must look your best at all times*. And to do that you have to get rid of everything that doesn't work for you. If your closet is cluttered with clothing that makes you look your worst, then obviously you cannot look your best. So the time has come—assuming that you are serious about wanting to change your life—to start throwing all those clothes away that are holding you back. It always interests and fascinates me to see what people are wearing in supermarkets. I can't just look. I carefully study and am amused!

Green-bag it all!

I mean that, quite literally. Get yourself a fresh supply of those big green plastic trash bags—and begin stuffing all that sorry, tired clothing into bag after bag. Eventually, we are going to stock your closet with new things, things that will make you look your best, but to make room for the new, we must first throw away the old and the useless.

Green-bag it all. Throw it away. Get rid of it.

But before we do that, I want you to play a game with me. I use this game at my Presentation Salon/Seminars, and I call it the Robert Panté Body, Wardrobe, and Grooming Game. The object of the game is to make you aware of where you stand as far as how you look, and particularly how valuable a contribution your closet and its contents make to that question of how you look. A closet is a living, vital thing and always in the process of becoming.

I am going to ask you ten questions. I want you to answer them, as honestly as you can, with a simple "Yes" or "No."

Here are the ten questions:

1. Do you feel that you are always dressed appropriately?
2. Do you dress each day as though your life depended on it?
3. Do you feel comfortable around people who are well-dressed?
4. Is the daily act of getting dressed a pleasure?
5. Do you use your wardrobe and your grooming as a tool to get what you want?
6. Is every item hanging in your closet something that makes you feel terrific and attractive?
7. Are you attracting everything you want in the areas of sex, money, and power?
8. Is your physical presentation working for you in attaining your goals?
9. Do you feel that you have put out 100 percent in every area of your presentation? Hair? Makeup? Grooming? Body? Clothing?
10. Are you willing to look sexy, wealthy, and powerful?

Those are my ten questions. How many "No" answers were you forced to give? And please be honest—if you lie about this, you are only fooling yourself.

If you did not have a single "No" answer, then give this book to a friend—you are already a winner and a member of the fast-lane set.

One "No"—you are definitely success material.

Two "Nos"—you have an edge on the competition.

Three "Nos"—you are on the right track.

Four "Nos"—you are taking too many shortcuts.

Five "Nos"—you are just getting by.

Six "Nos"—you are not quite making it.

Seven "Nos"—you are in the slow lane.

Eight "Nos"—you are not even on the highway yet.

Nine "Nos"—you are not even in the car.

Ten "Nos"—if you're a man, put on a pair of high boots, your shorts, then cover yourself with a raincoat, and make a beeline to your nearest haberdasher. If you're a woman, it's time to put on your high-heeled shoes, a good pair of panty hose, wrap yourself in your warmest outer coat, and get to the closest quality clothing store.

As I said, the key to your presentation is your *attitude. Your attitude determines your altitude.* In most cases, what you wear is the basis for much of your attitude. Your closet, therefore, is the front line in the war to change your attitude and move you from the losers' column to the winners'.

Thus, it is in your closet—and, additionally, in the drawers of your bureau and wherever else you happen to stash your clothing—that, together, we are going to start building that new, magical you.

So let's go to work.

Caution is the retardant—your boldness is not presumptuous when you're dealing with the facts!

Start with the big things—your suits or dresses. Count them. Let's say you have twenty things that qualify as major items of apparel. I've found twenty is about average for women, ten to fifteen for men.

Next—being superhonest with yourself—count them again. But, this time, just count the ones that really *work for you.* By working for you, I mean those suits or dresses that fit perfectly, that are contemporary and stylish, that make you look smashing, that would be appropriate for the kind of life-style you want to live. That make you credible, believable, trustworthy, and appealing. That, in essence, make you look well-dressed. *And a well-dressed person, I believe, is one whose clothing takes him or her through the spectrum of a day's experiences appropriately—a week's experiences, a month's experiences.*

Now is your hour of destiny—closet division. Count those major items of apparel you have that make you look and feel like a well-dressed person. What did you come up with out of the ten to twenty you started with? Four perhaps? Five? I think you are probably being generous but, O.K., let's say that you have five outfits that you feel really and truly *work for you.*

Keep those five. But the others are holding you back. Those others have no place in your life anymore—that new life you are going to create. Those other outfits are clothing for your dark and unsuccessful past, dreary and unattractive, not clothing for your bright and successful future. Eliminate them!

There's no place for sentiment in a closet. A closet isn't a hope chest or a museum. It is, or it should be, a highly functional place, an adjunct to your life. It should be full of useful, practical, helpful items of clothing.

So dig into that closet with ferocious barbarity. Which are the pieces—suits, slacks, dresses, blouses, shirts, ties, scarves—that you never wear? Are they uncomfortable? Too heavy or too light? Do they look inexpensive? How about that suit, the one with the wide, boxy shoulders and the too-wide lapels? Or that dark green corduroy jacket left over from your college days? You haven't worn either of them in ten years, so why keep them hanging around? How about that tartan-plaid skirt that is pilling from waist to hem? Or that knit dress that looks too matronly on you and adds inches to your figure? They may bring back lovely memories, but save memories for your scrapbook and keep your closet full of the future, not the past.

Into a green bag with them!

At this point, I suggest that you start making out a list of what you would like as replacements for those ex-clothes of yours. Chances are you won't be able to afford to get everything on your list immediately. So start out by arranging that list in the order of need; a priority system of apparel. Start with the things you feel are most essential, most immediate in your scheme of things, and work your way down to those items you would like, but can realistically wait for a bit.

Next step: the other things in your closet—the casual clothes— slacks and sport jackets for the man, slacks and casual jackets for the woman—and coats and raincoats and whatever else is crammed in there. Follow the same procedure that you used for the major items.

Ask yourself how many of those things still *work for you?* How many of them are *now*, fresh, smashing? O.K.—those you keep. But the ones that fail to pass the test are goners. Show them no mercy. Off with their heads. Green-bag them!

I can hear somebody out there moaning, "If I throw all those things away, I won't have anything left to wear." That could be true—but I want to tell you this: Better you go out wearing a pair of shoes, socks or panty hose, and a raincoat than in some of that stuff we just threw away. Your life will soar, believe me, with those clothes out of your life. Make a clean break of it, as you would with a relationship that has gone sour.

And keep adding things to that list of what you are going to get as replacements—what you need to replace those gone and forgotten duds!

Move on to your other belongings.

Shirts. Blouses.

Keep the right clothes—the ones that *work for you*. The rest? Deep six them. Green-bag them!

More notations on your replacement list, things you need now, followed by things that you hope to add as time goes by.

On we go to your socks, stockings, shoes, underwear, ties, belts, scarves. Everything. And, with all of it, apply the same rule—if it works, keep it; if it doesn't, out with it!

I want you to go through your clothing, everything you own, piece by piece, item by item, shoe by shoe, bra by bra. Keep the attractive, throw away the unattractive.

I want you, when you are finished with this vital inventory, to wind up with your choicest things left in your closet and in your bureau drawers—plus several green bags crammed with those things that have been holding you back. Give it to the needy. Dig a hole and bury it. Throw it in the trash, or just burn it.

I want there to be nothing left for you to put on except clothing that makes you look more appealing, alluring, important, affluent, reliable, trustworthy, smashing. I want there to be nothing left for you in that closet of yours but items that say to the world that *I am here!*

I want you to wind up with a closet full of clothes that *work for you*, clothes that are smart and advertise to the world that you are someone to be reckoned with.

The true test of a person's closet is this:

Go to your closet in the morning, swing or slide open the door, reach in with your eyes shut and pull out something. Put it on and go out the door without even looking in the mirror. If you can do that *and yet be absolutely positive that what you are wearing is great*, then your closet is a winner's closet.

Another.

When your only concern, as you pick out something to wear, is whether or not it is clean and pressed, then you also have a winner's closet. That means that you don't have to stop and consider whether or not the fit, the color, the fabric, the appropriateness is right. That's a workable closet for a winner.

If you are unsure of something—whether to keep it or throw it away—then put it on and model it for somebody you trust, or at least for yourself. *You can't wear anything that makes you feel doubtful!*

Your clothing must always be behind you, figuratively, not be something that is always in the foreground of your mind and your thoughts. You must be so sure of your clothing that you don't have to think about it. If you are thinking about your clothing—"Is this the right dress for this sort of affair?" "Should I have worn a white shirt or a colored shirt?"—then it is doubtful, and you can't be full of doubt and feel confident.

Back to the closet. In my experience, when I have assisted friends or clients to survey their wardrobe, I've found that at least 80 percent of what is in their closets can be and should be thrown away.

With a good many of the things you have in your closet, once you get started it's easy. The decisions are clean-cut. You've really known, deep down, for a long time that those things are useless. But after those simple, clear-cut decisions, it gets tougher. Maybe there are some things you still wear from time to time. But you have to ask yourself if they really do anything for you, or just keep you from being locked up for indecent exposure.

The closet is the place to start when you decide to make a change in your life and move over from the slow lane to the fast. Once you've done that, once you've green-bagged all the losers and begun to replace them with winners, you have taken the first bold and forthright step.

Now it is time to take a good look at the body those clothes are going over.

As your physical image changes, your self-image changes, and you relate differently to others and your environment.

Moshe Feldenkrais, Ph.D.

Keep the parts fitting

6

Assessing Your Physical Self

YOUR BODY: DOES IT GIVE YOU PLEASURE OR PAIN?

You have undoubtedly often heard the expression: "He (or, just as often, she) wears clothes well." Probably you've used that expression yourself.

People who make that statement generally mean it to be the ultimate compliment. They are saying that the person who wears clothes well has a superb *total presentation*. But let's think about that phrase a bit more.

What that phrase really is saying is that that person has a great figure, attitude, and mannerisms to display the clothes. This is known as "body magic." Attractive, vital bodies can serve as a shortcut in getting to know others.

With a few exceptions, we were born with perfectly shaped bodies, and if we don't use them properly they will show the neglect. What we don't use, we lose. Some of your best features aren't inherited—they are developed and molded.

Our culture is one that adores handsome physiques on men and stunning figures on women. There is no doubt about it. Well-proportioned, vitally alive bodies receive respect, admiration, and attention. We frequently choose people to interact with because of their physical appearance. It may seem a cold fact, but it is still a fact we have to face—others judge us by how we look. And no matter how bright or witty or loving we are, what they first see is our physical presentation—our body. Attractive, good-looking people have a *halo effect* on others; they look like they can do other things well, too.

Your body can be your vehicle for realizing your dreams. Do you want a VW bus or a sleek Jaguar? The key here is agreement: getting the largest amount of people to want to be on your side. Remember: Beautiful bodies are not just for the few who were born well proportioned, as some believe, it is everyone's gift to develop. Your physical bearing can open doors, captivate passing strangers, and renew interest in long-term relationships. I can't emphasize this point enough: People most often determine your future with them based on their first encounter with you. Be irresistible.

You were ruthless with your outdated clothes. Now be just as Spartan in appraising your body—its merits and its shortcomings. We want to fine hone your inherent beauty, reduce bulges, tone muscles. In other words, increase your chances of immediate acceptance by others. The fact is, you can have a wonderfully attractive body.

If you are tall, that's an added plus, but height is not as vital to a powerful presentation as is trimness. Some of our most attractive people today are not particularly tall. But there is a need to slim yourself down if you have even the slightest tendency to bulge at those bulgeable places. Keep it lithe and lively. Looking like a million in a maillot or a pair of tennis shorts puts you in the mainstream.

Can you recall a time you tried to slip into a skirt that suddenly seemed to have shrunk? Or pulled up a pair of trousers only to find they wouldn't zip shut? Or had a blouse or shirt that wouldn't button completely? The option is either to go up a size or to do something about those extra inches. And remember, whether we like it or not, as your size increases, chances decrease. What chances? Name anything— promotions, sex, relationships, being noticed, making friends—it affects every aspect of your life. So I say let's do something positive about it. Why have the squat VW bus when you can have that sleek Jaguar XJS.

If you think you should lose weight—and if you need to lose, you know it—then go out and lose some pounds. Millions of people have done it, and there's no big secret to doing it. It just takes setting priorities. It's your life-style and self-image that can eliminate those extra pounds and inches. If you need some help, see your doctor or buy any of the dozens of diet books that are on the market. I'm not going to recommend one over the others; if it works for you, then it's a good book. The only thing is that whichever one you choose, you have to stick to it. If books don't appeal to you, you might investigate some of the positive, result-producing weight-losing seminars.

Ditto for exercising. If you think exercising will energize and reshape—and it probably will because it reshapes most people—then by all means start exercising. Jogging or running or walking or aerobic dancing or jumping up and down on one of those indoor trampolines—it doesn't really matter much which exercise you choose. Whatever makes you feel good is good for you, and will help you shed a few pounds. And it feels great having additional energy. Fitness increases productivity. *Bodies that move increase in value.*

My point in this chapter is to tell you that it is time for you to assess your physical appearance with as much honesty as you surveyed your closet in the preceding chapter and will assess your mental state in the following chapter. This assessment is absolutely necessary.

It's time for you to really see those truths. And it's also time for you to "see" your figure, too.

First: look in your mirror. What sort of a figure is there staring back at you? Is this your optimum shape and form?

Is it a neat, trim, svelte person—someone who wears clothes well? If it is, great! You can skip the rest of this chapter and move right along to the next one.

But if that reflection in the mirror is definitely overweight, out of proportion, and not erect—then it is the right time for you to do something about it. No matter how marvelous your wardrobe is, clothes won't look their best on you because your body will distort the lines.

Don't be ashamed of not liking your figure. Please stop putting so much attention on what you don't like. Literally, lighten up.

You can kid yourself by buying things designed expressly for "full-figured gals," but the only person being kidded is you. You still look like a "chubette" and that is the precise first thought that pops into somebody's mind when they first meet you. That stranger isn't going to think of some charming euphemism like "full-figured"; he is going to think "fat."

I like to think of a human being as consisting of matter, and all matter needs refining. If your mirror says peel off some pounds, then start refining that matter and reduce that cellulite, *peau d'orange,* or just plain fat.

Don't think you can lose all the weight you want overnight, painlessly and magically. It will take a while, but if you start right away, you'll begin losing gradually, a pound or two a week, and that adds up to a nice loss over a period of time. If I gave you a million dollars for each pound you lost in a month, how many pounds would you lose? Check your priorities.

If your willpower is so weak that you simply cannot do it by yourself, then there are two alternatives I would recommend.

The first is to place yourself under a doctor's care, and let him curb your appetite. He will probably have you come in every week or so so he can monitor your progress. It's more expensive than doing it yourself, and no more effective, but it is perhaps the only way for those people who can't do it alone.

The second alternative is to go to one of the so-called fat farms, where they have crash programs for losing weight. Win the body game!

Slim it. Trim it. Gym it.

And you'll probably wind up with a bonus—not only will you lose weight, and thus wear your clothes better and look better, but undoubtedly you will feel better, too.

As a body specialist myself, having worked with thousands of people in my movement courses, I observed these truths about people and their bodies:

1. Our attitudes are the framework of our form—cut loose and release your feelings and your body will form more attractively.

2. Your healthy, vital living body creates your relationships—they are either rich and full-bodied or wimpy and strained.

3. People who demonstrate a great deal of vibrancy and stamina challenge the world, or feel in harmony with it—they don't give in to life's disappointments and setbacks.

4. Bodies that are upright, balanced, flexible, and forward-going are a result of attitudes of fulfillment, self-love, and an urgency to reach for the heights of human achievement.

5. Loose joints, open countenance, and expressive bodies show a greater ability to have loving relationships and to live in the world with a wider reality of life.

While you are considering your physical appearance, you have to realize that the physique is only part of it. It is a large part, of course, but not the whole enchilada. Being slim and trim is not all there is to your physical presentation.

There are several other things—things like your skin, your eyes, your hair. They are all wonderfully important to the overall look of a person, to *your* overall look.

To a woman, her hair is perhaps the second most important asset she has, next to her body. If the hair is not coiffed correctly, her entire presentation can be ruined. You ladies have to be very careful in your choice of hairstyles, and hair stylists. I've seen more women cry in beauty parlors than at dentists—because if their hair is ruined, they know that their whole look is ruined too.

Just as this isn't a diet book or an exercise book, so it is also not a hairstyle book. Hairstyle is such an individual, personal thing that there is no way I can advise anyone, sight unseen, who reads this book on what sort of hairstyle is best for her (or him). In my Presentation Salon / Seminars, I often have some of the leading hair stylists with me to advise my female and male clients on what to do about their hair.

A few general tips:

Keep it simple. That, I think, is the best possible advice. Those towering, overpowering, or straggly hairdos that are so popular with so many ladies who think they make them look exotic and sophisticated, really do just the opposite—they just look out of place. Hair should be something that enhances the face—an appropriate frame.

Keep it youthful when you are young, but don't try to stay with a particularly youthful hairdo when the rest of you has outgrown it.

Keep the color alive. Get a little help with your hair color: hennas, rinses, cellophaning, tints, streaking, dyes, whichever best enhances your particular style.

As for makeup, keep that tasteful, too.

All people—men and women, young and old—can have healthy skin. If yours isn't as fresh as it can be, consider a full facial cleansing. Men should not feel that getting a facial is unmasculine; it isn't. Getting your face cleaned professionally has nothing to do with masculinity. It is simply a means to an end, and the end is to get your face looking its very best—and there are plenty of rugged he-men who do it regularly.

There comes a time in every woman's life when she ought to consider having her makeup styled, or restyled, by a top professional in the field. Again, at my Presentation Salon / Seminars, I often have makeup experts accompany me to advise the ladies on how to improve their facial presentation. I am constantly amazed at what a few deft strokes with a makeup brush or an eyeliner pencil can do for a woman's face. Time after time, clients are completely transformed—the pale little blonde becomes a ravishing beauty simply because her makeup has been renovated.

Of course, I think the worst sin in the area of makeup is to overdo it. We want to see *you*, not someone painted up to obscure the real *you*. Send in the pretty faces, but don't send in the clowns.

There are a few women—but very few—who look good without any makeup at all. For most, however, there is a need. How about having your eyebrows and eyelashes tinted every two months? Makeup is a delicate, tricky business. Really, it is an art. So you want a genuine expert to help you. Design a fabulous face for yourself.

This might be the proper time for me to talk, briefly, about plastic surgery, or, as it is sometimes called, cosmetic surgery. Some people hear those words and immediately are turned off. They think that plastic surgery is just for people with gross deformities, or, at the other extreme, for Hollywood stars who may be governed solely by vanity.

That's not true. Millions of American men and women benefit from plastic surgery every year. Some people, as they get older, look older than they feel, and there is absolutely no reason in this day and age why that should be so. We can be stunning, and we can travel in the fast lane, no matter what our age is. But if we look older than we are, we might run into people who won't give us a chance. Each year more and more men in business are turning to plastic surgery.

In his book *Dr. Bellin's Beautiful You Book*, the noted plastic surgeon says:

> While most of my patients are already well-balanced, cosmetic surgery can strengthen their self images, relieve certain types of depression, and reinforce positive aspects of their personalities. This is especially true in present-day society, where appearances and first impressions are extremely important, and where youth is equated with energy and creativity.

Perhaps a minor cosmetic operation—safe, and not too expensive— can remove those lines around your eyes or those bags underneath your eyes that are giving you an old-before-your-time appearance. Maybe your entire face is sagging and a plastic surgeon can, with a nip here and a tuck there, magically restore the youthful firmness to the face.

Cosmetic surgery, of course, is not merely for the restoration of lost youth. If you are unhappy with your big nose or your wide-ranging ears or the size of your breasts, then by all means do something to change them. In this marvelous, enlightened time, anything is possible, thanks to the skills of today's plastic surgeons.

"When you look good, you feel good," Dr. Bellin writes, "and you're apt to be happier and more productive as well. Thus, when we make people more beautiful we actually improve the quality of their lives. We even perform a kind of surgical psychiatry."

In the same area, I want to discuss excessive hair in embarrassing places. Have it removed. A beauty with a hint of a moustache or a few wisps of hair on her chest is crimping her style. The urban man with unnecessary hair poking out his nostrils and ears and between his eyebrows needs clipping.

Today, through electrolysis, that hair can be gone. For men, baldness is the opposite problem. Some men aren't bothered when their hair falls out. ("It's not that I'm bald," said comedian / writer Abe Burrows, "it's just that everybody else is hairy.") Lots can be done to enhance the condition. Today's toupees are good, and there are other ways and other methods of adding hair to the head. But it's better to wear a bald pate than to wear an ill-fitting, amateurish-looking "rug." The eye is immediately, and negatively, drawn toward a toupee that is an obvious toupee. Better a head full of skin than a head full of obviously phony hair.

We all age, and some of us show greater signs of maturing than others. And to some people, this is traumatic, but it doesn't have to be that way.

Aging is something we can greatly refine. Put your age on hold by maintaining a healthy body. Some of the wonderful new body correction and enhancement techniques available are: Rolfing for structural integration, Feldenkrais for functional integration, and the chiropractic and Heller structural methods. All are administered by the hands of expertly and skillfully trained practitioners.

Your body is you. Your face is you. And they constitute your sales tools as you go out into the work force every day to make an impression on people you are meeting for the very first time. So you owe it to yourself to keep those tools looking as good as you possibly can.

On Madison Avenue, in the heart of America's advertising empire, they will tell you that people buy things for one or more of only six reasons. And those six reasons are:

1. PRIDE
People will buy something because it makes them proud to own it. A prestigious car, for example.

2. PLEASURE
People will buy something because it will make their lives more pleasurable to have it. A good mattress, for example, or a better-tasting coffee.

3. PROFIT
People will buy something because it will help them earn a better living. Good tools or a more efficient typewriter.

4. COMFORT
People will buy something because it will make their lives easier if they have it. A new washing machine or stronger detergent.

5. SECURITY
People will buy something because it brings them a safer, more secure life. Good car tires.

6. FEAR
People will buy something because if they don't have it, something bad may happen to them. Soaps that prevent body odor, tooth paste that stops decay.

Remember that every day because, when all is said and done, you are a marketable person, too. You are "positioning" yourself every day with as much enthusiasm as Madison Avenue ad men sell soap. You have to appeal to your "buyers"—the people you are meeting for the first time and trying to convince—and the reason you should is that it will be a *pleasure* for them to get to know you. Maybe later, you can also appeal to their *pride* or *comfort* or *profit* or *security*. (Let's not win them over through *fear!*)

Initially, however, it is *pleasure* that must attract them, or nothing will. Therefore, you have to make yourself an attractive commodity, so it will appear to them that, by making your acquaintance, they will be deriving *pleasure*.

The first impression is your *advertisement for yourself*.

Do your best to give yourself an edge.

Fine-hone and groom all of you that is physical. Master the art of magnetism. Revel in your beauty.

There is magic and irresistibility in looking your best.

Your body is the bridge between you and the universe. It is the medium of expression for your expanding sense of who you are—the point in time and space at which you get to express and experience love.

7

Assessing Your Mental Self

WHO'S IN CHARGE, ANYWAY?

O.K. There you are. You've thrown away all those old clothes, all those worn-out, blah clothes, and there's nothing left in your closet but what you want. You've slimmed and trimmed, so now you are the kind of person who wears clothes well.

What next?

Stop and think. It is not only the clothing and the body you put inside that clothing that makes you a winner, but—and possibly just as important—it is *that attitude that you have in your heart and head.* You hold the key to an entire world of opportunity for yourself; winning boils down to who wants it the most.

You must first recognize the fact that you are deserving. You rate the good life as much as the next man, or the next woman. And don't merely *tell* yourself that you are deserving, but *convince* yourself of that fact absolutely and mean it.

And you *are* deserving. Everybody is deserving. Why not? Why shouldn't you have the best of everything? There is no one in this world who is born unworthy. There are no second-class citizens, in my scheme of things. Everyone deserves the good life—including *you!* It is a matter of upgrading your life-style.

Suppressing your desires and fantasies is bad for your skin and causes you to lose your hair . . . The fast lane is waiting.

You know, Napoleon was trained by a professional actor how to act like an emperor. Before you go out there to conquer the world, there are some things you have to recognize about yourself. In many of us, these things, these ideas and notions, can hold us back.

Breaking through

So it's high time that you realized that:

1. YOU CAN'T BE AFRAID OF BIGNESS

Understand, please, that having it all is your birthright. Some people are afraid of getting too much, of accepting too much, of trying too much. You have to get rid of that attitude. Think big. Realize that if you can handle a small job, or a small pleasure, then you can handle a big job, or a big pleasure—it's just a touch larger, that's all. You can handle it, even if it seems insurmountable. It may take a little while to get the hang of it, but even the act of trying can be fun.

2. KNOW WHAT YOU WANT—AND WHAT YOU DON'T WANT

Too many people go awry, get off the track, because their goals are diffuse and indistinct. Set your sights on specific targets and go right for them. And, just as important, don't waste time, energy, and motion going for targets that are valueless. Be positive and assertive, not negative and wishy-washy.

3. CLEAR AWAY ANY FUZZINESS IN YOUR HEAD THAT MAY STAND IN YOUR WAY

You may have—we all have—some ideas and beliefs and explanations and reasons and excuses and alibis lodged in your mind that could block your path. Clear all that garbage away and concentrate only on that one pure, undiluted goal—your success. The fast lane requires a driver who keeps his eye on the road ahead. People with too much claptrap in their heads are reckless drivers and don't belong out there where the speeds are high and the competition is tough. A self-directed, disciplined mind will get you what you want.

4. TAKE SOME CHANCES

Sometimes the best time to take a risk is when it seems you have the most to lose because a person who stands still during uncertain times is actually sliding backward—losing ground while others are moving ahead. Now I'm not suggesting that you do something foolish, but what I am suggesting is that there are certain risks you have to take. Maybe you won't always know what the outcome is going to be. As long as the odds are in your favor—or at least even—then take a flyer once in a while. You have to have confidence in yourself, of course, and in your ability to triumph at least 1 percent more than half the time, but a good, well-calculated gamble is worth taking here and there. Daring is a plus quality in a person. You don't have to compromise your life and your possibilities. Oftentimes our best is not enough, so we have to expand our best.

5. HAVE A GOAL—BUT THEN SHOOT FOR SOMETHING EVEN BIGGER

Get in touch with the desire that's in you, in all of us—to *have it all*. Don't be satisfied to settle for anything less than the best, the most, the greatest. Second best leaves us yearning.

6. ALWAYS KEEP MOVING, STRIVING, REACHING

As a human being, our business on this planet is to get from one place to another. Once we get to that other place, we have to set ourselves another, more distant goal. Life is a succession of mountains; climb one and there is another one waiting, generally bigger and more formidable than the last. Where you are now is not as good as where you can be tomorrow.

7. YOU MUST INSTINCTIVELY KNOW THAT YOU BELONG IN THE FAST LANE

This is so important. You can't get there if you feel somehow guilty for winning; if you feel unworthy or insecure. You have to *know*, even with a shadow of a doubt if it happens to be present, that you belong up there with all the other winners. If you feel out of place and very uncomfortable, you won't want it to last. Prepare yourself for fulfillment; stop bracing yourself for defeat. Play for keeps!

8. IF YOU FIND YOURSELF ON A SIDE ROAD, TURN AROUND AND START OVER

Often, the fast lane seems to take us on detours that turn out to be wastes of time. As I have mentioned earlier, winners fail more than losers because they dare more. And so you will find that you sometimes go off on tangents. As soon as you recognize that it is a tangent and not the main road, turn around, retrace your steps, then pick it up and go forward again. You may lose a little time, but you will gain a lot of experience.

9. LISTEN TO EVERYONE, BUT OBEY ONLY YOURSELF

People are always eager to give advice. Losers are the biggest advice-givers of all; they haven't done it themselves, but they can always tell everybody else how to do it. Listen to whatever anybody tells you because you never know when you may hear something useful and valuable. But don't do what people tell you to do unless you, yourself, are convinced that that is the right thing for *you* to do.

10. YOU CAN'T EXIST IN THE FAST LANE UNLESS YOU ARE IN CHARGE

Don't let yourself be consumed by the chase unless you can willingly let go of it. Enjoy it, participate in it, play it to win—but be willing to let it go. Most people think you should never lose sight of your target. That is nonsense! Zen archers, once they have focused in on their target, let it come to them. You should approach your goals in the same way: set them, then trust them and let them come to you.

11. KNOW WHAT YOU WANT—AND GET IT

You can't get what you want until you know what it is. So, first set your sights on specific goals and objectives. Aim for them, shoot for them. *Reach them.* (Successful people know that as you approach your goals it's time to set newer, bigger ones.)

As you can see by reading these eleven suggestions they all have one thing in common:

They all involve you and what goes on inside your head. They all concern the need for you to motivate yourself. They all require that you think positively and decisively.

For many of us, that is as hard, or harder, than losing thirty pounds. A lot of us are born indecisive, shy, retiring, unenthusiastic, insecure, withdrawn. Those qualities will never transport you into the fast lane. So you have to change your ways of thinking and acting.

W. Clement Stone, one of the giants of the motivational field, calls this a PMA—Positive Mental Attitude.

"If you haven't learned the art of self-motivation with PMA," Stone writes in the magazine *Success*, "it isn't too late to make a change. A metamorphosis is *a change of physical form, structure or substance: a striking alteration in appearance, character or circumstances; a marked and more or less abrupt change in form or structure.* The alteration in appearance is associated with a change in habits.

"Man is the only member of the animal kingdom that can AT WILL cause a metamorphosis with himself—because he can permanently change his habits of thought and ACTION, his attitude from negative to positive. *Why not you?*" (Italics are Stone's.)

Why not you, indeed?

People often say, "Well, but" (and any time you start out saying, "Well, but," you've already lost)—"Well, but I can't do it, I can't change because of what I am, because I have to face the truth about myself, I'm not so hot, I'm not very much."

That defeatist attitude will, of course, get you nothing but defeat.

I like the old saying among gamblers: "The dice don't know you lost the last throw." Every roll of the dice is a new roll, a fresh roll. It doesn't matter if the dice have come up craps for a dozen times in a row—the thirteenth roll is a brand new roll, and the odds are just as good this time that you will roll a seven or an eleven as they were the first time.

With people it's the same thing. Every roll—every time you meet somebody new—is the first time. Every stranger is just that—someone you have never met before. This is a brand new roll, a brand new contact. This person you are meeting has no way of knowing about your previous misses—unless your conduct tips them off. But if you go into this meeting with your head up, with every cell oozing confidence, they will be impressed by you, and you will emerge from that meeting a winner.

Remember, the way you are treated, the way you are received, the way you are looked at is a result entirely based on the way you present yourself. It is how you look and what you say and do and the attitude you project that determines—totally, absolutely, and finally—how you will be treated.

Act apologetic and you will lose.

Act certain and you will win.

Maybe you have a history of losing. But history is just what the dictionary says it is—"the branch of knowledge dealing with past events"—and from now on let's concern ourselves with your future. O.K., maybe you've suffered a lot in your past. That's over and done with. That whole concept of "long-suffering" is old hat—we have moved ahead, and today is the era of short-suffering. Or (even smarter) no suffering at all.

"Don't look back," the great pitcher Satchel Paige reportedly said once. "Something may be gaining on you."

Look ahead. Keep your eyes fixed on the pot of platinum and prosperity that is out there waiting for you. When you're losing the race, run faster. And when you're winning, that's the time to go faster still. Slow down and coast only to refuel. When push comes to shove, keep going.

Winning is simply a state of mind. An attitude. You have to be assertive to win. Some people think that "assertive" is a bad word, that being assertive is an unattractive quality. Don't confuse assertiveness with pushiness or belligerence. Assertiveness merely means establishing a goal and going after it with rightful determination.

Being a winner is doing what you want to do, when you want to do it, and how you want to do it—at least 51 percent of the time.

Start out with a single objective, something that has eluded you. Perhaps it is a simple thing, such as wanting to dine at a particularly fine and elegant restaurant.

Remember, as you present yourself to the maître d'hôtel at his desk, that he does not know of your previous fear—"The dice don't know you lost the last throw"—unless you show it through indecision and timidity. Be direct, in charge, decisive, and know it belongs to you.

Winning once is a start, and a very good start. Keep it up and you will become a winner in everything, a total winner. Being at the top is simply winning in a series of individual encounters.

Students of sports will tell you that the best athletes in the world are probably the decathlon and heptathlon performers. Those are the men and women, such as Bruce Jenner, who participate in a series of ten or seven events—all different sorts of track-and-field events. To be a total winner, these athletes have to be individual winners. Winning is fine, but they have to win again and again and again to get the gold medal.

Winning becomes a habit, even a delightful passion. When you realize that you can win—even if it is just something as simple as going to that elegant restaurant and carrying it off with consummate cool— then you begin to treat yourself as though you deserve it. It becomes a way of life after that. The more you experience winning, the easier it becomes to win. It is a very good habit to develop.

Be willing to rehabilitate your ability to be insecure. This strengthens you. Remember how you learned to walk as a child—you fell and got up again and fell again. Life is alive when it is a series of gains and losses. Be sure, however, that every loss becomes an ultimate gain.

Your personality is a complex thing. You have many natures. We all do. Our one, overall personality is composed of dozens of facets, hundreds of our own individual quirks and idiosyncracies. And that's interesting because it makes us the individuals we are.

To make that final, exciting, lasting move into the fast lane, develop these three important human emotions:

1. YOU HAVE TO PERMIT YOURSELF TO BECOME ANGRY

You have to tell yourself, "No, this is not where I belong. I am being cheated and robbed of my rightful place in the world. I don't belong here—I belong somewhere else, someplace better." Get mad about the injustice of it all. You are deserving, and you aren't getting everything that should rightfully come to you. O.K., get angry. Experience emotion. But direct that anger and that emotion into constructive avenues. Don't glare at whoever or whatever it is that is holding you back. Rather, look ahead at where you can be.

2. YOU HAVE TO CREATE EXCITEMENT

Anger first, then excitement. Excite yourself into action. Get yourself aroused to the point where that anger is channeled into constructive paths. If you start moving toward your goal, then your goal can start moving toward you. Involve others in your plans; get them excited about your intentions.

3. YOU HAVE TO BECOME ENTHUSIASTIC

Anger first, then excitement, then enthusiasm. There is a big difference between excitement and enthusiasm. Excitement says, "I must do something about this situation I find myself in." Enthusiasm is your magical elixir. Anger first—so you know you *must* make a change. Excitement next—to propel you into turning that anger into positive channels. Enthusiasm next—to entice your appetite for the wonderful things that will be yours as you triumph.

Just be careful that you don't let the anger turn inward into your heart and soul, and eat away at you and turn into jealousy and envy. And be careful that you don't let the excitement turn into futile daydreams and useless reveries that turn you away from the need for action.

Turn the anger and excitement into useful, positive emotions, that lead to the enthusiasm you must release before you can begin to alter the direction of your life.

You can be the winner you are! "To be what we are, and to become what we are capable of becoming, is the only end of life" (Robert Louis Stevenson).

If you want to win, you must know where you want to go and how to get there; be honest with yourself and your dreams; be able to focus on your objectives; be enthusiastic and involved; be full of hope and confidence; be in control of yourself at all times; aim for the top; be inventive and imaginative; be open, direct, and frank in your dealings; be competitive but not bitchy about it; be willing to learn even when you are asked to teach; be organized; be satisfied with your accomplishments; and, above all, look like a winner, in your dress and total presentation. Learning how to dress well is a form of education in personal development.

It's all in your attitude. Your total participation is a function of your *attitude.*

> People are always blaming circumstances
> for what they are.
> I don't believe in circumstances.
> The people who get on in this world are
> the people who get up and look for the
> circumstances they want, and if they can't
> find them, they make them.
>
> GEORGE BERNARD SHAW

PART IV

Taking Action

A "star" in her own right! *Photo by Stephen Ladner*

"Smart people" dress all out. *Photo by Stephen Ladner*

A "simple statement" of an elegant life! *Clothes by Barcelino, San Francisco.*
Photo by Suzanne Estel

"Romancing" in comfort and style. *Clothes by Polo Shop, Stanford Shopping Center, California. Photo by Suzanne Estel*

8

Dressing to Win

THE INTENT TO EMPOWER

Winning, as we have already concluded, is a state of mind; an attitude that gets results.

But, remember, we also concluded that strangers see us and form immediate opinions and impressions based on how we look. And those first impressions are difficult—perhaps impossible—to dislodge. It is, therefore, imperative that we dress well if we want to experience life at the top. To win, we must *dress to win*. It's the polish that can help turn a dark horse into a front-runner.

How you dress to win is really the heart of the matter, the key to opening the door to a good life. The way you spend and circulate your finances says a great deal about your ability to accumulate and attract wealth.

There are three main points about dressing to win:

1. SIMPLICITY
2. ELEGANCE
3. ORDERLINESS

Let's consider these three items, one by one.

SIMPLICITY is a very valuable quality in many things, not only clothing.

Hiag Akmakjian, the noted photographer, has said that his goal in taking pictures is "to achieve a technique so transparent that it appears an absence of technique."

That is simplicity. You want to dress so well that people do not really notice how well you are dressed. It should just be there, like the sky and the clouds, everything blending together with you and your physique so perfectly that it looks as though you were born with that suit or that dress on your back.

A good way to test the simplicity of your outfit is to try to describe it to a friend over the telephone. If you can describe it quickly, easily, and vividly, so your friend can readily visualize it, then you are wearing something simple. On the other hand, if your friend has trouble getting a mental picture of what you are wearing or is confused about it, then, obviously, what you are wearing is too busy or too complicated. Change it.

Simplicity means freedom from distractions, such as too much trim, too many decorations, buttons, unusual stitching, strangely shaped pockets or lapels. Simplicity means a basic design that is classic or simply contemporary, not extreme. Simplicity implies a perfect fit. Simplicity demands that the color, fabric, and pattern all be basically harmonious and complementary.

Simplicity makes a *direct, positive impact* on whoever sees you. Complexity only serves to *confuse* and *distract* the people with whom you come in contact.

Example: For a man, a classic wool or cashmere navy blue blazer is the purest simplicity. It can be worn with tan, gray, or white / off-white slacks. The result is a very clean, trim, and simple statement. However, take that same blazer and combine it with slacks that have a vibrant pattern—plaids or checks or broad stripes—and the message is complicated. In all cases, balance, harmony, and proportion of fabrics, patterns, and textures are the keys for obtaining simplicity. If not, the outfit has lost its essential simplicity. And yet, on the third hand, that same classic blazer can be combined with faded denim jeans and even some cotton wash pants and the statement is again simple, although now it is more casual and sporty.

Example: For a woman, a basic brown-striped wool day dress with a plain brown leather belt and complementary colored pumps topped by an off-white blazer is a clear statement of simplicity. However, take that same dress and combine it with ankle-length boots and a wide multicolored sash, topped off with a print sweater underneath a beefy textured blazer of tans, rusts, browns, and gold—the look gives off mixed messages. And again, on the other hand, that same classic day dress can be combined with a long, narrow, camel-toned coat-jacket, strappy black evening shoes, a change to black-printed hose, a change of day earrings to larger, hooped evening earrings, a wider waist-clinching black belt, and two additional buttons left open and we have an evening dress that can go anywhere.

Simplicity means avoiding outfits in which there is an improper matching of colors, an improper mixing of fabrics and accessories, an improper combination of quality apparel with cheaper garments, a mixed statement of taste, or a confused statement of yourself.

Simplicity means shunning the cutesy-pie, the gimmicky, the faddish clothing. And, similarly, shunning outfits that speak more loudly than you do. Empower people—don't overpower them.

Simplicity, simply, is dressing with a clarity of purpose and with the good taste to express that clarity in a straightforward manner.

ELEGANCE

I wrote earlier that we are all *Living Human Treasures*. Elegance is dressing up to that role. A treasure is something of value and deserves to be dressed in something that looks valuable.

Elegance is hard to describe, and yet I find it easy to recognize. You see someone dressed elegantly and you immediately react positively. Yet you might have great difficulty describing precisely what that person is wearing. An elegantly attired person is characterized by dignified richness and grace; by refined, restrained luxuriousness; by a sense of appropriate propriety and fastidiousness; by a simplicity that has become opulent. And like everything that is above the ordinary, it is not easy to analyze but so easy to feel wonderful around it!

Elegance, like simplicity, is a quality that is not confined only to clothing. There are elegant homes and automobiles and furniture and jewelry. And, of course, elegant people.

Dressing elegantly combines style, fabric, colors, and quality accessories in a way that automatically empowers the wearer. To the beholder, an elegant person is awesome, and yet not frighteningly so. You see someone dressed with elegance and you know, automatically, immediately, that that person has arrived.

I would like to share with you this beautifully passionate, entertaining and informative description of "elegance" from Jacqueline de Ribes as quoted in *Interview Magazine*. Jacqueline de Ribes is definitely one of the most elegant women living today, as is the gentleman who interviewed her: Reinaldo Herrera.

> *Reporter:* You've always been considered a paragon of elegance. As a paragon you must have certain definite ideas of what elegance is or should be in itself.

Jacqueline de Ribes: First of all, I must say that elegance fascinates me because there's something eternal about it. If fashion is temporary, elegance is, for me, the emerging factor when you compare it to the inconstancy of fashion. It is eternal. Whatever the trend of fashion is, you find it if you wish to discover it. For instance, I was looking at an old issue of *Vogue*, and you can see even in the fashion of twenty years ago what was elegant and what was not. For me it's very clear. It's a sort of continuity of elegance that fascinates me. There is no ease without naturalness. Nothing is false or overdone in elegance, but it can sometimes take study. Without going as far as the famous Beau Brummell, who was the elegant of all elegants in the early 1800s, he used to say and has put in rhyme:

> My neckclothes form, of course my principal care,
> for by that we criterions of elegance swear,
> And cost me each morning some hours of flurry
> to make it appear to be tied in a hurry.

I love those lines because often I catch myself starting over and over in tying a bow or draping a scarf and being late for the sake of natural elegance. It's an attitude. A frame of mind. An intuition, a refusal, a rigor, a research, a knowledge. The attitude of elegance is also a way of behavior. English people of the nineteenth century used to make the distinction between the "gentleman" and the "tailor-made gentleman," which meant someone who behaved like a gentleman compared to someone who dressed like one. Also, one could say that this gentleman had an elegant attitude in such and such circumstance, which meant that he had the right attitude, the generous attitude, the largess—not just that he was wearing the right costume or a beautiful suit. Elegance makes no noise. It's calm, peaceful, tranquil yet remarkable in the sense that you've noticed it. It inspires respect and admiration but never astonishment. Jean Cocteau used to say, "Elegance is the art of not astonishing."

Also, you have to be at ease in your own elegance. It can only be obtained if you're natural. It's a very important thing to be natural. When I say, "knowledge, research, refusal"—one must be slightly sophisticated really, to be elegant. And the refusal is that I still think that elegance must be in your mind, that you must be trained to enjoy refinement. Your eye must know and see the details and the differences and you must understand that simplicity and sophistication are great friends.

What more could I add?

ORDERLINESS

This is the sum of simplicity and elegance.

To dress simply and elegantly you have to be orderly in your approach to what you wear. The orderliness begins, literally, in the closet—you want to have everything you own arranged in an orderly, methodical, systematic manner, so that nothing becomes wrinkled, so you don't overlook something and completely forget that you have it, so that everything has room to breathe freely, so that you know exactly what you have and what is available for duty.

With that accomplished, you can put together an outfit for every occasion, quickly and systematically and without emotional upset.

One more note on the importance of orderliness. When you are planning your outfit, for whatever occasion, remember that each item you select to become part of your costume adds to the total picture. If every item is harmonious, then the outfit has an orderly look. There can be no room for confusion in the well-dressed person's outfit—no mishmash.

Those are the three main facets of tasteful dressing. But as important as it is to remember what to do, it is equally important to remember what *not* to do. Those are the three opposites to the three plus qualities we have already discussed, and you must guard against these three— instead of simplicity, some people dress *garishly;* instead of elegance, some people dress *sloppily;* instead of orderly, some people are totally and resolutely *disorganized.* And there is another factor that must be strongly resisted—*cheapness.*

What is this fascination people have with the inexpensive? Oh, I grant you that thrift has its place. I applaud those sterling virtues, frugality and thrift. They are, and always have been, admirable qualities, and Benjamin Franklin would have been just another kite-flyer without them. But keep them under control. Their place isn't in your closet if you have any illusions about living prosperously. Whoever heard of a well-dressed miser?

Dressing to win means—and there's no way around it—spending a significant portion of your money on your clothing. If you have dynamite outfits, you can dress to win—*when it counts.*

In reality, when you buy the best quality of clothing it may turn out to be a bargain in the long run. It will last longer. If you shop wisely, that one socko outfit will be good and still stylish years from now. When you buy cheap, you get cheap. Cheap outfits begin to look rundown and wear out quickly, and that advertises you as being second or third class. And so you feel second or third class, too.

If I only had a limited budget, I'd buy two really great suits and wear them over and over, rather than have a wardrobe of several not-so-great suits and wear them sparingly. Maybe people will notice the fact that you are wearing the same suits—but at least they will notice you. And that's much better than wearing something different every day and having the world not want to remember that you've passed through.

Why do you want to dress well? The chances are that there are one of three reasons—three goals you have in life—or a combination of two of those three. And they are MONEY (affluence), SEX (appeal), POWER (clout). *You either run the sex, money, and power in your life or it runs you.*

MONEY is that which gives us more chances to enjoy the good life that our planet, and particularly this nation, has to offer—having a great home, marvelous vacations, a high-caliber education, eating in super restaurants, buying great cars and other luxuries, contributing to charities that help out the needy among us. Some people may criticize that goal as being materialistic, but only those who haven't developed a money consciousness and see the good it does. (More about this in a later chapter.)

SEX is—well, you should know what it is by now. In this particular context, however, I want it to mean the ability to intrigue and attract sensually.

POWER is being able to command or have an influence—whether it be people or organizations or ideas. *It is the ability to actualize your intentions and goals more quickly.* Powerful people are allowed to take charge, and things happen. Power is the ability to make a difference in how the world spins. Power is the gift of empowering others, and doing it in such a way that those others feel great from being around you. Power is perceived capacity. Power is the demonstration of the active principle of love.

Winners are those people who have all the money, the sex, and the power they want—when they want it. Winners travel in the fast lane, where money, sex, and power are theirs because they have placed a high value on the enjoyment of them.

But think about the people you admire who already have the money, the sex, and the power they want, and in full measure. Conjure up a vision of them right now. Picture them in your mind. What do you see?

To begin with, they are almost certainly well dressed. You never envision a millionaire, a powerful person, a sexy person, dressed sloppily. You almost certainly picture him or her in the best-made, best-fitted, best-looking clothing your imagination can dream up.

So you can look on your clothing as a means to the enjoyment of three ends: affluence, appeal, and clout—clothes are your passport. They are the visible tools you can use to get you where you want. Your total presentation—clothing, body, face, attitude—opens the possibility for you to triumph by permitting you to convey to the world a greater sense of presence, authority, believability, and likability.

Winning is largely a matter of self-confidence. And the best illustration of supreme self-confidence I know is this story:

In some forgotten time, in some forgotten, far-off land, there was an island civilization. The people on one island went to war with their neighbors, who also lived on an island. They agree to meet on a third island, neutral territory, and fight it out. So the peoples of both these islands piled into boats and sailed to the third island for a fight to the victory.

The first people sailed in a flotilla of three boats, and when they arrived at the island, their leader's first command was this:

"All right, now. *Burn our boats!*"

All his subjects thought he had gone mad, and they questioned him.

"Sire, if we burn our boats, how will we be able to sail home? Why should we burn our boats?"

"Because," the leader replied, "we will go back with *their* boats!"

Now that is what I call real confidence. I do not have any information about how that leader was dressed, but I would be willing to wager my ticket on his boat that he was dressed to win. You don't get to be leader unless you dress to win. Look at our military higher echelon.

Sometimes, people come to me and say, "Robert, I want to look powerful. Make me look powerful."

I can't do it. Nobody can do it. Power comes from within. You only look powerful if you are not apologetic for who you are. And so I can take those people and place their feet on the edge of the fast lane, making sure that they are dressed for agreement. Beyond that, however, it is totally up to them. They have to *feel like winners* before they can begin to exert any power. *You won the first game—you were the first sperm to reach the egg.*

People cannot be winners unless or until they feel and think like winners. Until they behave like winners. It all comes down to having the basis and the foundation for the obvious to come. Dress beyond your current job and life-style.

That old saying, "Clothes make the man," is *not* totally true. *Clothes do not make the man or woman—they make you more impressive.* After that, you have to do it with every facet of your persona.

Oscar Wilde said, "I have the simplest of taste—I am always satisfied with the best."

That, of course, is the heart and soul of the question of dressing to win. The best. Start there, start with the best, and you are well on your way. One great outfit can act as a catalyst.

Don't be afraid to say to the world, "Notice me," by dressing in a way that commands notice and attention. Don't be afraid to say to the world, "I have something to offer you," by wearing clothes that command respect and admiration. And yet—this is a fine line—your clothes cannot be so blatant and bold that they *plead* for notice. It takes fine taste to make that tricky, narrow distinction between the simply bold and the boldly simple.

Maybe the word for dressing with the elegant simplicity should be "smart." But the trouble is that no two people agree on just what "smart" means. Defining smart is as slippery as defining "love."

But, undaunted, I'll give you my own definition. I think "smart" means a clever use of tones and hues of color, the use of natural fabrics that harmonize and are compatible and play on one another. And, of course, those very important accessory touches and the just-right fit that gives the outfit your signature. Lastly, and most importantly, the body attitude of the wearer makes it "smart."

So that's my definition. But "smart" is a quality that really doesn't have to be defined. You *know* when someone is smart because he or she is wearing an outfit that makes people turn around and look, without having their eyes pop out.

Dressing to win means dressing to win *throughout the day*, not just at some special occasion. Some people think it's important to look good at work but, when that part of their day is over, they rush home and put on the most awful things you can imagine. Maybe they are winners at work, but they are losers the rest of the time. Or the opposite: There are folks who dress spiffily for social events but, at work, look like Living Human Horrors instead of Living Human Treasures.

You can't be a part-time winner, any more than you can be part-time pregnant. *Your clothes must take you through the spectrum of a day's experiences.* They must take you through a total day—work, lunch, dinner, sports event, elegant event, home entertaining, whatever is on your agenda.

A winning dresser learns (mostly by observing) the nuances of dressing to create satisfactory results.

The whole idea is to carefully observe well-dressed people in social and business settings. Note what colors they blend, what fabrics they choose, what accessories definitely enhance their look of importance, of having arrived. I often ask successful, well-dressed people where they bought an effective article of clothing. Try it, they love the compliment and will often go out of their way to steer you to their sources. This is the best way to learn to dress yourself with a similar panache. In this way you will learn to wear particular fabrics. Silk, for example, is the fabric for when you want the feeling of a second outer skin, and the sense of sensualness. In this way, you will learn when wearing jeans is just right, and when wearing jeans diminishes your image. You learn when a man should and should not wear a tie. You learn when a man can safely wear a sport jacket-and-slacks combination, and when a suit is mandatory. You learn when a man must wear shoes that lace, and when it is perfectly acceptable to wear a loafer.

Learning those things is the same as learning the proper vocabulary. For a while, being careful of what you say to whom and when and where is a tricky business and requires thought and effort. But after you have been doing it awhile, it becomes easy; an exercise in second nature. Similarly, the nuances of dressing well quickly become second nature too.

Some examples of the small things you'll learn, as you observe others, that combine to form the big things that contribute to your becoming recognized as a fine dresser, a winning dresser, are these:

1. When you wear a sweater, be careful. Sweaters have a way of looking great at one moment, sloppy the next. They *must* look as they were designed to look, whether snug or loose, full or tight. (Obviously, you have to buy them carefully; cheap ones lose their shape.)

2. Also in the casual area, sport jackets for both men and women frequently pull and bind, which causes the body to look stuffed into them. Or the reverse, they hang too loosely and flop about. Either effect is unbecoming and unflattering. Sport jackets have to be fitted precisely—and, again, if you buy them cheap, a good fit is practically impossible.

3. Pants—trousers and slacks for men; slacks for women—should all be fitted so that they allow the leg to extend easily and gracefully, and so that they permit sitting in a comfortable position. Too often, men and women wind up with pants that almost make sitting an unnatural act. Nothing looks quite as unattractive as sitting down and having your trousers scroonch up so tightly that when you stand up, you have deep creases up your lap.

4. For women, a good-fitting dress is, of course, something that is basic and quite essential. A dress should hang gracefully, flow smoothly, swirl if designed to swirl, be stark and straight if that was the designer's intention.

5. A winning dresser learns to use the elements of color in creating different and unique means of expressing himself or herself. Here are three options that are timeless in their usefulness, that consistently reappear year after year in designer collections for one reason: They make a statement.

A. MONOCHROMATIC Color Scheme: This results when each item of clothing (top and bottom) is of the same hue and color. It is choosing colors from a single family of colors. Using repetition, as in a beige blouse, a tan pair of slacks, an off-white sweater, accented with a light tan-colored belt with a large gold buckle, shoes of matching tan leather.

This look gives a sophisticated, monied air to the wearer. This would also be true of a gentleman wearing an entire outfit of khaki, blue, or taupe pieces. Some people consider this look boring. On the contrary, properly used, its subtleness permits the wearer, rather than the clothes, to be foremost in the total picture. The secret is in proper balancing.

B. RELATIVE Color Scheme: In this mode of dressing, the wearer selects and chooses colors that are related and harmonious, such as blue, lavender, fuchsia, and violet. Or yellow, orange, and rust. Or apricot, coral, and pink. The idea is a gradual blend and osmosis into its most natural next-of-kin color tones. This imparts a feeling of softness. For example, a charcoal-gray wool suit with a mild-toned silver-smoky-gray silk shirt and a scarf tied into a cravat—it too in shades of gray, black, and silver. Or imagine a striped silk day dress with soft, full-length sleeves where the stripes are alternately lavender, violet, and fuschia and the belt is plum colored.

C. DRAMATIC Color Scheme: Here the wearer deliberately chooses contrasting colors to create an impactful, dramatic effect. A white suit with a black blouse, or a red wool-jersey dress with a bold black-and-white-striped belt are examples here. Or a green cotton sport shirt with a bright orange T shirt showing through, completed with a canary-yellow pair of summer linen pleated slacks. Dramatic results when color juxtaposition demands that the wearer be reckoned with. (All three color schemes permit solid or patterned fabrication.)

These things are all factors that will become second nature; you will instinctively know what fits you and what doesn't, what goes well with your coloring and what doesn't, what style flatters you and what doesn't.

You will come to understand that every single thing you put on—from your underwear to your overcoat—helps create that statement you will be making. Even such a small thing as the watch you wear or carry, is as important as the dress or suit you have on your back. People notice whether it is gold or tin, simple or gaudy, sporty or smart, thin or thick. For a woman, the handbag she carries is almost like toting a sign. It can say, "I am classy," or "I am tacky." It *must* blend—not always match, but blend—in with the balance of her outfit. Fabrics, too, must blend. Sizes must be true. I think the total effect of a woman's outfit can be made or broken by the handbag she carries.

With a man, I believe the tie is the one, single item that too often invalidates his image. A man can wear the best, most powerful blue suit, neat shoes, perfect shirt—and spoil the whole picture with a tie Aunt Agatha gave him for Christmas, the one with the ducks flying in V-formation across his chest. I like ties that are either solids or English-style school stripes or very simple, neat foulards. Don't go cutesy or garish or sexy or loud with your tie, unless you're dressing up for some flashy party.

We all know when we see someone who is dressed well. When you go to a party, or any affair, all you have to do is listen to the swirl of conversation around you, and you will quickly pick up comments from people about how others are dressed. Our peers are critics of our costumes. They are often vocal about it, when we give them permission to tell us the truth about how we look. That's because our peers are governed strongly by that most important value judgment—they sincerely want us to look our best.

Over the years, I have collected some representative ad libs from people I have overheard in the act of becoming clothing critics. You might be intrigued by some of them. These are all favorable comments, which indicate to me that the speaker feels the person he or she is commenting on is admirable. These are women referring to men:

1. "I feel more attractive when I am seen with him."
2. "I want to pinch his buns. What a hunk!"
3. "Look at him—I wonder what his story is . . ."
4. "I would go *anywhere* with him!"
5. "He can buy my clothes for me any day."
6. "Isn't he adorable, oh, how cute!"

And now we have some comments from both men and women, referring to women:

1. "Wow, she's stealing the show—"
2. "She knows how to put herself together. She's a beauty."
3. "She's a classic."
4. "You can tell that that lady doesn't shop at Goodwill."
5. "She looks fantastic; I wonder where she got it?"
6. "Now that's the kind of woman I'd like to take out!"
7. "I've never seen her in the same outfit twice."

Now, do you see the general trend of what they are all saying? There is something about their dress that is impressive. It excites you or moves you or gets your attention. It's never boring or too flashy. It gets your attention and praise—you notice and admire them.

Good clothing is a frame for the person's presentation, it is not the presentation itself. Good clothing enables you to introduce the real you, whereas if the clothing is too forward, too pushy, then the real you is forever back there somewhere in the shadows. Good clothing is good style.

Style in a garment is the signature of the designer. Many designers have such distinctive styles that whatever they design is immediately recognized as being theirs. Some styles obviously don't look well on everybody. Certain designer's clothes require that the wearer be tall or have some other distinctive physical characteristic. Certain styles express a strong personality, which may not mesh with your own. You have to be careful, in wearing designer creations, that that particular style looks well on you. You have to know yourself and your personality so that you don't wind up wearing a style that contradicts yourself. No one designer is perfect for everybody; even wonderful Levi's jeans, probably the most universal style ever created, look uncomplimentary on some folks. Choose styles that convey your personality and marketing purpose.

You have to build your own style, perhaps starting with the style of some noted designer and then going beyond that. Make your own style by taking the works of a designer and changing them, with accessories or with the power of your personality, until they become no longer his, but yours.

Then you will have your own personal style, an offspring of your own personality. It will become you, speaking out completely about who you are and what you are. It is your own spirit expressing itself through your appearance. It is your imprint on the mind, soul, and heart of everyone you come in contact with. *It is when you take your own raw identity and forge it and polish it and smooth it until it becomes your own alter ego, your own second self.*

Style, therefore, should and must be unique unto you. Copy anyone slavishly and you are subjugating yourself and simply mirroring another person's image and taste.

Pathfinders are never predictable. Winners never ape fashion, they use fashion to add to their own sense of style.

The ultimate secret of dressing to win is dressing as the best, with the best. Why the best? Because the best is the most truthful, the best is the most sincere, the best sings!

"It is a funny thing about life," the late literary lion W. Somerset Maugham wrote. "If you refuse to accept anything but the best, you often get it."

The best allows the *you* that is inside to shine through. The next-best, the second-best, the run-of-the-mill, or all the way down the scale to the absolute worst—they all have the knack of taking the attention away from the real you. The best is what you were born to have.

And, of course, the best always begets the best.

Wear the best and you will receive the best treatment, get the best smiles, be shown to the best tables, attract the best people, make the most money, and enjoy the greatest success.

Most people who don't succeed fail because they don't look like successes. More—they don't look like they *want* to succeed or *know how* to succeed or *could handle* success if it happened to come their way.

Get an edge. Look as though you belong.

Here are a few tips that I think underscore your new dressing-to-win personality:

1. Dress as though you have always dressed well. Don't look as though this is all new and surprising to you. It may not be easy at first, but try to look as though you belong in the best clothing and, furthermore, that you feel comfortable in the best clothing and have always belonged in the best clothing.

2. I'm almost embarrassed because it is so obvious it shouldn't need to be said, and yet it is necessary to say it. And that is—*be clean!* I am always astounded and amazed when I see someone beautifully dressed, but with dirty fingernails, flaky scalps, soiled clothing, or some other indication that they believe cleanliness is next to nothing.

I once had a lady who attended one of my Presentation Salon/Seminars and she kept asking, over and over, "Mr. Panté, I want to know why men don't like to stay around me very long." She seemed attractive enough, but when I got close to her I understood her problem—she simply smelled bad. And as lovingly as I could, I told her the truth. No matter how attractive a person is, if their personal habits are repulsive, they will repulse everybody else. And so—*keep it clean!*

3. If you are in doubt about whether or not to wear something—don't. In the first place, your doubt will always show itself, and thus reduce your confidence in yourself. And, secondly, you should only wear something that you are absolutely positive works for you. "Almost's" don't make it.

4. Given a choice between dressing as a "conservative" or as a "trend-setter," consider for whom you are dressing: the host and hostess, the event, the other guests. In short, your choice should largely be determined by the social milieu you'll find yourself in.

5. Avoid the pretentious, the exaggerated, the coy, and the cute. Gimmick items can be fun for the wearer and introduce a sense of play or "campiness" into an outfit; reflective sunglasses, Mickey Mouse watches, T shirts with bow ties and cuffs painted on them, scarlet-lined opera capes, etc. In a sense it's like costume jewelry—there is a time when it is so right and does a perfect job. You must know what you are about however. Flash, sparkle, and "cutesy" may advertise you as foolish. Be smart and know when to play it down.

6. Make sure that everything that is connected with you reflects your good taste, your class, your winningness. If you carry something

for your work, be sure that you carry something classy. Keep your papers or whatever in a neat attaché case or, for the ladies, one of those feminine answers to the male attaché case. If you have to wear eyeglasses, keep them simple and functional and no-nonsense. They should reflect what you are about. (If you use anything in your job—from a pen to a clipboard—be sure it fits in with the rest of you. No dime store pens.)

7. If you are accompanied by a date or an escort, make sure that he or she knows the rules of the game you are playing. Nothing worse than a classy lady walking into a fancy affair with some stud with his shirt open to his navel, or a classy guy walking into the same affair with a lady who looks like a working hooker.

8. Men, no matter how hot it is, don't be the first to strip. Nothing makes you look cheaper faster than to enter a fancy restaurant or a dignified meeting and, without waiting to be asked, taking off your jacket and draping it over the back of a chair. There you are, sweaty armpits on display, and everyone else is still in their jackets. If the host, or the highest-ranking official, takes off *his* jacket first, then it's O.K. to follow. Go with the general consensus or initiate the taking off of jackets by asking if it would be O.K.

9. Last stop, before a big meeting or a heavy date or any sort of important function, should be in front of your mirror. A quick inspection to make sure everything is all right. Men, run your finger up your fly, to double-check the fact that it is zipped up all the way. We've all experienced the embarrassment of forgetting that little item, and if it happens at the wrong time, it could be distracting. Make a habit of that final check. Women, make it a point to check your makeup, tuck in your blouse, straighten your skirt, perk up the entire look to make an entrance.

All of the above information is, as you have probably sensed, designed to make you look perfect. But—and here's the tricky part—you don't want to look unapproachable. That may sound like a contradiction, but it really isn't. It is possible to look too unbelievable. Be approachable.

The total effect to achieve is that you should look classically adventurous. Look memorably exciting—and yet always comfortable. Use your clothing as a tool to help you get where you want to be, to do what you want to do, and have what you want to have.

That's all clothing is—a set of tools, a means to an end, a comfortable feeling. Maybe the people you meet will never remember precisely what you were wearing when they try to recall it later on, but they *will* remember the overall impression they received from you.

Let your image always consume people's memories.

9

The Art of Shopping

THE STATE OF MIND OF THE SUCCESSFUL SHOPPER

I don't know if I'm correct when I call this chapter "The Art of Shopping." Is shopping an art? Or, rather, is it a science? Or is it, most likely, a bit of both? The only thing I am absolutely certain of is that if you want to get the most for your dollar in this world, you must learn how to be an effective and efficient shopper. You must learn how to find the right store for you, the right salesclerk in that right store, and then the right merchandise in that right store with the assistance of that right salesclerk. Art or science, it can be a difficult but vital business. Shopping can be expressed in the terms of an equation:

$A + B + C = X.$
A is you, the shopper.
B is the store.
C is the clerk.
And X, the sum of those three parts, is a satisfactory and happy purchase.

As with any mathematical equation, if one of the components is missing or altered, the whole result will be thrown off. In our equation, A is always constant—you, the shopper, must always be part of it. But the elements of B and C—the store and the clerk—can vary. If one is wrong, then the entire equation is wrong. A + B + J doesn't equal X, and neither does A + Y + C.

What all this proves is simply that in order for you to get exactly what you want when you go shopping, you must become part of a triumphant triumvirate—you + store + clerk. And all three must be working together toward the same goal, that of finding you the merchandise that will best satisfy you. By the way, the retail community is a very committed group of sincere professionals who are upgrading their merchandise and do all they can to train their sales personnel to give the best service.

The question, of course, is how do you (A) find the right store, (B) and the right clerk (C) so you can go home happy and well dressed.

A few principles must be stated immediately. I have said them before, both in this book and in my Presentation Salon / Seminars, but I feel they must now be repeated in connection with this chapter on the art of shopping.

One of these principles is that what seems to be a bargain may not necessarily be a bargain. For a bargain to be truly a bargain—it must be something you feel wonderful wearing. *A bargain is not what you pay but what you receive.* Too many shoppers go stark, raving crazy when there is a sale in a store, and they see something that is marked down from $60 to $27.50—and they become intoxicated with the mere idea of saving money and, with some sort of reflex action, reach out and grab it. It is only later, back home, reflecting on that "thing" they have bought, that they realize it isn't anything they wanted in the first place.

I have often said that *"Only the rich can afford cheap clothing."*

Clothing for centuries has been probably one of our most significant and meaningful status symbols. Probably the cavemen had a pecking order, and the finest skins were worn by those at the top of that order. Later on, in the Middle Ages, the importance of clothing as a status symbol was acknowledged by law. In some countries, it became illegal for people to dress above their station. In the later part of the fifteenth century, in England, there was this law on the books:

"No knight under the rank of lord shall wear any gown, jacket or cloak that is not long enough, when he stands upright, to cover his privities and his buttocks, under the penalty of twenty shillings. No knight under the rank of lord shall wear any shoes or boots having pikes or points exceeding the length of two inches, under the forfeiture of twenty pence."

Status gave those fifteenth-century English lords the privilege of wearing short jackets and long, pointy shoes. And underlings who wanted to go for the fast lane and bought themselves short jackets and long, pointy shoes ran a fearful financial risk. If they were discovered, they would be fined—and twenty shillings and twenty pence in those days was a lot of money to a poor man. Debtors' prison would most likely be his fate.

Today, we have no such penalties. Today, a man who wants to look like a lord—or like some other successful individual—can wear clothing exactly like that lord or that individual wears. No fine awaits him if he is caught at that masquerade. The result is that many of the lords of our world today—and our "lords" are usually business people— find their regalia usurped by just about anybody. And, in realizing this they have taken to wearing copies of poor people's clothing. It is a kind of reverse snobbishness. The eccentricities of a Howard Hughes— sneakers, old pants, rumpled shirt—are a perfect example of this type of mentality. Since they are dressing like us, the reasoning goes, then I have no choice but to dress like them.

But they do it with a difference. A new trend is emerging with today's super-rich. They dress down, all right—jeans, T shirts, all that— but they give that costume their own privileged touch. Their jeans are custom-fitted. Their denim jackets are whipped up with special styling. Their tough-looking boots are fabricated from only the choicest leathers. So they manage to carry off that clothing attitude, but with a definite upper-class imprimatur. In short, the lords and ladies of today are having it both ways—dressing down but living it up, and doing both simultaneously.

That's why I say that only the rich can afford cheap clothing because cheap clothing wears out more quickly and advertises you as cheap.

I will assume, for the sake of argument, that you are not one of the super-rich. So you can't afford to be a clothing eccentric. You still have to make an impression, and as I have stressed often in this volume, the first and best way to make a socko impression on your audience is to dress with dash. Save the poor-boy clothing for those very rough occasions, hiking in the woods or digging up your front lawn. Otherwise, be sure that you *always look at your peak.*

Bargains are rarely going to help you. Shopping may be an art or a science, but bargain-hunting is purely a matter of luck. There may be some skill involved in being able to recognize a real bargain when you stumble over it, but the basic question of finding bargains boils down to a combination of good fortune and persistence and time that might be better spent multiplying your money rather than saving it.

In most cases, the people who go out to those big sales come back big losers. Oh, they may be carrying a suit or a dress or a pair of slacks or something with them that is a great find, but in the majority of cases that stupendous, colossal bargain may prove to be a total disaster. Don't forget that what stores—in almost every case—put out as sale merchandise is merely a collection of stuff that hundreds of shoppers have previously pawed through and rejected. Or else it is genuinely cheap goods, which will fall apart or shrink or fade or turn different colors the first time it is sent to the laundry or the dry cleaner or gets wet or is exposed to the sun. Cheap, in most cases, is *cheap.* Or else it is simply something that is bought only for the price and has no style to it, and consequently, you will very quickly tire of it.

I have said often that the dollar is not made to stretch—it may rip or it may tear, but it simply does not stretch. And yet the shopper is often conditioned from birth to look for sales, to buy anything that has had its price cut—or to put off what they really want until later.

There are, of course, some genuine sales, times during which stores really and truly mark down the prices on a lot of their better-quality merchandise. A sale mentality can deprive you of first choices, however. Note if this sale attitude is consistent with other areas of your life. You may be missing out on first-choice everything!

In most cities, the top-flight stores have annual or semiannual sales, and they are famous for them. If you are one of those dedicated bargain hunters, you will make it your business to learn those dates and save your shopping until that sale comes about. The most frequent date, of course, is immediately after Christmas. But other stores have odd dates that do not seem to bear any relationship to other business practices or other seasonal events. They just are when they are.

Another factor for wise shoppers to understand is that there are three kinds of stores at which they may do their buying. There is, first and most noticeable, the large downtown metropolitan "super-great" department store with its "finer" clothing departments, or its suburban branches. There is, next, the local clothing store where you can occasionally find some quality items. And, finally, there is the crème de la crème, the specialty shop.

Each has its place in your marketing menu. I would suggest you do some shopping in all three types of establishments.

A parenthetical note about "casually smart" (call it "dressy sport" if you wish) clothing at this point: It's hard to find anywhere. In my shopping research, I have found that only about 15 percent of *all* stores— big, middle-sized, small—carry what I would call genuinely good casually smart clothing. Of course, the top echelon of stores do. I don't know why this should be, but it is: Perhaps it is because casually smart clothing is a new horizon that is now emerging for more people. Further, when you can find this kind of clothing, it is usually sold for top dollar because it is usually specially conceived and designed. But more and more of the local clothing stores are beginning to carry this merchandise.

However, when it comes to your top-quality clothing—the men's suits that are for business or important social affairs, women's suits and dresses for work or important after-work engagements—avoid the nationally recognized cheap chain department stores like the plague, as well as those hokey local clothing stores, and make a beeline for the finest quality specialty shops and "super greats" you can find.

And, as a man who has explored most fine stores in the United States and Canada, I feel that I am in a very good position to make some specific recommendations to you. All of the stores that I list here as being in the top echelon are a strong sampling of this "fine" quality. Obviously, this list cannot be all-inclusive; there are undoubtedly some magnificent smaller stores still waiting to be recognized on a national level. The following list points the direction for the shopper wanting to up-grade and maintain a level of superb dressing.

Top Quality Stores

Alan Cherry—Toronto
Alex Sebastian—Costa Mesa (California)
Alion—Honolulu
Amen Wardy—Newport Beach (California)
Andover Shop—New York City
Ann Taylor—New York City
Anthonie's—Bloomington (Illinois)
At Ease—Newport Beach (Virginia)
Atilla—Honolulu
Avventura—Chicago

Balliets—Oklahoma City
Barney's—New York City
Barra of Italy—New York City
Henri Bendel—New York City
Bergdorf Goodman—New York City
Bigsby & Kruthers—Chicago
Bijan—New York City, Beverly Hills

Bloomingdale's—National
Bonwit Teller—National
Brisson & Brisson—Montreal
Britches—Georgetown (D.C.)
Brooks Brothers—National
Bullocks Wilshire—Los Angeles
Butch Blum—Seattle

Cache—Chicago
Capriccio—Scottsdale (Arizona)
Carol & Mary's—Honolulu
Carson, Pirie & Scott—Chicago
Charivari—New York City
Charles Gallay—Los Angeles
Chez Catherine—Toronto, Palm Beach
Chipp—New York City
Chocolates for Breakfast—Honolulu
Collection III—New Orleans
Creeds—Toronto
Cuzzens—Dallas, Houston, Las Vegas

David Stephens—San Francisco
Dayton's—Minneapolis
De Lisi—New York City
De Noyer—New York City
Designer name shops—National
D. Fine—San Francisco
Dimensions—Philadelphia
Donato—Toronto
Dresner—Troy (Michigan)
Dunhill—National

Estell—Montreal
Ethels—Honolulu

Fabrice—Montreal
F. G. Bodner—Houston, Miami,
   Bal Harbour
Filene's—Boston
Firuze / Farnoosh—San Francisco
Frederick & Nelson—Seattle
Frost Bros.—Texas

Garfinckel's—Washington (D.C.)
Gauchaux—New Orleans
The Gazebo—Dallas
G.G.'s—Sausalito (California)
Gene Hiller—Sausalito (California)
Gianpietro—New York City
Giddings-Jenny—Cincinnati
Giorgio—Beverly Hills
Giovanni's—Chicago
Grege—Montreal
Gucci—National

Harold's—Palm Beach, Minneapolis
Hattie—Birmingham (Michigan)
Helen's of Course—Seattle
Holt Renfrew—Montreal

Jacobson's—Birmingham (Michigan)

Jerry Magnin—Beverly Hills
Jimmy's—Brooklyn
Jimmy's—New Orleans
John Leavell—Dallas
Jones & Jones—McAllen (Texas)
Jordan Marsh—Boston

Donna Kendall—New York City

L'Elite—Houston
La Griffe—Montreal
Lilly Simon—Montreal
Lina Lee—Beverly Hills
Linea Pitti—Washington (D.C.)
Little Daisy—West Coast
Lord & Taylor—National
Loretta Blum—Dallas
Louis—Boston
Lou Lattimore—Dallas
L'Uomo—Montreal

Macy's—San Francisco, New
   York City
Madison Avenue stores—New
   York City (60th–75th streets)
I. Magnin—National
Maison Blanche—New Orleans
Maison D'Amir—Westwood
Marc Fidani—Toronto
Marcello Tarantino—Toronto
Mario's—Portland (Oregon), Seattle
Mark James—Vancouver (Canada)
Martha—New York City, Palm
   Beach
Maxfield—Los Angeles
Miss Jackson's—Tulsa
Montaldos—mid-South states
Mr. Guy—Beverly Hills

N. David—Portland (Oregon)
Nan`Duskin—Philadelphia

Neiman-Marcus—National
Nicole Dante—San Francisco,
  Bellevue (Washington)
Nordstrom—Northwest states

Orpheus—San Francisco

Paul Stuart—New York City
Pegasus—Philadelphia
M. Penner—Houston
Perkins Shearer—Denver
Pino's—Seattle
Polacheck's—Milwaukee
Polo Shops—National
J. Press—New York City

Rafael's—San Francisco
Ragazza—Portland (Oregon)
Rich's—Atlanta
Robbie Casey—Odessa (Texas)
Robinson's—Los Angeles
Rodeo Collection—Beverly Hills
Rodeo Drive stores—Beverly
  Hills
Roger Johns—New Orleans
Jackie Rogers—New York City
Ron Ross—Tarzana (California)
Rubenstein Bros.—New Orleans

Sakowitz—Houston
Saks Fifth Avenue—National
Saks-Jandel's—Washington
  (D.C.)
Sara Fredericks—New York City,

Palm Beach
Satel's—San Antonio
Sonny's—Milwaukee
Stanley Korshack—Chicago
St. Germain—San Francisco
Swanson's—Atlanta

Theodore—Beverly Hills
Tootsie's—Houston
F. R. Tripler & Co.—New York
  City
24 Collection—New York City,
  Miami

Ultimo—Chicago

Walter Fong—San Francisco
Wanamakers—Philadelphia
Weinstein's—New Orleans
Wilkes Bashford—San Francisco
Woodward & Lothrop—Wash-
  ington (D.C.)

Yves Saint Tropez—Beverly Hills

FINE CUSTOM SHIRTMAKERS

Arthur Gluck—New York City
Beck and Sobel—New York City
Joseph Rudee & Son—San Fran-
  cisco
Michael Weinstein—Seattle
Nat Wise—Beverly Hills
Sulka—National
Tony Colleta—Akron (Ohio)

There are more good stores, some in smaller cities. If a store works for you, then you have to call it a good store. After all, you must be the final judge. I have simply listed the ones where I have had success shopping, so I feel justified in recommending them to you.

My feeling is that when you are out, looking for the best, looking for something that will make you burst with joy and confidence, then you should settle for nothing less. I like to think that a genuinely fine specialty shop is, in reality, a museum of fine clothing. And fine clothing can be—indeed should be—works of art, such as you find in museums.

Approach the act of shopping for your first-string clothing with that attitude, as though you were going out to buy a work of art, and that your body is the easel on which it will be displayed. People are looking for really special items. They want to build a wardrobe, not just have clothes in their closet.

Dr. Aldo Gucci, the founder of the world-famous specialty shops bearing his name, is supposed to have said, "Quality is remembered long after the price is forgotten." If he said it, bravo for him. Whoever said it, I applaud the thought. It is certainly true. I know it is with me. Even in my earlier years, when I was in need of expanding my clothing allowance, I bought the finest. And, after a while, I honestly had forgotten what those garments cost—but I never forgot how great they felt on me, and how great they made me feel when I wore them.

Take Gucci's advice—and mine. Shop for the best, remembering that there is always a way open for people who are going to the top, so don't let those payments frighten you away from buying the best. Somehow, someway, you'll manage. I truly believe that you will be rewarded financially for the daring you exhibit in buying the best and making yourself look your best. It is the old cast-your-bread-on-the-waters philosophy. I believe you will find that by looking your greatest, your income and your potential will multiply rapidly. Later in this book, I will quote some letters from clients of mine who did just that, with amazing results. *If you buy above your station, above your current level, you will experience an exhilaration that will thrust you forward.* You will find yourself benefiting many times over for your foresight and your courage. You are making a breakthrough, and almost everyone at the top has, at one point or another, made a similar breakthrough. Take a risk and win big.

I want to suggest to you the value of acting on inspiration while shopping. You may see something you like on your very first stop on a shopping tour but not buy it because you think you may find something you like better later on. And, all too often, you never find anything nearly as good, so you have missed your opportunity.

When you see something you admire and like—buy it! You may not see anything half that good again. Of course, it is possible that you will see something you like even better later on, but the odds are you've just seen what you know you want. You can always buy that second thing too, so you will have two things you like a lot. And remember, every time you wear it you reinforce the feeling, the knowledge, the certainty that you do know how to spot a great find. So obey those inspiring impulses. They are usually correct.

However, there is the opposite side to the suggestion that you act with inspiration, and that is that you should never rush into anything, or be stampeded into anything. Just as you should obey your inspiration to buy, so also obey your impulse *not* to buy. Don't let anyone or anything—a hotshot salesman, a bargain-basement price tag, a friend who is with you and restlessly urges you to hurry—push you into buying something that you are not positively sure of. Unless you, yourself, are absolutely, definitely, totally, 100 percent sure that that is what you want, *don't buy it.* Use your *no* power. If you do that, then later your *yes* power will be stronger and you will feel more confident.

If you want it, get it. If you fall in love with it, get it. If you can't live without it, get it.

But if you just can't make up your mind, leave it alone!

O.K. Let's suppose you have found the store you want to shop in, either through one of my recommendations or through personal observation or through the experiences of friends or business associates or relatives. I suggest you visit that store. Get the feel of the place. Observe the layout of the merchandise and the various departments. Note the designers being featured. All this scouting is so that you feel relatively at home. And, therefore, nothing will interfere with your single-minded purpose—buying terrific clothing.

There is another and perhaps more important aim in visiting the store. And that is to see if you can spot a particular salesperson who will be *the* one you want to wait on you.

How will you recognize the one you want?

There are a few clues to look for. Before I allow anyone to serve me in a clothing store, I first observe the store's clerks for some time. I watch the way they look at me squarely in the eye, greet me, and handle other customers. I want them to know that they have my undivided attention, and I have theirs.

I like to watch the clerks as they wait on others, before I commit myself to any one of them. Are they helpful? Are they overly obsequious and fawning and subservient? (I don't want clerks pushing things on me, but neither do I want them agreeing with everything I say and just being yes-men or yes-women; there are times when a dissenting opinion is valuable.) Are they mere sycophants? Above all, does it look as though they know what they are doing?

I size them up as individuals, as human beings. Are they, themselves, well dressed? Are they dressed in a manner I consider to be in good taste? (Obviously, if they are wearing things I consider dreadful, then their opinion is one I wouldn't trust.)

When I find one I think will work best with me, I find out his or her name. The best way to do that is to go up to him—or her—and say, "I am coming back here soon to shop, and I would like you to serve me. What is your name?" Generally, they will give your their card. And—another useful purpose of the direct approach—they will probably tell you which days they work and which days they are off, so you can be sure to come to the store when you will find that particular clerk is on the job.

To get good service, you also have to be a good customer. That merely means being a decent person—polite, considerate, humane. You will want them to assist you, but you are not contracting a slave. Don't expect them to respond favorably if you are the sort of person who thinks a customer has a right—some even think it is their privilege—to bully the salesclerks. They don't appreciate that kind of treatment, nor do they merit it. Your salesperson is in training for sainthood—I know, because I used to be one!

Remember, too, that a clever salesperson is a natural-born psychologist. He or she has been dealing with the public so long that they probably sized you up correctly the moment you set foot in the store. Don't try to play the snob or the phony. Be yourself. Be honest with the clerks. Treat the salesclerks right, I have found, and you will be the better for it.

The salesclerk is on the front line with clothing possibilities. They know—or should know—their merchandise, and they pretty well know, at first glance, what you would look best in. If you can find a really good salesclerk in a top-notch store, chances are you can virtually put yourself in his or her hands and come out of that store looking fantastic. Some of them are as expert in the field of fashion and clothing as the highest-paid fashion-magazine editor.

When you go shopping, start out looking good. That gives the clerk the idea of *how good you are capable of looking.* If, on the other hand, you come into a store dressed shabbily or shoddily, a clerk will have to use great flights of imagination to picture you dressed in the better things they have on their racks and shelves. When you are dressed well, you give the clerk a point of reference; a starting point. It saves everybody a lot of time and energy. (Women—don't shop for clothing without full face makeup, or the clothes may look more vibrant and alive than you.)

O.K. We have shopped for the right shop, and we have shopped for the right clerk in that right shop. And we are approaching the whole purchasing expedition with the proper mental attitude. Is that all there is to it? No. There are what I call the Seven Keys to Successful Buying, and these must be studied and considered. They are, in my opinion, essential when it comes to shopping successfully.

The Seven Keys to Successful Buying are these:

1. OPPORTUNITY

Go into that store and place yourself in the hands of that clerk, your newly discovered favorite salesperson. And then make absolutely sure that your mind is open and receptive. You have to give yourself the *opportunity* to win.

For many of us, strange as it may seem, the act of shopping is traumatic. That's why so many people dress poorly—they do not shop well. Something gets in their way. Perhaps stores and clerks and the whole shopping process intimidates them. Perhaps they consider the act of shopping a bore and a waste of time. Perhaps they are simply tightwads, and the thought of spending money, even on themselves, is offensive.

They just never give themselves the *opportunity* to acquire good clothing, clothing that will help them move into the fast lane. I do not want to imply that shopping is the most important act a human being can aspire to, but I do suggest that it must be worthy of your most serious attention. It is not, or should not be, something to be undertaken frivolously. It is a necessary step if you are to look your best. Clothing doesn't come leaping out of a store and jump on your back! The requirements of our civilization demand that we go into a store and pick out the clothing we want. Of course, there are some wonderful specialty-mail order catalogues such as L.L. Bean, Neiman-Marcus, and Victoria's Secret where the really particular shopper can select items that fit his or her special needs. If we approach that duty with an open mind, with eager anticipation, then we are giving ourselves the *opportunity* to become men and women of taste and distinction.

When you are in a store, and a salesperson approaches you with one of the time-honored opening gambits—"May I help you?" or "Is there something you are looking for?"—what is your initial reaction and response? I have found that, under ordinary circumstances, people answer those questions with one of these lines:

"No, thanks. I am just looking."
"Not just yet. I'll call you if I need help."
"No, thanks. I am just browsing."
"I'm waiting to meet a friend."
"I'm waiting to meet my sister."
"I don't need anything right now."

Other times they answer an affirmative "Yes" and seize the *opportunity* when the salesclerk says, "May I help you?" Maybe you know you can't buy that day for one reason or another, but you just want some idea of what is on hand and how much it costs. The clerk will give you something of a guided tour if you answer his or her question affirmatively.

In my years of shopping with and for others, I always find that when my clients say "yes" to a first-rate article of clothing, they always feel wonderful afterward. And they look wonderful, too. They have grabbed *Opportunity by its capital "O."*

Opportunity, you know, is a fickle and forgetful thing. You must recognize it when it comes along and hang on to it with an iron grip. It doesn't hang around too long. Seize the moment.

I have come to know many incredibly successful people, and when I asked them for the secret of their success, inevitably they said they took advantage of their *opportunities*. The *opportunity* to augment your wardrobe is one of the biggest and most important, when it comes to self-improvement. Don't let it pass you by. *Opportunities* related to money, sex, and power usually have an initial discomfort about them.

Start out by making a detailed "select" list of what you need, just as though you were rounding out a table of carefully chosen dinner guests. List the clothes you need, and perhaps have a separate list for those things you don't exactly need, but might like to have, should you happen to see something great in those areas.

You are the master of your shopping fate. You direct your own shopping success. When you get to the store, and you see something you know will be just right for you—buy it!

2. TRUST

You have to *trust* somebody when it comes to shopping. Maybe it's yourself, your own good taste, your own knowledge of what looks best on you. If you do not have that *trust* in yourself, then you must rely on someone else. Perhaps it is a spouse or parent or offspring or friend, someone whose taste you respect and who you know will have only your best interest at heart. Or perhaps you will choose to use a salesperson, which is when your selection of the right salesperson becomes very important. Or you may want to hire and *trust* a professional wardrobe consultant, which would be a wise choice while building your confidence. Use this person as you would a stylist.

You are going to be faced with a moment of truth. You will be trying on a garment—a dress, a suit, whatever—and you will have to decide then and there whether or not to take it. You will stare at yourself in the mirror. You will check with that other person you *trust*. You will search your soul. And then you will have to say a simple "yes" or "no."

You have to have *trust* that you are doing the right thing by either buying it or rejecting it.

So make up your mind and stick to your verdict. Stop the habit of returning merchandise; it decreases your self-confidence and certainty when you make purchases later on. (Kill the thought that "you're being taken" or "you may be making a mistake.")

And that's why you must *trust* somebody and learn that that *trust* is reliable. You have to go home with that purchase grasped firmly in your hands, and you must know, beyond a reasonable doubt, that you are carrying a brighter future in that package. You have that glorious feeling of "I did it! And I'm glad I did it!"

3. ATTITUDE

I am going to tell you a fable, which is even more fabulous than most fables because I invented it. Once upon a time there were two magnificent suits (or dresses or slacks or whatever). Two magnificent blue suits. And one day two men came in and each one bought one of the suits. And the two identical blue suits said good-bye to each other and they were somewhat sad because they were being separated, but somewhat happy because they were going off on great adventures.

Three weeks later, to the day, by a truly amazing coincidence, the two suits were reunited in the dry-cleaning plant. And Suit A said, "Hi, there, Suit B. Isn't life wonderful? I've been living the most incredibly exciting life with my new master. How's it going with you?" And Suit B said, with tears on his lapels, "You want to hear trouble? I'll give you trouble. Life is full of worms. I'm unhappy. I wish I were back on the old rack in the good old store." And Suit A said, "That's the worst thing I've ever heard, old friend Suit B. What's the matter?" And Suit B said, "It's all in my master's *attitude*. It's all wrong." And Suit A shook his jacket sadly and said, "Oh, you poor fellow. I feel for you."

End of fable. And the moral of the story is that if you want to keep your clothing happy—and, more importantly, be happy yourself—you have to have the right *attitude*. How you think and feel and act in your new outfit determines whether it will be a success or a failure on your back. Clothing needs you, as much as you need clothing, if it is to become a winner. Performance is what it is all about. *Clothes do not make the man or woman, they make you more impressive.*

So, while you shop, ask not only what the clothing can do for you, ask also what you can do for the clothing. It must be a truly working, happy, flourishing partnership, you and those garments you are considering buying. When you try on something, get a sense of what wearing it in certain situations will be like. Try to experience how it will be for you two, you and that garment working in tandem toward the common goal of making you a winner. See if it helps give you that winning *attitude*.

And, once you have bought it, wear it with confidence, with self-assurance, with that same winning *attitude*. If you do, both you and your garment will be happy.

4. SELECTIVITY

For every garment in a store that deserves your vote of approval, chances are there are a dozen you must turn down. *Selectivity* is terribly important. Don't be rushed into anything. In my experience, 70–80 percent of all garments in the run-of-the-mall stores are wrong for just about everybody. Yet somebody buys them. Just make sure that somebody isn't you!

You have to be able to say no, just as strongly and as full of spirit as when you say yes. There are a great many articles of clothing for sale that deserve a rousing *no!* I think many of them should be burned at the stake, or drawn and quartered, or destroyed in some other permanent way. I believe in capital punishment for unworthy clothing. And I certainly feel that the discriminating buyer—that obviously includes *you*—must learn the gentle art of *selectivity*. You must learn to train your eye and your sense of appreciation so you can separate the wheat from the chaff, the good from the inferior. You must come to know yourself well enough to know, in an instant, if some garment the clerk offers you is right or wrong for you. And, if it's wrong, you must have the moral strength to say *no* immediately and firmly.

Above all, don't let yourself be persuaded into buying something you have strong doubts about. With clothing, you need not be absolutely, completely, 100 percent positive all the time before you buy. But most of the time you will be. Learn *selectivity* and you will quickly become accomplished and successful at shopping.

5. ENJOY

Shopping, some people feel, is one of life's more unpleasant chores. The whole concept of having to go out and buy something strikes them as about on a par with a weekend in the Sahara Desert, without a hat. It doesn't have to be that way, and it needn't be that way. Learn to look on shopping as an adventure, a fun experience, something for you to *enjoy*.

And today's stores, by and large, do make the shopping experience an *enjoyable* and pleasant one for you. If they don't, search out the ones that do. *Enjoyment* is especially true with the classiest stores. In many of the ultra-ultra shops along Beverly Hills' very exclusive Rodeo Drive, at Wilkes Bashford in downtown San Francisco, at Ultimo in Chicago, at Louis in Boston, at the Gallerias in Houston and Dallas, and in the prestigious stores in New York City and other major shopping meccas, they serve their customers tea or wine or soft drinks, and some have bumper-pool tables and other entertainments. The philosophy behind that is simply to relax you, to make you feel comfortable, so you can *enjoy* the shopping experience. I find that those among my clientele who do *enjoy* it are, in most cases, more successful shoppers than those who do not. The *enjoyers* take their time, savoring the moment, while those who hate the whole idea of shopping try to get it over with as fast as possible. If you rush, you miss out on the fun.

So, don't rush it. Take your time. *Enjoy* it and you will come away with winning clothing.

6. DESIRE

You have to approach a shopping excursion with a great avid, eager *desire* to buy something. Maybe it's only one small item—a necktie, a scarf, a blouse—or maybe it's an entire new outfit, or even, perhaps, your whole new spring wardrobe. Don't approach a store aimlessly, drifting without purpose from department to department, from display to display. Approach it, instead, with an overwhelming *desire* to come away with a particular purchase. Have a vision of what you want when you shop.

If you go out with a specific goal in mind, you will almost always succeed, and then your moment of unwrapping will be a glorious one.

"Aha!" you will say to yourself, or to anyone within earshot. "Look at this necktie (scarf, shirt, blouse, whatever) I got. Isn't it great!" I want you to experience the *desire* to have it all. I want you, at least once in your life, to go out to a top-flight store and have the *desire* to buy yourself the most fabulous, exciting, and truly outrageous outfit you have ever seen on anyone's back. And come home with it on your back!

Desire something—and then put that *desire* into action.

7. SATISFACTION

The last of my seven keys is the key one: to buy something you are certain will give you a true sense of *satisfaction*. I consider *satisfaction* the sense of fulfillment that makes you feel great and, further, makes those who come in contact with you feel great, too—turned on by your vibrancy and your charm. When you are *satisfied* you become a new and contented person, and that feeling radiates out from you like a magnetic field. It is contagious.

To get that feeling—and give that feeling—you have to be completely *satisfied* with your purchases. You have to know, in your mind, your heart, and your soul, that each piece you have bought goes into the completion of that piece of fine art, that *Living Human Treasure* known as *you*. You will have the further *satisfaction* of knowing that you are a successful shopper. In today's civilization, the shopper is something like the hunter of bygone cultures—he went out on a vital quest for himself and his family, and if he was successful, his return was a time of celebration. We don't have to do that today, but we can get the same *satisfaction* out of shopping—it is a quest that takes time, talent, luck, and perseverance, and the successful completion of that quest is a time for inner joy and great personal pride and *satisfaction*.

Today's shopper is investing in himself or herself and his or her future. You are spending money (perhaps a great amount of money), and it is as much an investment in your future security as though you were investing in stocks or bonds. And so, when you return from a shopping expedition with the inner confidence and knowledge that you have spent your money wisely, then you have every right to feel a sense of *satisfaction*.

The bottom line is that you have won in an arena where winning speaks loudly to the rest of the world about who you are and where you are going. You are perfectly justified if you strut a little when you return home. When you go shopping, remember that you are going for your own personal gratification and your own personal *satisfaction*.

As you shop, or prepare to shop, there will certainly be some questions that will concern you. Really, there are three main problem areas for all of us, as we set out to add anything major to our wardrobe. And those three areas are *design, fabric,* and *color.* You might say only one area—style—because style is the sum of design, fabric, and color and how you add your own personal flair. But let us look at those three big question marks and analyze them, one by one, before you jump into the shopping fray.

1. DESIGN

The most important facet of any garment's *design* is its basic shape; its silhouette. Try to visualize the garment you are considering without its color, without its trim, without its texture—merely that basic, fundamental shape. It's a little like building a house. You work from a plan, a blueprint, which simply gives you the details of the house's basic shape and construction. It is only much later that you start thinking about color (paint, wallpaper) and trim (pictures on the wall) and texture (wood or stucco exterior). And if you can do the same thing with a garment, you are much better off. Of course, you will eventually have to give serious thought to the garment's color and fabric and those other details, but your primary consideration must be the silhouette of that garment, and whether or not that design is a good one for you.

One silhouette may bring you admiring glances and envious stares, while another one simply bores the people you meet. One shape says youth; another speaks of maturity. One form is playful; another is deadly serious. One design extols the human form; another tries to hide it.

You must know what image you want to project, and then find the silhouette that accents and enhances that image. And, before you go into a store to try something on, you should have that vision clearly in your mind, the vision of the message you want to express with the design of the garment you plan to buy. And don't let anything or anyone seduce you away from that vision, or a better one—not a salesperson or a marked-down price tag; not a pretty color or some other garment that woos you away from your goal and purpose.

Proportion is an integral part of design. The proportions of each outfit must be in harmony, balance, and symmetry with your own body type. The parts of the whole must complement one another. A delicate ratio must be established. The interdependent relationship of the top of an outfit with the bottom must balance with your body width and length. The particulars—such as lapels, collars, size and slant of pockets, cuff and sleeve lengths, skirt or pant length or rise, amount of blouson, too severe or too loosely fitted garments, tie and bow length and size— can either enhance or diminish the wearer. Fabric texture tremendously influences proportion. Accessories—their size, physical properties, and colors—must enhance, not overpower, the outfit and wearer. Lastly, from every angle your proportion, body shape, and all-around appeal can be as aesthetically pleasing as a Rodin or Michelangelo sculpture.

2. FABRIC

Fabric and texture often dictate seasons, or are dictated by seasons. They often dictate appropriateness for day or evening, the mood you want to feel and express. Some fabrics say "Poor" and others say "Rich." As you prepare to buy a garment, you should know in advance which fabrics you would accept, or at any rate, which fabrics you would not accept.

I have said frequently, both in this book and elsewhere, that I urge you to wear natural fabrics—cotton, wool, linen, silk. Most fashion experts agree with me about the poorer image projected by people who wear synthetics.

"The movers and shakers of Washington," says Barbara Blaes, one of our capital's top image consultants, "do not wear polyester."

I do want to say here, however, that synthetic blends have their place. Obviously, they are becoming increasingly important in the general clothing picture in America and the world. In a recent article, Gerald P. Elden, chairman of the board of the Man-Made Fiber Producers Association and president of Hoechst Fiber Industries, expressed the case for synthetics very well.

"Man-made fibers," Elden wrote, "such as polyester, nylon, rayon, and acrylic, have been refined and improved so much that they can be 'engineered' and tailored to fit specific apparel needs and provide desirable characteristics in a finished garment.

"For example, modern technology has been applied to achieve stretch fabrics. Polyester and spandex are now being added to cotton and other fibers to give more comfort to top and bottom weights. Used in woven fabrications, stretch has moved beyond the swimming pool and exercise floor into men's active wear, sportswear, and tailored clothing."

Yes, synthetics do have their place. I wouldn't go so far as Mr. Elden and urge my clients to buy "tailored clothing" of synthetic material, but certainly in some applications it is very worthwhile. In the gym, of course, the stretchability factor of synthetics is very desirable. Also, in linings synthetics perform very well. However, the really well-dressed man or woman sticks with all-natural fibers. You wouldn't think of wearing polyester underwear!

And so, when you shop, think of the *use* you are going to put any garment to, and try to plan to buy something made of a fabric that will assist that purpose.

For sportswear: synthetics, if you do a lot of active playing; cotton for comfort; linen for good looks.

For daily wear, evening wear, and other occasions: wool, cotton, linen, silk, leather and suede, and other natural fabrics.

3. COLOR

Wear the color or colors that work for you! Color has power!

You are the best judge of that, maybe the only judge. But you must be very open and very objective. Colors are tricky things. It most often is the hue and intensity of color that makes the necessary and sophisticated difference. Some colors that you may love and adore may look ridiculous on you. A man could, for example, consider forest-green to be a sight for well eyes, colorwise, but he would look like an overgrown zucchini in a forest-green suit or even a forest-green shirt in most conservative business situations. Obviously, that is an extreme example, but you get the idea. You have to look like what you are—a Living Human Treasure—and not like something that was thrown together by a monkey with a paint-by-numbers kit. You have to blend, not clash. Stop dressing matchy-poo and blend your clothing colors. Colors can stimulate and soothe, cheer and enhance, entice and captivate.

What I mean when I say "blending" is:

You have to have the talent and skill to utilize unusual color and fabric combinations. Not just the cliché combinations—brown and yellow, red and white, blue and gray—but combinations you don't see every day—gray and tan, brown and black, green and coral, red and purple.

Don't be afraid of color, but don't go color mad. Keep it under control, yet use it. It's a narrow line I'm asking you to walk, and if you don't feel as though your own taste is keen enough to trust, then you will have to put your trust in somebody else—a friend, a relative or salesperson—providing that someone has knowledge that goes beyond suburban save-a-dollar thinking. This is true for the color specialist. If you are going to use one, find one who offers more than simply giving you color advice and make sure he or she has sophisticated taste.

One more thing about color and shopping. Leave those color swatches at home. Not that piece of fabric you're using to match your shoes with your dress but that packet of color swatches a color consultant gives you. If you must refer to the packet, do it before shopping. Clerks have told me that there is nothing that turns them off as quickly as a customer who is constantly putting his or her color packet up against a garment on the rack to see if it matches the advice given.

Men, you don't need to try to extend hair color, eye color, or skin color when it comes to picking the color of a business suit. That idea can be totally eliminated. Nothing says believability and authority more than the true blue suit no matter what the color of your eyes, hair, or complexion.

When you go to a store with the knowledge of what you want from the standpoint of garment, design, fabric, and color, then you and the salesperson, working as a team, have an easier time in finding the perfect garment for you. The clerk knows (or should know) what is in stock, and you know (or may have an idea of) what you want. Together, you'll find the perfect garment if it exists in that store.

If, however, you start out vague and indefinite, the salesperson will be put at a disadvantage to assist you. I am not here to urge you to rush through your purchasing so clerks can get rich quick. You will get better service if the clerk feels that you are not going to take an unnecessary amount of time because you have nothing better to do that day but kill time in the store.

In some of the better establishments these days, you will find men and women who are sometimes called "dressers," sometimes "wardrobe experts," sometimes even something as prestigious as "image consultants." If you decide you want to use their services, then I suggest you take my earlier advice about clerks and watch a few of these people in action. Look closely at how they, themselves, are dressed and, if possible, at some of their customers, and be open to be guided by their taste, matching it with yours. The private image consultants have come into their own. These entrepreneurs, in most cases, have extraordinary dressing skills, fabulous taste, and many resources at their disposal. They owe no allegiance to any store and are well informed on where to go to find exactly what you want.

Finally, before you go out on your next shopping expedition, I want you to consider your attitude.

Like anything else in life, if your attitude is negative, the results of your shopping expedition will almost always be negative as well. The way you think, and how you think, will most certainly be reflected in what you buy. Your attitude determines your altitude.

Many people, as I have said, hate to shop. It is, to them, one of the worst of all possible human experiences. They feel it is something to be gotten over with as quickly and painlessly as possible. And they look it, too. They wear things that are mismatched, out of style, ill-fitting, unattractive. They look like has-beens that never were.

There are others, at the extreme other end of the shopping spectrum, who love to shop for shopping's sake. They look it, too. I can spot them just as easily as I can spot those who hate to shop. The "shopophiles," who always seem to be wearing those very special sweaters, coats, shirts, shoes, and so forth, look as if they have an "in" with each store owner. Everything they wear is exquisite.

Somewhere in between those two extremes can be you. Don't hate to shop; think of it as an adventure in finding your best image. And enjoy shopping; it is a means to an end, the purchasing of your needed wardrobe. Recognizing and acquiring a great piece of clothing is almost as thrilling as having created it yourself.

I have often gone shopping and bought the first thing I tried on. My theory is that you should try something on and, if it works, buy it. No need to keep looking if you've already found something that works.

And yet, on other occasions, I have literally spent hours in a fruitless hunt for a specific item. Those times may be long and arduous, but they also are informative and purposeful—never a loss. They give me up-to-the-minute knowledge of what is happening in the big world of retail clothing merchandising.

It is, as I said earlier, like a hunter off searching for food for his clan or family. The hunter may find game quickly and triumph, or he may be out for weeks without success. And, similarly, the shopper may win quickly or never win at all on that particular day.

But if your goal is the fast lane, you *must* learn how to shop well. It is an essential part in the process of turning your life around. You cannot be well dressed without good clothing, and the only way to get good clothing is to buy it.

10

Assembling Your New Wardrobe

THE MAGIC OF OWNING JUST THE RIGHT PIECES

It all starts from the beginning, like everything else. If you want a great garden, you have to start out by planting something. If you want a great wine cellar, you have to first buy a bottle of wine. And, if you want to build a marvelous wardrobe, you first start by buying an article of clothing.

But it may seem insurmountable to you, this business of assembling an entire new wardrobe. Where to begin? What should you buy first?

Starting at the beginning, why do we wear clothing in the first place? Probably, our primitive ancestors first threw an animal skin over their backs to keep warm, and basically, that is the chief utilitarian purpose of all clothing to this day. Perhaps next, a few millennia later, came the desire to show off a little. Somebody, an early furrier, used two animal pelts instead of one, and that looked nice. And that was the start of the desire that is now so prevalent to wear clothing that flatters.

Finally, not very long ago as archeologists reckon time, came the need to wear clothing for the sake of modesty.

So clothing serves three purposes in our culture—protection from the elements, appearance, and masking our shyness.

We will assume that all clothing you get today automatically qualifies as protection from the elements (although some of the wonderful things some ladies wear today won't help much in a blizzard) and also qualifies as garments to preserve modesty. Here we are naturally concerned primarily with clothing that aims to enhance and improve our appearance. Let the world's finest designers combine to create a wardrobe for you of unprecedented quality and appeal.

As you set off to build a new wardrobe, don't begin your quest worrying too much about the cost of things. Remember, a bargain is not what you pay, but what you receive. *I think it is much better to buy the cheapest thing in the most expensive store than to buy the most expensive thing in a cheap store.*

Excellence in developing a wardrobe is never an accident. It is achieved as a result of vigorous insistence on the highest standards of craftsmanship. It requires an unswerving expectancy of quality. Excellence is contagious. It infects and affects everyone who sees you. It charts the direction of your path. It provides vitality and zest to your outlook. Excellence in selecting a wardrobe must be nourished and continually revised. Wardrobe excellence is the result of a creatively conceived and precisely planned effort. Its results inspire! It electrifies! It unleashes an impact that influences every aspect of your life. In developing a wardrobe of excellence you must be imaginative, adaptable, and vital. It requires of the dresser a constant state of self-discovery and discipline.

I suggest that you align with—and emulate, in terms of how they dress—people who have a vision, men and women of style and purpose who triumph. My friends who ski tell me the way to learn to ski well is to get behind a really proficient skier. My friends who play bridge well tell me that the way to learn to be a crackerjack bridge player is to sit down at a table and play with real experts. And the same principle holds true of dressing for the top—if you want to learn to dress well, watch how the really well-dressed people do it. Get behind them, just as the skiers get behind the top skiers. They don't mind being copied or imitated; as the old cliché says, imitation is the sincerest form of flattery. Hire a professional dressing consultant if you desire quicker, surer results.

So let's start our shopping trip.

Logic tells us that we should start with the major item, then add the accessories that go with it. For a man, that means we begin by buying a suit. It wouldn't make any sense to buy a tie first, and then try to build a total outfit around that tie. No, buy a good suit first (unless you are a highly skilled or experienced dresser). Pick out the major item, then fit the accessories around it. (Orderliness, remember?)

First, make a list of your needs. Or use mine. I believe that an outfit for a man should be assembled and purchased in this order (specific suit, tie, and shoe designs are covered in Chapter 11):

1. Suit
2. Shirt or shirts
3. Tie or ties
4. Shoes
5. Belt or belts
6. Socks
7. Underwear (when needed)

That's the daytime, go-to-business outfit. Next, a casual or sport outfit. And, again, you start out by buying the major item first:

1. Sport jacket
2. Slacks
3. Shirt or shirts
4. Tie or ties (if desired)
5. Shoes
6. Belt or belts
7. Socks
8. Underwear (when needed)
9. Sweater or special suede, leather or fabric vest (if desired)

All right, back to the daytime outfit. We are agreed that the suit comes first. But there are a lot of suits out there. They sprout up in stores like weeds.

What suit should you buy? My vote would be to aim for a navy or midnight-blue suit. I believe there is still nothing that conveys power and success as quickly and convincingly as a really fine, rich-looking blue suit. I call a good blue suit a *power-blue suit*. (No, not powder-blue—power-blue!) It may sound easy to go out and buy a blue suit, but it requires knowing what caliber suit you want. As a matter of fact, in my experience the two items that are the hardest for a man to find are a quality black belt and a quality blue suit.

So look and shop until you find that great blue suit, and coordinate the shoes, belt, shirt, tie, and socks with it.

Actually, there are four things I want you to consider when you are buying that most-important suit:

1. The color. As I have said, I prefer blue. Not a gaudy blue, but a serious, subdued blue. Plain but, if you prefer, just a subtle hint of a

stripe or a pattern. The great designers all create styles that are harmonious, sophisticated, easy to describe. The styles must look persuasive on you, of course. Start putting them on.

2. Then there is the question of suit design, which is not quite the same thing as style. (More detailed descriptions and photographs of each suit type are included in Chapter 11, so you can have greater confidence and know-how in selecting your next suit.) For men there are:

A. AMERICAN CLASSIC TRADITIONAL (Conservative Sack)

This is your typical Brooks Brothers look. Its keynote is "conservative." Understated clothing with a natural-shoulder, minimally shaped fuller-cut jacket with armholes somewhat low—a symbol of American businessmen for years—never seems to become obsolete. Presence is given to the wearer mainly by this suit's traditional acceptance, not by its unique structure and form. It has been tested and has proven itself. Suit colors are the classic business blues, grays, tans, and earth tones— with very slight changes.

B. AMERICAN UPDATED TRADITIONAL (British-American)

This more fitted look is more style-oriented than designer-oriented. Some of the design specifics are: rounded, slightly shaped shoulders with slight padding that contours to the man's silhouette. The jacket is a little longer, the waistline more definite and shaped, the jacket skirt often side-vented, and the lapels are wider and notched. Most trousers are shown with a cuff, but they're not mandatory. The color combinations for this look are exciting and unusual, often mixing your usual blues, grays, and browns, with shades of purple, greens, and whatever happens to grow on a mountainside or in a valley. A rich sense of color and texture is often evident but not always. (The American designers for this style: Ralph Lauren [Polo], Alexander Julian, Garrick Anderson, Alan Flusser, Cesarani, Jhane Barnes, Jeffery Banks, Chester Barrie.)

When you read and see fashion statements like: "herringbone jacket features an overplaid in oxford-shirt pastel colors; it's worn with pleated flannel trousers; wool-mohair knit tie; authentic Harris Tweed jacket in an offbeat seafoam worn with a wool argyle sweater, wool ripcord trouser; cotton oxford shirt, and pure-silk rep tie; or crisp checks, bold blazer stripes and tasteful windowpane and glen plaids"—you know you've arrived in American Updated Traditional Land! It is clothing that is conservative at heart, with underlying individualism and adventure.

C. EUROPEAN "V" WEDGE (Classic or Trend-Setting)

This is a more closely fitting suit with narrow, square shoulders and fitted hips, higher armholes, and slimmed down, tapered jacket sleeves. An appearance of "dress-up" is how many Americans classify this look. However, well-dressed men who are considered to be "dapper" by their colleagues often are seen in this type suit, which conveys more flair. In many cases these are higher-quality suits. The Classic European is not severely tapered or too broadly shaped. It is a tremendous suit to enhance the physique of an aging executive and adds vitality and "up-rightness" to the wearer. (Such designers as Brioni, Zegna, DiMitri, Corneliani, Yves Saint Laurent, Cerruti, Nutter, Devenza, add well-worn names to this category.)

The Trend-Setting European has its emphasis on fashion. The suits are more severely styled, often with built-up, narrow, square shoulders, wider lapels, and higher, tighter armholes with tapered sleeves. The jackets are either single- or double-breasted and generally side-vented or non-vented. The trousers may or may not be pleated, but are seldom cuffed. Styling and fit seem to be the two characteristics that set this European look apart from the Traditional American Conservative design. In styling, because it is in the forefront of design—you can see the "personality" of each designer. The suit fit flatters because of the way it is cut to the body. You need to be trim to wear this design to its full advantage, although a *slightly* overweight body will appear to have lost five to ten pounds just by putting on the jacket.

This style allows a wide range of colors in addition to the blue, gray, and brown possibilities: blacks, creams, dark, and subtle fashion tones. There are also interesting pattern combinations as well as fabric combinations—raw silks and other "nubby" natural fabrics. (Such designers are Armani, Versace, Basile.)

The key for keeping each of these categories in harmony is balance within the look. It may be proportional balance between the coat lapel of four inches, the shirt collar of approximately three inches, and the tie of three inches. Any of these looks mentioned could be you. All three are good designs. Each makes a different statement about the person wearing the suit.

Design is a matter of appropriateness. Some suits are more appropriate for daytime than evening wear, for winter than summer, for country than city. So be sure that not only is the style becoming to you, but that the design—the shape, the silhouette, and the form—is good for the purposes you intend the suit to achieve.

3. After you have settled on color, style, and design, you have to consider fabric. And, in my lexicon of clothing, there is no question here—natural fabric, which for men's suits almost automatically means wool and cotton for business, silk, linen, wool, and cotton for other occasions.

4. Lastly, I want you to ask yourself, as you make that vital

purchase, this key question: Would Robert Panté, or a friend whose clothing you greatly admire, buy this garment for you?

Everything on those two lists must be bought with care. Don't think that because you've always bought the same kind of shoes from the same shoe store clerk in the same shoe store that you must keep right on in that groove. This is a *new you* and I think a *new you* merits and deserves top-quality shoes.

Shoes are very important, not only for their appearance but because if they are uncomfortable, your entire presentation will be adversely affected. Nothing makes a man (or woman) look worse than when his feet are killing him; that discomfort makes his whole body look awkward. And—this is a personal theory—if your shoes are not flexible then you age more quickly.

The following is an excerpt from a wonderfully informative article in *United Magazine,* December 1981, "New Status for the Business Shoe," by Alex Carpenter:

> There is no question that the shoe you want to do business in is a leather one. There are several good reasons for this, apart from the fact that vinyl and polyurethane substitutes never manage to look sufficiently like the real thing. Leather is a skin, which means it "breathes," allowing air to enter and moisture to escape. This is important: adult male feet can produce as much as half a pint of perspiration a day. Also, leather is suggestible: it conforms to the shape of a foot with wear, then stays that way. As a result, leather shoes become more comfortable as they grow older. It's smart to select shoes with leather linings and soles as well as uppers. Leather soles, especially, give a pair of shoes a sleek, all-of-a-piece look, and they are highly resistant to punctures.
>
> As for types of leather, you'll most frequently encounter cowhide, which can be stiff or soft depending on the quality of the hide and how it is tanned. Soft is best, of course, and is almost as status-conferring as calfskin. Both types—calfskin and top-grade cowhide—are sturdy and scuff-resistant, and wonderfully pliable while still being supportive of the foot's complex anatomy. The other major leather type is cordovan, which is not really leather at all, but a layer of subcutaneous cartilage taken from the rump of a horse. Though durable and rich-looking, it doesn't breathe; consequently, cordovan shoes can be extremely hot in summer.
>
> Construction is as much an issue as materials. Essentially, you want a shoe that's stitched rather than cemented together, or God forbid, injection-molded. The most familiar technique, as well as the most expensive, is the Goodyear welt, a kind of grooved ledge, almost always of leather, that runs around the front part of the shoe at shoe level; stitches through the upper portion of the shoe anchor the welt to the insole, while

egant evening

siness

ort and casually smart

Men's Shoes. *Walter Newberger for Wilkes Bashford.*

separate stitches downward through the welt hold the shoe in place. Well-constructed shoes are sturdier than any other kind.
(Reprinted courtesy *United Magazine,* carried aboard United Airlines. © 1981.) East / West Network, publisher.

And when well-fitted they are great feeling and long lasting. In addition to the black and brown shoes, burgundy, tan, taupe, and all natural shades of earth colors have their place in today's varied business sectors where men perform the business of multiplying profits. The new entrepreneur has more shoe options based on the nature of his work and professional encounters.

When you come to buying the sport jacket, be very careful. There is a tendency among some men to go wild and crazy with sport jackets. They buy things with all sorts of loud and gaudy colors, all manner of freakish patterns. I have a private game I play, and it always works. I can tell everything about people by the kind of plaid they pick out. If I were to give you a hundred dollars and tell you to buy a plaid shirt or a plaid blouse, I could give you a pretty good character analysis based only on what sort of plaid you brought back. I could tell the kind of education you have had, what sort of person you are, even what kind of life you lead. Avoid big plaids, checks that are too bold, stripes that are overpowering. You are buying a sport jacket for a human, not a blanket for a horse.

The jacket—whether it is the suit jacket or the sport jacket—is the key to your appearance. The test of a really good jacket is whether or not it looks good in black or white. If you can visualize it in either solid black or solid white, and you still like it, then buy it. But that test will eliminate some jackets that rely for their style and appeal almost entirely on color and pattern. The really superior jackets would look good even in black or white, so apply that test to any jacket that you are contemplating purchasing. It's the silhouette, cut, and shape that count most.

When it comes to purchasing pants a good-fitting pair of pants goes a long way in making a man look attractive and feel sharp. Such problems as having one leg longer than the other; extra large calves and thighs, narrow waists, bowleggedness, flat bottom, etc. all add to caution when buying and being fitted for the right pair of pants.

In an article in *Esquire* entitled "A Gentleman's Pants" (February 1983) Ronald Varney explains what every man should know when choosing pants that you know will make you look and feel perfect.

> What a man should reasonably expect from a good pair of pants is a good fit. According to Vincent Bonasera, head of all tailoring operations for Brooks Brothers, "The most important thing to consider is the rise, which is the measurement from the waistband to the crotch." Most men are not aware of the rise, though it affects the way they feel in the pants and the way they look . . .
>
> The rule of thumb is that if a man is five foot six or shorter, he will need a short rise; five foot six to five foot nine, a regular; and five foot nine to six foot three, a long rise. This measurement is crucial. When you see a man in a pair of pants with a sagging crotch or with one that digs in like a sling, you know he has chosen the wrong rise . . .
>
> The standard procedure goes like this: The customer is asked to try on the pants with a belt. The fitter rolls up the right leg and asks if the gentleman prefers a cuff or a plain bottom. Then he asks, "Sir, would you like it to break on the shoe, or just hit the top of the shoe?" Whether the man wants a heavy break or wants to show his socks, the fitter makes sure the pants are not too short, easily the worst of all mistakes . . .

After length, any adjustments in the waist and seat that need to be made are done. Mr. Varney goes on to quote Chris Giannino, the head tailor at Paul Stuart, who says,

> "A pair of pants is the most important piece of the wardrobe. The average person spends more time selecting pants than in selecting the entire suit. Why? Because pants have a hidden message. They tell of your taste, your awareness of style. They should be tailored to conform with

the contour of your body and fall easily and comfortably. Of course there is more to it than that, such as the selection of fine fabrics, the subtle details, the lining, and the underpressing. The most important part, though, is the tailor's skill in making a pair of pants a piece of art."

When it comes to a necktie, remember what I said earlier: A man's tie is his signature. A man's tie can hang him if it is too outlandish. You can reveal yourself with your tie. It tells people what you are like, what sort of a personality you have, and thus those who meet you will—subconsciously or consciously—draw a lot of information from your tie.

Men's Ties. *Wilkes Bashford.*

For women, here is my suggested order or purchasing list, and here, again, my recommendation is to build your outfit around the major item first (specific dress, shoe, blouse, and coat designs are covered in Chapter 11):

1. Day Dress
2. Shoes
3. Belt (if the dress requires it, and it doesn't come with it)
4. Handbag
5. Other accessories, as needed
6. Underwear (when needed)
7. Coat, if your climate demands it

That's for one key outfit, the essential day-dress outfit. But, just as essential to a woman today is the outfit built around a suit. Purchase that in this order:

1. Suit
2. Blouse or blouses
3. Shoes
4. Belt
5. Handbag
6. Accessories, as needed
7. Underwear (when needed)
8. Coat, if your climate demands it. (The coat you already bought for the day-dress outfit may or may not fit over a suit. Check to see if you need an additional coat to go over your suit outfit.)

And, finally, women need a casual outfit, which should be purchased in this order:

1. Skirt or skirts
2. Blazer
3. Blouse or blouses
4. Shoes
5. Belt
6. Handbag
7. Accessories, as needed
8. Underwear (when needed)
9. Sweater or vest
10. Coat (maybe the same coat here, too)

Here, as with men's outfits, many things can do double duty. Some blouses can be worn with both the suit and the casual outfit.

Ditto belt and shoes, although sometimes a belt or a pair of shoes are so special that they must be reserved for one particular outfit. Handbags can definitely be carried with more than one outfit, don't be afraid to demand too much of them. As I have written earlier, you can spoil a great outfit easily by carrying a non-statement-making handbag. A beautifully designed handbag, "looking like superb luggage," always works.

For women, as well as men, there are a variety of suit designs from which to choose. (More detailed descriptions and photographs of these suit types are included in Chapter 11.) For women these are:

A. Classic Hip-length
B. Thigh-length Jacket
C. Short Jacket with Full Skirt
D. Long and Lean, Straight Jacket and Skirt

port and casually smart

usiness

legant evening

Women's Shoes. *Shaw's Shoes, Walter Newberger for Wilkes Bashford.*

E. Double-breasted, Thigh-length, Peaked-lapel Coordinates

F. Pantsuit

Women often have a much greater variety of appropriate clothing for work to choose from than men. These include: separates, day dress, day dress with blazer, matching coat and skirt with blouse. While I have listed the basic suit designs in Chapter 11, here we will examine these other possibilities further.

Once you have your clothing bought and hung in your closet, my suggestion for a logical next step may surprise you. But, in nine out of ten cases, I think the next thing you should do is to go out and get a good haircut or restyling. And I also urge my female readers to have their makeup professionally restyled at this point. Nothing enhances new clothing—a *new you*—more than a totally new hairstyle and, for the ladies, a new face (and a new makeup gives you a new face).

Wardrobe plans to convey a look that is *attractive, has strong presence, and carries clout* are (these suggestions are not initially to save you money but to make you money—in the long run they will pay off richly! The price of a garment is determined by the quality of fabric, the amount of hand-stitching, and the caliber of the designer):

The One-Star Plan

*FOR A MAN: (One Perfect Business or Social Evening Suit)
    1. One suit. Dark blue, two or three piece.

                                            $550–850
    2. Two dress shirts. One white and one light blue.

                                            $50–75 each
    3. Two ties. One rep and one foulard.

                                            $25–40 each
    4. One pair of shoes. Black or burgundy.

                                            $135–175
    5. One belt. Black. $50–75
    6. Two pairs of socks. Black. $5–15 each

The One-Star Plan

*FOR A WOMAN: (One Perfect Business or Social Evening Outfit)
    1. Suit and day dress. Blue, tan, burgundy, or gray.

                                            $550 (suit)
                                            $200 (dress)
    2. One blazer. $300
    3. Two blouses. $150 each
    4. Two pairs of shoes $150 each
    5. One belt $60–100
    6. One handbag $150 and up

This One-Star Plan for a beginning wardrobe collection is a guaranteed win/win. By having this initial set of clothing in your closet you have the "criteria" for all others to come. It is much easier building a wardrobe knowing the reality of cost. And you will have known quality, top of the line, designed clothing of the best fabrics, workmanship, and design. You'll definitely know what it feels like and looks like to wear and be seen in the best.

Two-Star Plan

**FOR A MAN:

For a man, to build a Two-Star Wardrobe, he wants to *double* the One-Star Plan exactly; with the same number of pieces, and possibly changing the color of the suit. Or if you definitely know that you look best and feel best in dark blue suits, buy another one, possibly with

*Approx. $1,200
*Approx. $1,500
**Approx. $3,500 additional

pin-stripes this time. Also, on this Two-Star Plan you want to add a wonderful blue blazer, single or double-breasted, plus two pairs of slacks and a sweater or vest. Increasing the wardrobe this way will give you much more versatility, and your clothing pieces will wear much longer.

Two-Star Plan

**FOR A WOMAN:
    For a woman to build a Two-Star Wardrobe, she wants to *double* the suits and day dresses to two suits and two day dresses, and add two skirts, two more blouses, another pair of shoes, another belt, possibly a hat, and a sweater. She will have a splendid full week of wearing a different outfit each day that is smartly tailored, and because of its high-quality fabrics and designs she will feel great mixing and matching and blending these outfits. She won't feel that they "don't quite make it." This often happens when you attempt to mix and match inexpensively made pieces of clothing. You've seen this attempt at mixing not-so-good's with not-so-good's—a disaster!
    Let's move on to my Total Wardrobe Plan for both men and women. It includes the things a man or woman ought to have if he or she is really going all out for that elusive fast lane.

Three-Star Man's Prosperity Wardrobe

1. Three suits. One blue, one gray, one tan.
                                    $550–1,300 each
2. Two sport jackets. One blazer, one tweed.
                                    $350–950 each
3. Eight dress shirts. Two white, two light blue, two tan, one gray, one striped.
                                    $45–250 each
4. Six ties. Two to go with each suit.
                                    $30–45 each
5. Five pairs of shoes. Three for work, two for casual.
                                    $150–225 each
6. Three belts. Remember, belts must blend or match your shoes.
                                    $40–150 each
7. Four pairs of slacks. Two with each sport jacket.
                                    $125–300 each
8. Three coats. A topcoat, a raincoat, a dark evening coat. (Men

----

**Approx. $3,500 additional

living in warm climates need only the raincoat unless they desire the evening coat.)

$450–1,250 each

9. Five casually smart sports outfits. Two of cotton, one of silk, two pairs of jeans. This includes shoes, shirts, pants, and a belt.

$500–1,000 each

10. One outer sport jacket of leather or suede.

$450–900

As you can see the minimum for a man to acquire this Three-Star Prosperity Wardrobe is somewhere around $9,000—that's the bottom figure, but it can go much, much higher. Don't think that's too much money; you must look at it as an investment in your future. Don't you consider it a good deal, to invest $9,000 and, in return, look great and reap the financial benefits?

Three-Star Woman's Prosperity Wardrobe

1. Three day dresses. Cottons, silks, or wools.
$115–300 each

2. Two suits. One for day, one for evening wear.
$550–900 each

3. Six blouses. Silk or cotton. $100–300 each

4. Two skirts. One straight, one fuller.
$125–300 each

5. Five pairs of shoes. For day, or evening.
$100–215 each

6. Two pairs of slacks. $125–300 each

7. Three blazers. One solid, one tweed, one white or off-white.
$300–550 each

8. Three belts. $35–150 each

9. Three handbags. One for day, one for evening, one for fun.
$150–500 each

10. Two hats. One for business, one more adventurous.
$75–300 each

11. Three evening party dresses. Two calf-length, one floor-length.
$450–3,000 each

12. Three coats. One heavy one for day, one raincoat, one evening wrap.
$350–1,500 each

13. Six casually smart outfits. One silk, one leather, two cotton, two jeans.
$400–600 each

14. One short sport coat. Something like a fur chubby.
$750–3,500

15. Two pairs of earrings. One for day, one for evening.
$225–1,000+ each

16. One gold necklace and two bracelets.
$250–1,000+ each

That is the basic investment. Obviously, when it comes to jewelry, the sky's the limit. And, in the area of coats, if a lady chooses to add a mink or some other really great fur, that would, of course, up the ante considerably. But that basic wardrobe, again figuring on the low side of all those estimated figures, comes to close to $11,000, a shade higher than the men's wardrobe. The life expectancy of a woman's wardrobe is somewhat shorter than a man's. Except for coats and jewelry, which can be expected to last some time, women should figure on replacing a third of what they have at least once every year and a half.

Four-Star Plan

****FOR MEN AND WOMEN:

The Four-Star Wardrobe is quite simple. First you double the number of pieces that make up your One-Star Plan, and your Two-Star Plan, plus your Three-Star Plan. That is easy. For men you now have a change of business clothing for *each day* of the week for *two weeks* plus casual wear. For women you have a change of clothing for *each day* of the week for *three weeks* of work and casual wear. Now is where the real excitement comes in buying clothing—it is the Five-Star Plan.

Five-Star Plan

The Five-Star Plan brings into your wardrobe those fantastic evening clothes for dining, dancing, concerts, and all those wonderful events that announce "come dressed to the nines."

*****FOR MEN:

For a man you want to add these complete outfits to your already winning wardrobe: one tuxedo, single or double-breasted, two- or three-piece, tuxedo shirt, self-tie or ready-made black bow tie, an additional pair of black shoes—they need not be patent leather—and a handsome set of tuxedo shirt studs in onyx, gold, platinum, or even have some made out of your family antique rare-jewelry collection. In addition, you will want to purchase a double-breasted, European-cut suit in any of the dark evening colors—blue, black, or wide-striped gray wool.

Also, you may want to add a velvet jacket with striped morning pants or solid silk, black pants to your collection. It is a total of three more complete evening outfits that are your entrée to all formal, dress-up, elegant affairs.

*****FOR WOMEN:

For a woman you will want to expand your already fantastic wardrobe by adding, for evening, a great fur coat that says *you have arrived*. Two floor-length gowns; two shorter leggy cocktail or dance dresses; two silk-pant outfits; two dinner suits, and accessories to go with each stunning outfit, including a pair of smashing diamond or precious stone earrings and a necklace that will launch the security guards into action.

When you are assembling wardrobes such as these, you should, of course, make sure that everything you buy conveys your message. You don't want to buy items that will contradict each other. *You, as a person moving upward, are always thinking and acting on course, and so your clothing should always be purposeful.* Be consistent in the message you convey.

As you shop for your wardrobe, when you are looking at the creations of various designers to find the ones best suited to you and your body, remember that what distinguishes one designer from another is primarily the *silhouette* or *attitude,* of the creations. *A silhouette can create strong presence, can fabricate interesting body contours, can convey a powerful, esthetic pleasure.* On the other hand, the unflattering silhouette can make a person look less than totally impressive. When you are testing different designers, remember that it is the attitude of the entire garment that makes the difference, so at first be aware of the immediate impression that strikes you. It is this message that will be conveyed to others. Concentrate, as you look at yourself in the mirror, on the basic silhouette and how it looks on you. Know what you want to say.

In that regard, buying a garment can be like buying a house. Clothing experts will tell you not to concern yourself with all the details when you are clothing shopping. Instead, look at the basic design of the garment—will it hold up? Does it have the capacity to become a classic? Or are you more concerned with its present usage? Both have their place in your wardrobe. Try on several creations from each designer to make sure that those silhouettes really work for you.

That's another reason why I keep hammering at that theme of mine—shop only in the finest stores. Those stores will have enough tasteful creations by enough different designers so you will have plenty of opportunity to try on sufficient garments to make a judicious choice. In less-well-stocked stores, they may only have one or two creations by each designer, and only a few designers, and that's not enough to allow you to be fair to yourself.

The One-Star, Two-Star, and Three-Star Wardrobes that I have suggested in the previous paragraphs are basic. Certainly you can augment them in many ways; ways that allow you to express your own taste and personality.

Sweaters, for example. Many men and women—myself included—love to wear sweaters. I think you can build a small collection of top-quality sweaters that will give your wardrobe variety and distinction. Sweaters punch up the way you look in leisure settings.

And jeans, too. I suggested a couple of pairs of jeans in each of the Prosperity Wardrobes above. But maybe you will choose to add more than just those few pairs. Fine. I'm a pro-jeans person. *I believe that great jeans are to clothes what potatoes are to a meal—essential.* For a man with flair, there is no better all-around casual party outfit more exciting than jeans, coupled with a velvet jacket or wool sport jacket and a silk shirt.

And boots at the other end. It takes a certain savvy to carry that off, but it can be a powerful and winning outfit.

What about fabrics? Almost all of the natural fabrics have their place in a contemporary wardrobe. My own personal taste as to which fabrics can be used for what purpose is as follows:

Broadcloth—blouses
Camel's hair—winter coats, jackets, sweaters
Cashmere—sweaters, jackets (blends)
Corduroy—sportswear
Cotton—shirts, blouses, casual slacks
Crepe—evening dresses
Denim—sportswear
Foulard—scarves, ties, dresses (if small patterns)
Lace—anything sexy or romantic
Leathers—shoes, gloves, handbags, belts, jackets, slacks, sportswear
Nylon—oh, if you insist, some blouses
Polyester—only in small percentages in blends, and only with great care, in some sportswear
Satin—evening wear, luxurious and heavy
Shantung—never to work
Suede—always social, often business
Tweed—suits, jackets
Velvet—sexy, evening
Wool—coats, suits, jackets, ties

A few final suggestions, based on my years of experience of seeing how people look and advising them on how to look their best at all times:

1. Whatever you buy, apply this yardstick to it: Is it appropriate for the use I intend to put it to? If not, pass it up!

2. Whatever you buy, make sure it looks as though it was made for you, and not just something that looks good on a model or mannikin. You are part of the real world, and your clothes should look real too and believable to others. Your social group will determine this.

3. Clothing is not and should not be considered an investment, like a painting, a diamond, or a chunk of gold. It is an investment in the sense that it assists you to a brighter future. But it is, in itself, not intrinsically an investment. Clothing is to be lived with and enjoyed, and eventually worn out and discarded without a backward glance. Keep creating an empty closet and filling it.

4. For men, the age-old question: double-breasted or single-breasted jackets? That, my friends, is your choice. It all depends on what is right at the moment and, more importantly, what looks good on you and what feels comfortable on you. Buy both!

5. Don't always buy clothes just for the moment. You may want to buy things that have a sense of timelessness, but you don't want to die never having worn those fashionable clothes of your lifetime. Don't be a slave to fad or fashion, classic or traditional. Be as open-minded about clothing as you are about your life.

6. For both men and women, the crowning glory can be a made-to-order suit. It may be only psychological—ready-made suits by the great designers are probably every bit as good—but there is something about a made-to-order suit by a great tailor that is a top-of-the-line thrill. You are getting the finest fabrics and, primarily, getting a fit that is perfect.

7. It's O.K.—in fact, it's very good—to fall in love with a particular suit or a particular dress. Maybe it will be a case of love at first sight, as you spot something breathtaking in a store window, or love at first feel, as you run your fingers admiringly over something magnificent dangling from a store rack. Good. Perhaps it is something that is currently beyond your financial capabilities. If there is any way at all, short of criminal, then go for it despite the expense. It is worth the price for you to own at least one thing, to have at least one garment in your closet that is perfection. Then, when you put that something on, you will feel like royalty, you will feel like a millionaire, you will feel like the Living Human Treasure you are—and that will give you pleasure, and that joy will be obvious to everyone who sees you.

Wear rich, feel rich, exude rich.

Do you know how the best-dressed people got on that best-dressed list? They all started the same way—they went out and bought something. One item of clothing to begin with. (Those men and women on that best-dressed list also lead a life-style that is socially active. They participate fully.)

PART V

Categories of Clothing

11

Dressing for Work

LEAD, FOLLOW, OR GET OUT OF THE WAY!

Suddenly, the question of what people should wear to work has become important. There are the important and unimportant issues in life; and there are times when the clothing you wear is very important. As I write these words, I can look around and see several books—entire books!—on my shelves devoted to that single subject. They each add in *their* way to the storehouse of information available. "Bottom line" dressing has an air of continuity about it; and the appropriate bottom-line style of dressing is expanding—it's broader now.

I have talked about business clothing in my Presentation Salon / Seminars for years. It is also a subject I have counseled people about for years. Its time has fully arrived. Business clothing serves as a vehicle for action and interaction with others. Fading into the crowd or into the organization is not the surest way to succeed. Keeping a definite low profile may keep you out of trouble, but it doesn't always mean success. Highly motivated executives and executives-to-be will most likely move steadily. The tops in business today go after high achievement with everything they've got. Today it is O.K. to be upfront about your excitement for success. After all, with so many skillful and resourceful people available, one needs all the resources one can muster. In management, sales, technology, marketing, the arts, and personal services you want a clear-cut go ahead when you have something to say. If you are already making it—shift into a higher gear; if you want to make it faster—step up to a new level; if you haven't been making it—start now. You need to look inside yourself and answer the question, "What can I say with my clothing that will make a favorable difference in how people react toward me?" The way your clothing treats people determines the way they will respond—strike a profile for profit.

Use clothing as a larger vehicle for yourself—clothing that supports your behavior and intentions will eventually determine how you live.

The study of what to wear to work has gone so far that the famed Wharton School of Business of the University of Pennsylvania conducts an annual day-long seminar on executive dress, at which the school's two hundred or so candidates for the M.B.A. degree are told the best way to dress for success. There was even an article in *Money* magazine recently, called "A Man's Guide to Dressing Well for Business," in which the author, Charles J. Rolo, laid out rules for dressing. And, while seminars and lengthy articles may be interesting to attend and enjoyable to read, they do tend to leave out the actual experience of how to purchase clothing. *Actually, your buying habits may be more important than what you wear. I feel very strongly that your buying habits, coupled with your own input into the way you dress and the way you look, is absolutely essential if you are to avoid the trap of being a carbon copy of the entire world and looking like a filing cabinet!*

The main thing to realize is that when you go off to work you go off to contribute to things happening. Far and away more Americans are white-collar workers than blue—forty-seven million as against thirty-one million, according to the most recent statistics. This chapter is directed to them, to the white-collar workers, both men and women. They are the ones whose appearance is significant to their eventual success or failure, who must look good if they are (A) to do their jobs well, (B) make a favorable impression on the people they come in contact with, and (C) progress up the corporate ladder, which, presumably, is the understandable desire of most workers.

So the only definite rule you will find in this entire chapter is the rule of common sense:

Dress to conquer the world—every day.

That rule applies equally to any worker. There are, certainly, different types of workers, different dressing requirements. And each type carries with it its own image of success. The man who is an electrician may not aspire to become president of a bank, but his image of success—perhaps he might like to head up his own electrical company one day—is as viable and just as important as is the bank teller whose image of success is the bank presidency. There are as many different images of success as there are different jobs. Success does not have its own identifiable stamp. One woman's success is another woman's so what. But every man and woman has some image of success tucked away in his or her mind—and thus *must* go out every day determined to make the world notice, and the first step in that pursuit is to dress the role—be the part. There are countless ways to achieve status.

One of the most dramatic bits of evidence of the importance of dress in the business world I have come across was something I found in the Los Angeles *Times* one morning. It was an account of a woman's conference on options in architecture and related fields at Scripps College, in Claremont, California. The conference was covered for the *Times* by its distinguished architecture and design critic, John Dreyfuss, who proceeded to devote much of his space to a description of what the conference's keynote speaker was wearing. Dreyfuss reported:

> Then along came keynote speaker Julia Thomas. The president of Bobrow / Thomas & Associates, a Los Angeles architecture and planning firm, she created a controversial stir without opening her mouth.
>
> She did it with clothes. In extraordinary contrast to other speakers— both male and female—who dressed conservatively, usually in suits, Thomas walked on stage to give her address in black, high-heeled shoes, black stockings and a snug, short-skirted, highly fashionable black sweater dress cinched at the waist with a black leather belt.
>
> To dwell so on Julia Thomas' wardrobe would be pure sexism except that the wardrobe, combined with her natural beauty and the fluid way she moved around the stage, came together to arrest the attention of both men and women in the audience even before she spoke.
>
> Thomas' immediate impact was no accident. When it comes to dressing, she leaves little to chance.
>
> "I've passed the point where I need to dress like a lawyer before a judge," she said in an interview. "I want to show that women can be free to be women and businesspersons at the same time. That is why I carefully selected my wardrobe for this appearance.
>
> "I think it had the desired effect. And it especially pleased me that, after I spoke, one woman said to me that I made her realize she could be simultaneously feminine and successful in the business world. That's just what I was trying to say with my clothes."

And that is just what I will be saying in this chapter, to both men and women—clothing for work can be exciting, as well as functional. Men can be masculine and successful, women can be feminine and successful, and they both should dress to achieve those two objectives.

But you don't have to follow every precise rule, you don't have to dress like everybody else—witness Julia Thomas and her black stockings. That is hardly conservative, hardly what you will find recommended in any of the books on what to wear—and yet obviously it had the desired impact. It conveyed the impression that she was secure, successful, and, simultaneously, a very attractive woman. For many women executives, the whole dress-for-success boxy, "mannish" suit concern never quite fit in the first place. For others it definitely has its place.

You don't have to be a carbon copy of your office neighbor to be considered appropriately dressed for work. In fact, if you want to move up the ladder you should be distinguishable in some way from your neighbor. You should always be yourself—distinctively unforgettably *you* even if at times it looks "similar" to the other guy or gal. Even among "dress-for-success" adherents there are signs of relaxing the rules. Beautiful fashion blouses and accessories combined with classic or more feminine suits look persuasive and commanding for the office. The trick is to achieve that goal without going overboard and becoming a joke and not being taken seriously. Don't try to achieve individuality at the expense of good taste. Don't become so unusual that you become outlandish. Be authentic, but within acceptable boundaries. Be yourself, but just make sure that that person you are being is a very competent individual. If you dress with a "secure" look, you will make an important financial statement.

Many employers set standards of dress—the infamous Dress Codes of many institutions—but even those are generally broad enough so you have the freedom to express yourself within those boundaries. Your employer may require a suit, tie, and jacket for men, for example. That allows a man plenty of room to be himself and still live with that regulation. For women, they may demand a dress and forbid slacks (although, in many situations that kind of hide-bound rule is fast disappearing), but even that allows an imaginative woman plenty of room to look attractively herself. The best "formula" is to *look as though you deserve it,* and you'll make it. That look of having arrived.

"Walk through any office," says Janet Wallach, the author of *Working Wardrobe,* in an interview with Cheryl Lavin, "and you'll probably see *levels* of dress. The receptionist is probably right out of junior college, and she's wearing pants and a T shirt. The secretary is wearing a skirt and a blouse, maybe a jacket if she's smart. Jackets are important to women in business. If you're in a conference room, eye to eye with your peers or superiors, you'll want to look as broad-shouldered or commanding as they are." Women in management wear suits or a day dress with a blazer to signal their executive status.

Pecking Order. Left to right:

(A) CLERK   Michael Bertiaux for Cacherel; pocketed black wool skirt, gray-and-white pinstriped cotton blouse with white cuffs and collar. *Firuze / Farnoosh.* Shoes. *Walter Newberger for Wilkes Bashford.*

(B) SECRETARY   Pierre Cardin silk shirtwaist black-and-ivory-print day dress. Shoes: black patent leather. *Saks Fifth Avenue.*

(C) ADMINISTRATIVE ASSISTANT   Two-piece double-breasted brick-red suit with white silk blouse; silk foulard neck scarf. *Saks Fifth Avenue.* Shoes. *Walter Newberger for Wilkes Bashford.*

(D) MANAGER   Herbert Grossman three-piece wool plaid suit in black and white; off-white silk tucked blouse. *Saks Fifth Avenue.* 14K gold loop earrings. *Tiffany & Co.*

(E)   VICE-PRESIDENT   Black-and-white-striped silk dress by J. S. Scherrer; white wool jacket by Brioni. *Wilkes Bashford.* Shoes. *Walter Newberger for Wilkes Bashford.* Polished 18K gold flexible choker, geometric gold-and-black earrings by Angela Cummings. *Tiffany & Co.*

(F) PRESIDENT   Gray pinstriped wool skirted suit by Brioni, white-and-black-striped silk tie blouse by Pancaldi & B. Brown suede and snakeskin shoes. *Rafael's.* 14K gold earrings. *Tiffany & Co.*

"The clothing worn by employees," says author-lecturer-consultant Betty Lehan Harragan in an article in *Savvy* magazine, "has a definite influence on the working environment and, often, on the efficiency of the operation."

Naturally, therefore, what you wear is vital—to both your own future and to the efficiency and the environment of your place of business. You want to make it easier for yourself to do business. "The executive woman is not an enigma in the work force. She is here to stay. If you want to be an executive woman then you have to behave and dress like one," say Vicki Keltner and Mike Holsey in *The Success Image.*

Without becoming overly specific, I want to give you my recommendations for what your wardrobe for work should consist of in most "standard" highly professional offices. I call this a "business starter wardrobe," and I feel that any woman entering the business world should be sure that she has the following items of clothing available in her closet:

1. A jacketed suit with skirt and a blouse, plus an additional complimentary skirt
2. A day dress and blazer
3. A skirt and blouse, with blazer
4. A second jacketed suit with skirt and a blouse, plus an additional complimentary skirt (and slacks, if they are permitted where you work)
5. A second day dress
6. A second skirt and blouse, with blazer
7. Three additional blouses (these are your ammunition)
8. A day coat (top coat or overcoat depending on the weather— a great fur-lined raincoat always fits the bill here, as do chesterfield, full raglan-sleeve, classic tie, military officer's design, trench, smock, leather or suede, street-length coats)
9. Three pairs of high heels; two pairs of lower heels; classic pumps, spectator pumps, sling-back, or ankle-strap, mostly with closed toe, some open toe
10. Three belts
11. One important, expensive-looking day handbag that enhances all these outfits (rather than having six cheaper bags in different colors to match each outfit)
12. Hosiery in natural or light suntan shades, which are best for wearing in most offices. However, opaque, textured, ribbed, and sheer pantyhose can be worn where the office environment permits it.

You'll note the prominence of blouses in this assemblage of garments. That's because my own feeling is that, to a woman, a blouse is perhaps her most important single garment to create fresh new looks. A blouse, to a woman, is ammunition. It is the blouse that somehow seems to make the greatest impression and enhance all her other pieces of clothing. If you are just starting your job, get yourself five smashing blouses so that you can make a show of variety as you begin your career. Appropriate blouse collars are Peter Pan, tie, stand-off, mandarin, V-neck, turtleneck, boat neck, cowl, square neckline; you can wear long, medium, or short sleeves, with long preferred.

Fortunately, women's fashion within the business world has changed for the brighter. No longer must assertive and intelligent women look dismal and dreary.

In the February 1983 issue of *Working Woman*, an outright declaration of women's clothing independence as professionals was very accurately looked at by Elaine Louie. The essence of the article reads as follows, "The uniform is dead. Long live individuality. All kinds of successful working women are developing their own styles. These days, dressing for success can range from the classic suit to sophisticated separates . . ." What I believe is being said here is that ultraboxy, ultraconservative, mannish-tailored suits for professional women with the string tie or floppy foulard-print tie, that characterize the "uniform" for women who desire to make it in the business world, is not the end-all its advocates claimed for attaining success.

However, in about 50 percent of the cases for the professional woman the conservative suit, when made of quality fabric and executed by a designer of merit, definitely has its place in their wardrobes for those times when such a suit is required. It adds its own special "workability" to the business situation.

If you own a navy blue suit, now's the time to enhance it with a stunning yellow silk blouse, or perhaps a multicolored striped blouse. The bottom line is that there is absolutely no dogmatic way all women should dress from nine to five. The most suitable types of ensembles for women to wear in the professional world are suits—skirted or sometimes slacked; day dresses—simply colored or patterned; separates—blazers, pants, sweaters, vests, blouses, or skirts. The four basic suit lapel shapes are the notch, a strong lapel for business; the peak; the shawl; and the cloverleaf.

More detailed descriptions of these suitable ensembles for women are as follows:

A. CLASSIC HIP-LENGTH JACKET (with or without belt)
The silhouette is basically derived from the English and has a British look to it. The jacket should be fitted and the belt (if included) should never be too tight or wide. The silhouette is straight in line, and in most cases the lighter the material, the better the fit, since the excess material makes for a bulkier and harder-to-wear jacket. Best suited for tall or thin women.

Classic hip-length jacket without a belt

Classic hip-length jacket with a belt

B. THIGH-LENGTH JACKET
The silhouette is American classic and one that can be worn season after season. The look is usually double-breasted or four-layer single-button, and the length terminates around the beginning of the thighs. For those who are under 5 feet 3 inches, stay away from this particular silhouette as it will accent your shortness: likewise, those who are overweight; it will accent your thighs.

C. SHORT JACKET WITH FULL SKIRT
This particular ensemble consists of a straight, shirtlike (almost

Thigh-length jacket

resembles the shirt on your back), single-button jacket—usually hemmed around the beginning of your thighs. When teamed with a full dirndl skirt, the look tends to accent the bottom half of your body, slenderizing the top half with the lesser fabric silhouette. This duo can be worn for the office, but it is usually considered a separates type of outfit, so be

Short jacket with full skirt

careful not to wear it to an important business meeting or board of
directors gathering. When putting together a shirt jacket and a full skirt,
stay away from bright colors and bold patterns. The less noticeable the
pattern, the slimmer the look.

D. LONG AND LEAN, STRAIGHT JACKET AND SKIRT
    This particular silhouette is a fashion-oriented one and is best suited
for women who are not overweight. The jacket is usually double-

breasted, and the length terminates around the middle of the thighs, while the skirt is usually a straight silhouette and the length hits the middle of the calves. Although some fashion know-alls claim that the longer skirt slims down the body, this is not true. The longer skirt draws attention to the bottom half of your body and thus, if you have heavy thighs, heavy or unattractive legs, beware. Since this category is considered an updated fashion look, it is particularly well-suited for those who do not work in a conservative office environment.

Straight jacket and skirt

Double-breasted suit

E. DOUBLE-BREASTED, THIGH-LENGTH, PEAKED-LAPEL COORDINATES
Here the silhouette is youthful. The look is heavily European and is primarily better bought in European labels and from high-quality American designers. It teams exceptionally well with trousers. A slight variation here is an asymmetrical jacket with straight or full skirt or even pleated trousers. The jacket tends to close on one side with only a single button and must be kept buttoned.

F. PANTSUIT

The idea of wearing a pantsuit (matching jacket and trousers) to an office meeting or important function is a personal preference and perhaps even an office-attire matter. If your place of business does not have any objections to you wearing trousers and a coordinated jacket, great. Comfort is the key when wearing slacks. However, be sure that your jacket and pants are well-teamed and that if the jacket is gabardine, so are the pants—likewise with wool, linen, or silk. Although some people mix and match fabrics, those are often fashion-oriented folks who have an extensive background in apparel and are absolutely sure of the combination. If you are not one of these people, stay clear of mixing and matching. Go with the tried and the true.

Pantsuit

G. MATCHING COAT AND SKIRT WITH BLOUSE

This look is in the family of a coat dress and is also called a coat suit. The coat is a chesterfield coat with three buttons, plain and in a straight row. It is best to stay away from patterns, plaids, and strong colors. It can be teamed effectively with a skirt.

Matching coat and skirt with blouse

Day dress

H. DAY DRESS

A day dress suitable for office wear can be solid, multicolored, or patterned, but be careful to stay away from particularly bold or dramatic patterns and colors. The less adorned the more professional you will look in these: shirtwaist, coat dress, sheath, wrap-around, A-line, blouson, princess, knit or sweater dress, two-piece, and chemise.

Day dress with blazer

I. DAY DRESS WITH BLAZER
This look takes the day dress a step farther, adding authority and professionalism.

J. SEPARATES
When talking about separates let's first clarify a point. Separates are fine for the office, as long as they are well-coordinated and perfectly

matched. Sometimes, unintentionally, of course, women can make the mistake of haphazardly mixing and matching skirts, blazers, and blouses. Try to keep them simple and unadorned. The less ruffles, do-dads, and gimmicks, the better dressed you will be. Choose from several designs—straight, wrap-around, flared, A-line—and several details—inverted pleat; box pleat; knife pleat; front or back slit vent; shirred, tucked, or flat top; belt loops; pockets; kick pleat—front or back; and top stitching.

Separates

Separates

Separates

For a man, a similar "business starter wardrobe" is even simpler to describe. Just lay in a supply of:

1. Three suits (these can be two- or three-piece, depending upon what strategies you're using to get ahead). *Important:* Familiarize yourself with the rich color and "hold" of expensive fabrics— you want durable prosperity. Get one gray and two dark blue suits.

2. Seven dress shirts (three white, three light blue, and one striped *or* vary this combination as it suits your particular need in shirt color).

3. Seven ties (two pinstripes, two foulard small prints, two pin dots, and one insignia *or* vary the combination for ultimate results). Your tie is your signature, it's a badge of membership.

4. Two pairs of shoes (preferably laced; one pair black, the other deep burgundy or cordovan).

5. Two plain leather belts (one black and one deep burgundy with a simple, plain buckle).

6. Six pairs of socks (over the calf; black and dark blue).

For the young male executive, or executive-to-be, however, the difficulty comes in choosing exactly which suit to buy. There are three basic, but distinctive, types of suits, and all three are winners. These three types I call American Classical Traditional, American Updated Traditional, and European "V" Wedge.

A. AMERICAN CLASSICAL TRADITIONAL (Conservative Sack)
The look of this garment is primarily functional. The man who prefers this look is a traditionalist, a no-nonsense, stick-to-the-rules type of person. The American Classical Traditional is the blue-chip look, the classic banker/lawyer look. This is your typical Brooks Brothers look. Its keynote is "conservative." It never seems to become obsolete. It is a good old suit that works. To quote W magazine in an article on the "Wabbly Wasps": "Meet the apostles of the cult of the bland . . . The self-styled American aristocrats."
—usually single-breasted
—usually center-vented
—has a natural shoulder (little or no padding)

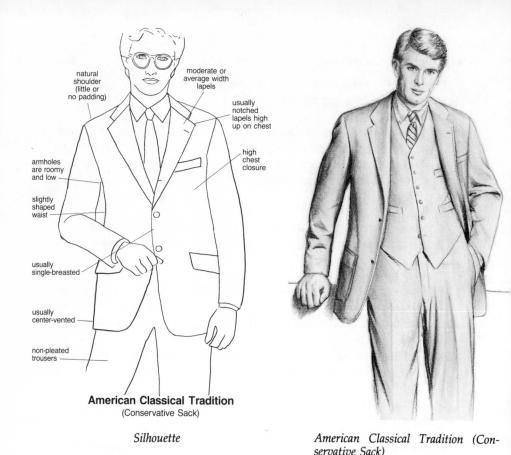

natural shoulder (little or no padding)

moderate or average width lapels

usually notched lapels high up on chest

high chest closure

armholes are roomy and low

slightly shaped waist

usually single-breasted

usually center-vented

non-pleated trousers

American Classical Tradition
(Conservative Sack)

Silhouette

American Classical Tradition (Conservative Sack)

—armholes are roomy and low
—has moderate- or average-width lapels
—lapels usually notched and high up on chest
—only slight shaping of waist
—high chest closure (buttons start higher up)
—trousers usually without pleats

B. AMERICAN UPDATED TRADITIONAL (British-American)
This look has become a classic since being introduced in the 1930s. Its emphasis, while still functional, is more gentlemanly, international. This more-fitted look is more style-oriented than designer-oriented.
—"more" shapely silhouette
—waistline more defined and shaped
—more likely to be double-breasted than American Classical Traditional but usually single-breasted
—usually side-vented
—slightly shaped shoulders with slight padding

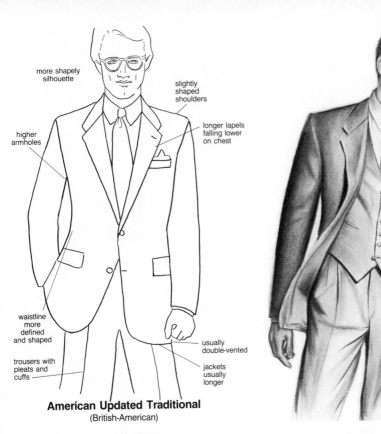

American Updated Traditional
(British-American)

more shapely silhouette

slightly shaped shoulders

longer lapels falling lower on chest

higher armholes

waistline more defined and shaped

trousers with pleats and cuffs

usually double-vented

jackets usually longer

Silhouette

American Updated Traditional (British-American)

—armholes higher, longer width lapels, usually notched, falling lower on the chest
—jackets usually longer
—lower closure (jacket closes and buttons lower)
—trousers with pleats and cuffs more common

C. EUROPEAN "V" WEDGE (Classic or Trend-Setting)

Here the look tends to add sophisticated presence to the wearer. It conveys a stronger sense of style, both in the silhouette and in the details. Rather than simply conforming to the shape of the body, the European "V" Wedge look strives to enhance the form of the wearer— it makes the shoulders broader, the waist slimmer, the body leaner. The double-breasted suit jacket often belongs to the European school of clothing. It is something that is not right for everyone, but for many it is great. The person who wears this style has individuality, flair, élan.

—"most" shaped silhouette with fitted hips
—single- or double-breasted

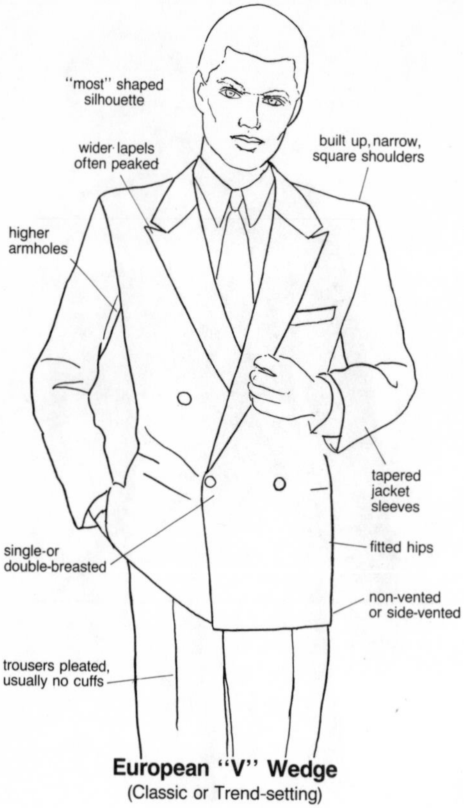

Silhouette

European "V" Wedge (Classic or Trend-Setting)

—non-vented or side-vented
—often with built-up, narrow, square shoulders
—higher armholes and slimmed down, tapered jacket sleeves
—lapels wider and often peaked
—low closure
—trousers may have pleats, but usually not cuffs

D. MORE CASUAL BUSINESS ALTERNATIVE (The Blazer and Sport Jacket)

Here, as you can plainly tell from the name, the look is sportier—although not completely sporty because we are still in the going-to-work part of our closet, and we are still wearing a tie. But this look is for slacks and sport-jacket combinations, which, in more and more situations, has become permissible. Blazers and sport jackets can be

More Casual Business Alternative (the blazer and sport jacket)

found in the three categories previously listed. Blazers and sport jackets differ from suit jackets not in shape but in:

—greater detailing—belted, gun patches, elbow patches, collar tabs, patched pockets, etc.

—wider range of colors, and textured fabrics

—extra millimeters of depth

—stronger patterns balanced against varying textures

In many professions today, the More Casual Business Alternative of slacks and sport jacket is every bit as acceptable as a suit—for teachers, actors, writers, designers, and art directors, sometimes for salesmen, scientists, and engineers. These, I suppose, are all what could be considered creative professions, and there seems to be a greater acceptance of the relaxed in clothing in these areas of work than in some of the more staid and conservative professions. The blazers can be single- or double-breasted, blue, black, burgundy, or gray. The sport jackets can be tweeds, herringbones, or plaids. I think this look is great, but be careful and only use it when you know for certain that there is a general agreement that it is considered acceptable attire where you are planning to wear it.

Please always be careful about falling into the too-much-of-a-good-thing trap. That way lies "preppiedom." If you wear the Classically Business / Casual outfit of slacks and sport jacket every day then, consciously or not, the people you associate with will begin to think of you as a preppie. So I would suggest varying your clothing diet and adding several suits that give you an authoritative, established look. Go from preppie to the big time.

I also want to warn you of a pitfall. I hear people in my Presentation Salon / Seminars say: "I chose this outfit because it's practical." This "practical" they speak of denotes *ordinary* rather than extraordinary. This compulsive drive to find practical items of clothing all the time restricts you from propelling yourself to the front of the pack. So I just want to caution you not to always think "practical" and end up thinking "small."

Until fairly recently, businessmen almost always dressed in the Ivy Look—from their crewcut hairstyle down to their penny loafers, with the button-down oxford shirt, the knit ties, the madras jackets, and the chinos. (And there was his mate, Mrs. Ivy, who had the female equivalent of that he wore, with the most prominent article of her attire being the pleated, plaid skirt.) The Ivy Look often included the camel's hair blazer (with the patch on the sleeves and the insignia emblazoned on the jacket pocket) and, to top it all off, the London Fog raincoat.

Remnants of the Ivy Look remain, and they can be fun and interesting. But today, fortunately, men and women generally give themselves more credit for individuality, more allowance to permit their private personalities to poke through. Uniforms have a way of squelching personality totally and preventing other possibilities from emerging, no matter how glorious the uniform is.

In some circles, the Ivy Look was replaced in the '60s, by another look—what might be called the Rebellious Hippy Look or its slightly neater cousin, the Almost-Hippy Look. The former was marked by a conscious effort to be different, and that difference became as much of a uniform as the uniform they were supposedly rebelling against. The washed-out jeans, T shirt, beads, moccasins, and long hair—that was the in thing to wear in some circles in that transitory decade. The Almost-Hippy Look was a sincere effort to polish this ultrarelaxed mode of dressing which usually sent off mixed messages. In most businesses, other than the entertainment and social-worker types, this look is inappropriate.

Let's talk about color, the color of your working clothing. For men, let me say again: blue, especially dark blue, conveys a sense of established power, authority, stability. It is hard not to trust a man in a navy blue suit. If we were to hide ourselves in America's boardrooms and peek at the members of the boards of America's leading corporations, I would be willing to bet we would find blue the predominant color, with gray a strong second (a gray suit also gives its wearer substance).

Most will be wearing solid blue, but some pinstripes and even a lightly plaided dark blue suit here and there would be seen. I think you can prove the importance of blue to yourself the next time you see a group of businessmen enter a restaurant for lunch or watch some other group of businessmen convening. Look at them objectively and I think you will conclude that the ones in tans, browns, olives, or grays will diminish in importance in your eyes, when compared to the ones in blue.

Blue is the color of winners! It is no coincidence that blue is the color of the ribbons for first-place finishers. Blue is solid, important, triumphant, authoritative. Gray is a strong underdog that is also in the running.

But color alone is not enough to guarantee your victory. We go back to what was said earlier about silhouette, about picking a suit that has the look, the proportion, the quality of fabric, the finish, and detailing of being the best. Your first-string suit should—*must*—give off a message of power and competence. It should almost be able to go out and get a job on its own, without you being in it—that's how strong that suit should be.

I would even go so far as to suggest that you buy several blue suits, as many as your budget can absorb. (Variety in color is not essential.) Do that rather than adding other colors that decrease your impact. And if at all possible, I would urge you to go to one of the following designers, especially for that one, that all-important, that top-of-the-line, that first-string blue suit for your important business appointments.

MEN'S SUIT DESIGNERS—equating *quality, design,* and *price* of the suit with well-known automobiles.

Kiton	Bentley
Luciano Barbera	

Brioni ⎱ Nutter ⎰	Rolls-Royce or Stutz
Zegna	Ferrari
Abla ⎱ Belvest ⎰ Devenza LeVorato	Mercedes
Armani (couture) ⎱ Canali ⎰ YSL (couture)	Maserati
Oxxford	B.M.W.
Chester Barrie ⎱ Hickey-Freeman ⎰	Lincoln Continental
Basile ⎱ Cerruti ⎰ DiMitri Ferre	Porsche, Jaguar
Corneliani ⎱ Givenchy ⎰ Hugo Boss	Citroën
Brooks Brothers	Chrysler New Yorker
Alan Flusser ⎱ Alexander Julian ⎰ Cesarani Garrick Anderson Polo (Ralph Lauren)	MGB, Toyota, Datsun 280Z

If you put yourself in a really elite dark blue or gray suit from one of those top designers, you are On Your Way! Your job, whatever it is, will find you leaving your competition behind and zooming up the ladder as though you were propelled by your own personal jet stream.

Within the four business classifications for men—American Classical Traditional, American Updated Traditional, European "V" Wedge, and the More Casual Business Alternative—is a range of totally appropriate and proven, distinctively different alternative moods and attitudes for men. And for women, the range of suits, dresses, and separates afford a comprehensive and exciting number of choices. Six modes of personal expression that work are:

Executive Looks—Great Eclectics.

MAN Gray wool suit with peaked lapels by Zegna; gray wool vest, gray shoes, gold tie bar, wine-colored silk tie and pocket handkerchief, striped shirt by Van Laack. *Wilkes Bashford.* Shoes. *Walter Newberger for Wilkes Bashford.* 18K gold pocket watch and chain. *Tiffany & Co.*

WOMAN Cashmere sweater and wrap-around shawl in fuchsia by Valerie Louthan; wool herringbone skirt by Brioni. Black shoes. *Wilkes Bashford.* Shoes. *Walter Newberger for Wilkes Bashford.* Strand of 8mm opera-length pearls. *Tiffany & Co.*

Executive Looks—Power Punch, Superstars.

MAN Two-piece blue medium-width pinstripe suit by Brioni, Daniel Schagen white cotton shirt, red-and-white pindot tie by Polo (Ralph Lauren). Black shoes. *Wilkes Bashford.* Shoes. *Walter Newberger for Wilkes Bashford.*

WOMAN Skirted wool suit in Chinese red by Arthur Chapnik. *Saks Fifth Avenue.* Black-and-white butterfly tied silk-and-cotton striped blouse, bone-colored shoes. *Wilkes Bashford.* Shoes. *Walter Newberger for Wilkes Bashford.* 18K gold Breguet strap watch and 18K gold Angela Cummings fan earrings. *Tiffany & Co.*

MASTER OF SUBTLETY AND GREAT ECLECTIC DRESSER

Ingenious harmony, esthetic, triumphant assurity, great eye-pleasing "blender" of shape, texture, color, and feeling. A truly distinctive identity.

POWER-PUNCH SUPERSTAR DRESSER

A giant at the top, imitated, wearer of the crown, impactful, awesome presence, monumentally authoritative, decision maker.

ORTHODOX FERVOR DRESSER

Icon of tradition, social restraint, ultraconservative, plainer lines, conventional demeanor.

Executive Looks—Orthodox, Conservative.
MAN   Three-piece navy blue wool suit by
Polo (Ralph Lauren), Ralph Lauren silk tie
in red stripes. White cotton oxford button-
down shirt, black shoes. *Wilkes Bashford.*
Shoes. *Walter Newberger for Wilkes Bashford.*
WOMAN   Black-and-white   double-
breasted houndstooth wool jacket by Stanley
Sherman, black wool skirt by Stanley Sherman. *Saks Fifth Avenue.* Shoes. *Walter Newberger for Wilkes Bashford.* 14K gold button
earrings. *Tiffany & Co.*

Executive Looks—Fast Riser.
MAN   Two-piece gray-plaid wool suit
Brioni, maroon foulard silk tie by Fer
Reed, white cotton Daniel Schagen shi
black shoes. *Wilkes Bashford.* Shoes. *Wa
Newberger for Wilkes Bashford.*
WOMAN   Gray herringbone coat dre
*Vicki Keltner with Strictly Business, Sakow
Gray suede pumps with lizard toe and h
by Lorenzo Banfi. *Rafael's.*

FAST RISER
> Streamlined attractiveness, competitive edge, exuberant,
> young, bold, energetically unstoppable, clean-cut.

FASHIONABLE / TREND-SETTER DRESSER
> Nudging the status quo, unexpected, unrestrained, daredevil,
> the exception to the norm in attaining the golden ring.

CREATIVE / FREE-SPIRIT DRESSER
> Unabashed, provocative, celebratory, joyful, you can't help but
> want them around and to make it big.

Your clothing is your calling card to success, and so it is imperative

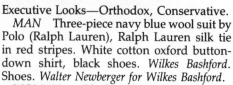

ecutive Looks—Fashionable, Trend-
tter.
MAN Zegna, double-breasted brown-
d-gray-plaid peaked lapel suit. Tan-and-
ige-striped shirt by Daniel Schagen with
ite collar. Rust-colored silk pocket hand-
rchief. Pancaldi, silk striped tie, gold collar
r. Black shoes. *Wilkes Bashford*. Shoes.
lter Newberger for Wilkes Bashford.
WOMAN Black wool crepe dress
mmed with rust cobra. *Rafael's*. 18K gold
sa Peretti free-form ear clips. *Tiffany & Co*.

Executive Looks—Creative, Free Spirit.
MAN Camel, brown, and ivory tweed
wool jacket, suede mushroom-colored vest,
white-and-tan-striped cotton shirt by Van
Laack, pumpkin silk knit tie, tan wool slacks
by Zanella. Camel suede shoes. *Wilkes Bashford*. Shoes. *Walter Newberger for Wilkes Bashford*.
WOMAN Cashmere dark gray long coat
and pants by Zoran. Cashmere knit top.
Black shoes. *Wilkes Bashford*. Shoes. *Walter
Newberger for Wilkes Bashford*.

that people take notice. Of course, if everybody in the world dressed
in that same, or a similar, top-caliber outfit, then the wearer would no
longer have a competitive edge. But that won't happen; there are still
too many people around who are dedicated Bargain Hunters, and they
would never wear the professional "status" outfits I have recommended.
These "coasting resisters" have to let go of yesterday's thinking or else
they will be the confirmed Make-Doers, and they will always be trying
to get another year's wear out of a suit that should have died and gone
to Suit Heaven a year or more ago. Or they are the professional Wild
Dressers, and they will be trying to get ahead in the world while
wearing their double-knit green jackets with the yellow trousers and

Hawaiian print shirts. Or they are the Steady Rebels, who wouldn't be caught dead in anything that made them look even remotely like they belonged to the establishment.

Choose to follow a strong leader or set your own direction. Have the innate sense of what is appropriate and will get you what you want.

The main elements that you align are *fabric, color, fit,* and *tailoring,* as well as the *shape* of the suit itself. Remember your military days? If you served in any of the armed services, you will surely remember how every man wore the same clothing, and yet each one looked different. It is the same with nurses and waitresses. Two people can take the same uniform—or the same dress or the same suit—and manage to look entirely different. We each have a personal way of expressing our brilliance.

If you look at the greatest successes in the world, particularly in the business community, you will generally find that they share one trait in common—they have all been unreasonable in their quest. They don't fit into a frozen mold. They are not dutiful, obedient followers unless that is what will do it. They are sometimes members of any pack that works. They are not content to trot along with the rest of the world, either in their thinking or in their clothing. They think with originality, they act with originality—and they dress with appropriate originality. They nearly always make themselves known in some way.

All of the above, of course, applies with equal weight to both sexes. Increasingly, women are finding their rightful place in the business world, as well as in the other professions. So what I have written about men is equally applicable to women. There is, for example, a female equivalent to the junior-executive uniform for men. And the women who wear that outfit—dark suit, white blouse, plain shoes—are playing it safe but don't necessarily move to the top ranks by doing so. *You must look powerful and not apologetic for who you are.*

It is an exciting road that I am suggesting you walk. I don't want you to become so outlandish in your search for clothing originality that you become objects of behind-the-hand snickering and ridicule. That's the other extreme, just as bad (perhaps worse) than being a junior-executive clone. You have to feel your way along that road. And you find that road through several methods. The chief method you want to use is your own keen sense of observation. During your first weeks on the job, see what the decision makers are wearing. There may be certain taboos in your place of employment. Perhaps the big boss has one of those phobias—maybe he doesn't like red, or maybe he has a thing against shoes that don't have laces, or perhaps he immediately assumes that any lady who shows too much leg is not serious. So you have to move slowly, at first, because the worst thing you can do is to break a taboo. And you have to check the territory, see what works for others, and what doesn't. Then you can simultaneously be observing fashions and stores and prices, and when you are pretty sure you know how you want to look, and why, then you can go out and start assembling your new wardrobe, the one that will give you a first-class ticket to the fast lane.

The quality of unreasonableness that I find in most of America's business leaders does not necessarily mean they are unusual when it comes to their clothing. A man (or woman) can be unreasonable within reasonable boundaries. It is possible for a man to wear the power navy blue suit I recommend, with all the accompanying accessories, and still be unreasonable—because he gets such a dynamic suit, a designed suit of the finest style and workmanship, that it stands out from the crowd. Unreasonableness does not require garishness; it merely demands that you not be mundane and that you insist on the absolute finest in everything.

I think it is much easier for a woman to be unreasonable in her clothing than it is for a man. Ladies have more latitude in what they wear than men. A man is virtually limited to the time-honored suit-shirt-tie, with perhaps an occasional sport-jacket-slacks-shirt-tie to alter the diet. But a woman can wear a suit. Or she can wear a dress (and, of course, there are an infinite number of dress possibilities). There are many acceptable styles and colors in dresses, and even women's suits come in many more cuts and styles than do men's suits. And then, too, a woman can wear combinations—a blazer over some day dresses; skirt or slacks (if permitted by the mores of your company) and blouse, with or without a jacket; low heels or high heels; maybe even a hat; and an infinite variety of things she can do with scarves and jewelry. In many cases what changes day into night is a dressier belt, dressier jewelry, shoes instead of boots, and the addition of a beautiful shawl.

Today, of course, there are more and more women who are combining careers and motherhood. For ladies who are applying for work, after having been away from the job force for some years to start their families, the dress for work for some appears to be confusing.

I have a few suggestions to make it less confusing. First, approach the job interview in a businesslike, I'll-get-the-best-job-for-me frame of mind. Try, for that brief period, to forget the fact that you are a mother and remember only that you are a person of skills and talent and that they would be fortunate indeed to hire you. Avoid bringing anything with you that smacks of home, hearth, hubby, and the kids. Don't have big, showy charms on your bracelet in the shape of souvenirs. Don't show the personnel people that you will take longer to adjust. Wear a *brand new outfit*, businesslike and attractive. You are there for one reason only—to sell them on how great a worker you would be—so don't let anything get in the way of that intention. I am assuming, of course, that you do have the necessary skills. Beyond that, you must then convince them that you are the type of person they want to have on their office team: efficient, attractive, enthusiastic, ambitious, serious.

And how you dress and look is at least 50 percent of the total impression you will make on them. Your skills, your background, and your manner of communicating make up the other 50 percent.

In many cases, a mother going back to work will have had a thriving career before maternity interrupted. She might come to the conclusion, as she prepares to seek out her new job that what she used to wear when she worked five years ago (or ten or fifteen) is probably still O.K. Maybe that's so—but probably it's not. Times change. In those five years (or ten or fifteen), during which you had your baby (or two or three) and saw them through their infancy, styles have come a long way. Maybe that old dark green suit that was so stunning back then is still in good condition, but probably anybody who sees it today will recognize it for what it is—yesterday's news. If you really want a good job, start out by getting a totally new job-seeking wardrobe. Make sure it is businesslike. What you want to project is a picture of a woman who is serious, pleasant, capable. You and your clothing together want to tell your prospective employer that you are right for the job, that you can handle it with ease, that you are the absolutely perfect person to fill that vacant niche.

Then, after you have passed that test and have been hired, it is time for a total closet reevaluation. The one (or more) outfits that you bought for job-hunting may be good, but you must have a full assortment so you don't look the same day after day after day. Go through your closet meticulously. Separate the non-working items—the dresses, skirts, blouses that won't be right for working—from those that are fit and able to become part of your everyday working wardrobe. Put them on a different rod, or in a different closet.

Try to put together five smashing outfits for your first five days on your new job. (Use any order you prefer.)

1. FIRST DAY: Suit with skirt
2. SECOND DAY: Dress with blazer
3. THIRD DAY: Skirt, blouse, and blazer
4. FOURTH DAY: Dress
5. FIFTH DAY: Suit, shirt, and slacks

Once you are committed to a return to the labor force, don't go about it halfheartedly. You have made a choice and elected to become a working mother. Obviously, you have confidence in the person who is taking care of your child, or in that child's ability to take care of himself or herself. So you are free to devote 100 percent of your energy and attention to the job and to your efforts to achieve personal success. Your choice of what to wear makes a considerable difference in whether or not you will be treated as just another employee or as someone who has a big future with the organization.

For a certain length of time, you will be what I call "A woman in transition"—making the major move from home to office. That transition can be a difficult one. Before you elect to try to find a career (or more likely, before you elect to return to a career), you were fairly free at home to look any way you wanted to look, dress any way you chose to dress. You took pride in your appearance, of course, but it was not as vital to your future as it becomes once you are back being a working woman. Perhaps you gained some weight. Not having to worry that much about your appearance, you picked up a pound here, a pound there. Now, however, your appearance is one of the utmost concern, so you must get rid of that excess weight immediately. Do it, if possible *before* you begin your job hunt. To look your best in skirts and tailored clothing, trim your figure. On the job, you may be doing more sitting than you have been doing at home. So it is essential that you slim down. I suggest that you begin a regular program of exercise—either at home or at a gym—so that the indolent office life doesn't result in you putting on even more poundage.

Incidentally, as a bonus for being slender, you will discover that there is a much larger selection of clothing available to slim women. *My own formula is that for every ten pounds a woman loses, there is approximately 20 percent more clothing for her to choose from.* If a woman is larger than size 12, she has less in the way of attractive selections. So slim down—not only for the sake of your appearance and your health, but also because slimness widens the possibilities of clothing open to you.

And while you are slimming and thus building a new you, think about getting a new hairstyle, too. Might as well do the whole thing.

With a man, his necktie is often his best chance to be original and totally different. I have said this before, but it bears repetition: *a man's tie is his signature.* And just as every man signs his name differently, so every man's tie can be his stamp, too.

There are seven types of neckties that I feel are permissible for the business world today. They are:

1. The plain tie.
2. The striped tie, regimental or old school, a narrow stripe against a plain background.

3. The foulard tie, or something with a similarly mild, inoffensive pattern.
4. The polka-dot tie, assuming that the dots are not too bold and the colors are subdued.
5. The paisley tie, small pattern.
6. The knit tie, almost always a solid color.
7. The bow tie.

But, with bow ties, a word of caution. Bow ties come and go in popularity. Some men—I would guess that perhaps 1 or 2 percent of the total male population—wear them exclusively. With certain facial types—primarily the long, thin faces—they look marvelous. They have a professorial look about them. I don't recommend bow ties as a rule, but I have included them in my list of permissible ties because I know that some men are madly in love with them.

You will note that on my list of seven permissible ties I did not include ties that light up at night, or ties that have nude ladies recumbent upon them, or ties that have funny sayings or political slogans emblazed on them. And you should know me well enough by now to realize that I do not and will not advocate poorly knotted ties. If you have unsightly and outdated ties, donate them to your local Red Cross; they can make dandy tourniquets out of them.

The tie is very obvious in a man's costume, and his shoes are of almost equal importance, although they may not be as obvious at first glance. Shoes tell the world a great deal about the wearer, so it is incumbent on you to be well and attractively shod. I would even go so far as to say that the casual observer can tell more about a man from his shoes than from his memoirs. A pair of shoes speaks eloquently about the wearer's education, financial status, social condition, ethnic origin, and personal preferences. And the socks that go with those shoes underscore all those traits. They should be at least calf-length so that no matter how you sit, no bare leg is visible above the top of the socks. Spend your money on first-class shoes. Not only do they contribute so much to your appearance and your image, but top-quality shoes are a sound investment because they go out of style very slowly, and a well-made pair of shoes will last considerably longer than a cheap pair.

When I earlier talked about the More Casual Business Alternative I mentioned that the wearing of sport-jacket / slack outfits are becoming more and more a permissible costume in business situations. That seems to be the case in some professions more than others—it appears generally allowed in education, science, communications, advertising, entertainment, and the like, while still frowned on by the financial, insurance, medical, legal, and affiliated professions. It does give men more flexibility, a bit more opportunity to express originality and many men find this type of outfit more comfortable than a suit.

There are several sport jackets that can be worn, but the blazer is far and away the most popular. A solid navy blazer with gray or tan slacks, and an elegant shirt and tie, make a wardrobe combination that is practically unbeatable. But there are also marvelous tweed jackets and plaids and herringbones, and if you don't let yourself get carried away and go overboard, they are all eminently acceptable, too. One word of caution: If the jacket has a pattern, be sure you team it with slacks that are solid or mildly patterned or vice versa. I would also suggest that, when you consider your shirt, allow a pattern in only one of the three (jacket, slacks, or shirt) and keep the other two plain, unless you have a highly trained eye that's savvy and allows for contrast to work. Patterns, no matter how muted, do have a way of clashing with each other if not selected with an "eye" for taste.

All of the above suggestions regarding sport jackets for men apply, with equal force, to women, too. The sport jacket-blouse-skirt (or slacks) combination is dynamite for the ladies, but just be careful you don't go too far with patterns, and be sure that you allow yourself a pattern that definitely evokes tasteful comments of praise. Too much pattern can add age to a woman's look, unless she is particularly skilled at coordinating and complementing fabric patterns.

Finally, in case you still harbor some lingering doubts about the importance of your dress in the context of business, consider a survey conducted by Dr. Judith Waters, professor of psychology at Fairleigh Dickinson University. Her subjects were potential employers in several major cities. She asked them to consider women as they look ordinarily, and again after they had been done over—clothes, hair, makeup.

The results showed that the same women were offered jobs with up to 20 percent higher starting salaries, based only on how they looked.

Isn't that a good investment—pay attention to your appearance and, in return, be worth 20 percent more money. And that's just for openers!

Dressing well for work is a major step in your movement into the fast lane. When playing at these high stakes it is no good measuring yourself against conventional standards, you need to measure yourself against available opportunities.

It's an exciting place to be, the fast track. In fact, if you are impatient to win big in business, it's the *only* place.

Fortune magazine, 1982

12

Dressing with Sophistication

CASUALLY SMART AND ELEGANT EVENING

Casually Smart

Casually Smart (also called "dressy sportswear") consists of the clothes that are suitable for informal entertaining or for being informally entertained; for shopping or sightseeing, for wearing to sporting events, for going to the movies or to informal parties, for wearing to classes— if you are a student. Casually Smart is the most flexible and variable part of your wardrobe and includes a wide variety of garments.

Among them for men are sport jackets, slacks, jeans, cords, cottons, sweaters, vests, polo and sport shirts, loafers, and boots. Casually Smart for women runs an equally wide gamut, everything from skirts, blouses, blazers, and other odd jackets, through slacks and sweaters, and on to heels and boots.

Casually Smart clothes are your fun outfits, clothing that is easy to wear, easy to move in, easy to live with. Casually Smart clothes are fun to buy, fun to wear, fun to look at. When you are in top-flight casually smart clothes you look delicious, people want to be near you and want you near them. A sensitive eye can spot them in an instant.

Casually Smart—Chic Women. Left to right:
(A) Giorgio Armani three-piece outfit: wool plaid jacket, off-white silk shirt-blouse, taupe wool skirt. *Wilkes Bashford*. Gold geometric earrings. *Tiffany & Co.*
(B) Laura Biagiotti winter-white knit sweater, beige silk-linen slacks. *I. Magnin*. 14K gold heavy link bracelet and gold looped earrings. *Tiffany & Co.*

Casually Smart—Distinguished and Elegant Men. Left to right:
(A) Allen Vanessi raw-silk-and-cotton boat neck, horizontally woven sweater, cream-and-beige-striped shirt, pleated corduroy pants in cream, plum ascot, woven leather shoes. *Wilkes Bashford*. Shoes. *Walter Newberger for Wilkes Bashford*.
(B) Brioni double-breasted navy blue wool jacket, cashmere off-white turtleneck, white wool slacks, tasseled cream-and-beige shoes. *Wilkes Bashford*. Shoes. *Walter Newberger for Wilkes Bashford*.

But note that in establishing the name for this category, I have actually given it two names—not only *casually* but also *smart*. The casual part of that two-word label is the fun part, obviously. It means informal, loose, comfortable. But I think it is very important for winners to remember that they must look smart as well as being casual.

We earlier decided that "smart" was a very difficult word or concept to define. It's like those people who go shopping for a painting and say, "Well, I don't really know anything about art, but I'll know it's good when I see it." I think we all recognize "classy" and "chic" and

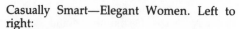

Casually Smart—Elegant Women. Left to right:

(A) Anne Klein white cotton-twill skirt, red cardigan, and royal blue strapless knit top, shoes. *I. Magnin.* Pearls. *Tiffany & Co.*

(B) Anne Klein white linen piqué blouse with jet buttons, black linen trousers, black patent leather belt by YSL. *I. Magnin.* Gold earrings and watch. *Tiffany & Co.*

Casually Smart—Casual and Down Home Men. Left to right:

(A) Gray worsted flannel pleated slacks, plaid shirt, knit striped rust tie, yellow cashmere sweater, loafers. *Wilkes Bashford.* Shoes. *Walter Newberger for Wilkes Bashford.*

(B) Brioni two-button single-vent tweed sport jacket with wool vest, yellow cotton shirt, silk striped tie, brown loafers. *Wilkes Bashford.* Shoes. *Walter Newberger for Wilkes Bashford.*

all those other slippery terms. And I think (and this is perhaps equally important) we all know and can recognize the opposite of Casually Smart—Casually Sloppy.

First, I don't want you to get this category confused with sporty; those are active, athletic, rough-and-ready clothes. I am speaking about a very special category. One that is deficient in most men's and women's wardrobes. It seems that only the elite, the prestigious, the cosmopolitan in our society, and those who aspire to the leisure class afford themselves the luxury of this look. It conveys the ultimate in quality, the finesse of the upwardly mobile, and people who play at the top echelon of our society.

Casually Smart—Glamorous Woman. Calvin Klein silken wool petite houndstooth check double-breasted suit with side-buttoned skirt, white cotton top with jewel neckline. Hat by Frank Olive. *I. Magnin.* 14K white-and-yellow-gold grooved choker and gold-stacked earrings. *Tiffany & Co.*

Casually Smart—Sharp and Hunky Men. Left to right:

(A) Linen-banded-collar shirt, black V-neck cashmere pullover, white linen trousers, black tasseled alligator loafers, Barry Kisselstein black lizard belt with sterling silver buckle and tip. *Wilkes Bashford.* Shoes. *Walter Newberger for Wilkes Bashford.*

(B) Polo shirt (Ralph Lauren) in rust, pleated gabardine slacks in tan, naked leather belt, yellow cotton knit sweater by Alan Flusser, tan loafers. *Wilkes Bashford.* Shoes. *Walter Newberger for Wilkes Bashford.*

This category, as you have no doubt noticed, clearly is burgeoning and exploding in America today. In Europe this concept of clothing has been building momentum for many years. Its depth of expression conveys refinement. It breeds an air of knowingness and luxury. It is a passport into a wide assortment of socially savvy people.

If you desire to be on the "inside track," you will cultivate this look. You'll be a notch above your yesterdays. It gives you an edge.

Learn to dress Casually Smart; it is the way you can accelerate your upward climb and move into a culture of brilliance and success.

So, when you begin to assemble your wardrobe and get to the casual area, remember to pay as much attention to the word "Smart" as to the word "Casual." I am always surprised when I see well-meaning, clever people who can manage to look classy in their business outfits but think that a casual occasion is an invitation for them to look grubby. They arrive at some casual affair in old, hokey clothing and figure that just because their host said it was informal, it's O.K. to look tacky. Movers and shakers don't do that.

It is very possible to be Smart at the same time as you are being Casual—and still be comfortable. Today's designers are specializing in creating informal, casual wear that is the ultimate in sophistication, smartness, comfort, and chicness.

Casually Smart "Chic" and "Spicy" woman

Casually Smart "Casual and Down Home" man

Naturally, in the casual area you can have more freedom of choice and selection than in the area of business wear. For one thing, you can do more with colors and fabrics. You can combine separates that give you a sense of freedom—I love the look, for example, of canvas shoes with jeans, a linen shirt or blouse, and a linen sport jacket. Man or woman, they both look great in that.

FOR MEN. Dressing Casually Smart covers the following territory. I have assembled this list to be used as if you were about to venture on a shopping spree.

1. Sport jackets
2. Sport shirts

Casually Smart "Elegant" and "Glamorous" woman

A special Casually Smart look for all types of men

3. Jerseys
4. Poplin, khaki, or corduroy trousers; wool, linen, silk slacks
5. Sweaters
6. New denim jeans or cotton pants
7. Leather or suede trousers
8. Outer wear: leather or suede jackets; sweater cardigans designed much like a blazer
9. Woven leather or cloth shoes, boots, and loafers

FOR WOMEN:

1. Skirts
2. Blouses
3. Sweaters
4. Slacks—wool, silk, cotton, linen
5. New denim jeans, corduroys, khaki-cotton trousers
6. Leather or suede ensembles
7. Outer wear: leather and suede jackets, blouson jackets, sweaters, and multicolored vests (length varies—waist, hip, or thigh)
8. High-heel or flat-heel shoes, boots

To add certainty as to what I mean, look at these outfits; they are Casually Smart:

Casually Smart "Distinguished and Elegant" man

Casually Smart "Sharp and Hunky" man

FOR MEN:

Visualize yourself in a pair of new jeans—yes, that's right, jeans—
a pale yellow button-down oxford shirt with a knit, solid rust-colored
tie. Now slip into a tweed sport coat in autumn brown, yellows, rust,
and forest green with leather-patched elbows. Push up the sleeves just
below the elbows and turn up the collar if you desire, pull on your
Lucchesi cowboy boots, and you're ready to go.

Here's another easy-to-wear, tastefully put together, outfit for going
to a movie, shopping, or attending a sporting event; khaki cotton pleated
trousers topped with a rich cobalt blue cable-knit sweater (no T shirt or
other shirt underneath) covered by a lightweight, caramel-colored,
zippered, cotton jacket.

On another occasion you might choose to wear a quality pair of
silk, linen, or wool pleated slacks in black, midnight blue, or pearl-
gray, with a white-linen shirt, topped by a 3-ply cashmere sweater in
colors of burgundy, winter white, or loden green. The outfit is finished
with an easily slipped into pair of soft, woven leather shoes.

FOR WOMEN:

I would like for you to see yourself putting these clothes on as I
describe them. A pair of gray flannel, pleated trousers with a raspberry
sweater, matching scarf, and a pair of low-heeled, black patent-leather
walking shoes. You might even want to add a raspberry-and-black
cashmere poncho. This is a happy outfit.

How about this when you go to have lunch with friends? A white-
on-white challis overblouse and black, fitted skirt with a snappy black
high-heeled pump, trimmed in white.

You might wear a wonderful pair of ivory-colored gabardine pleated
slacks, topped with a silk blouse in colors of gold, black, and ivory
stripes, with a large bow tied at the side of the neck, covered by a black,
raw-silk blouse-jacket. A strand of gold-and-ivory beads brings luster
and richness to your outfit. A pair of sling-back pumps or sensual
strappy sandals elevates you above the ordinary. That's Casually Smart!

We have added a new phrase "Casually Smart" to your language
of fashion. Please realize what a powerful edge this gives you. Women—
see yourself in a simple, sapphire-blue V-neck sweater with matching
gabardine slacks—you complete the look. Men—see yourself in an
olive-drab fatigue jacket, a pair of black-cotton slacks, and a white
turtleneck—you finish the look.

Casually Smart is the dynamic way of putting together quality
separates.

Casually Smart—Spicy Woman. Calvin Klein red-linen knit sweater with red-and-white-striped long and lean side-buttoned crepe de chine skirt. Shoes by YSL. *Saks Fifth Avenue.*

It boils down to mixing rich with rich.

The result is that you look as though you have arrived.

Elegant Evening

By definition, the word elegant is translated as tasteful luxuriousness and grace of style, design, and contents.

In the fashion world, men and women are dubbed "elegant" when they appear in public as a notch above the rest, when they have grace and poise and present themselves to others in only the most magnificent of style—with aplomb and assertiveness, with self-confidence and steadfast assurance, with naturalness.

Quite often, elegant clothing is reserved for formal events, although there is no reason on earth why a man or woman could not be elegantly attired in a day suit or a one-piece silk ensemble.

However, we are going to stick mainly to the use of elegant in terms of dressing up; in terms of formality. I am sure that each and every one of us enjoys dressing up and playing with costumes. It is, perhaps, an idea that is left over from our childhood, when little girls loved to play with Mommy's ball gowns and rummage through attic trunks looking for the most dazzling organza sheaths. Little boys played make-believe too, donning costumes of a macho nature and pretending that they were military generals or feudal lords.

There are few moments of anticipation as titillating and exhilarating as getting ready to attend an elegant affair. There is something about dressing in your absolutely very best, with every bit of you, from your shoes to your hair, at its ultimate peak, that turns me on. You are *you*— but yet you are a *super you!* You are holding nothing back. You are scrimping on nothing. You are all set to radiate, to shine, to scintillate. And, somehow, we all seem to develop a new and special glow, to go along with our finest, most elegant outfits. Everybody else at the affair seems to feel that way, too. You come on superstar. It is the end of innocence!

Personally, nothing excites me more than going to an elaborate and elegant affair, where everyone is dressed to the nines and looks smashing. The men, all spiffed up in their black tuxedos or white dinner jacket, and the women, well—I don't believe that any woman could possibly look unattractive when covered in luxurious fur or swathed in layers of chiffon. No matter where the soiree might be taking place—a garden, grand hall, a mansion, a swanky restaurant, a country club, or someone's home—people tend to look better when the lights are dim and they are decked out in their very best.

What type of clothing fits into the category of elegant fashion? First, before we get on to that particular subject, let's clarify the boundaries as to the sort of affairs where elegant clothing is deemed appropriate.

If you happen to receive an invitation to a dinner party, cocktail party, wedding reception, dance, opening night of the symphony, opera, or any other type of benefit for charity, it is most likely that the host or hostess will have noted on the invitation whether the correct attire is formal or otherwise. If the invitation reads: "Black tie, optional," then men must decide, after investigating what others who have been invited are wearing, whether or not to wear a tuxedo. In most circumstances, it would be safe to wear a tuxedo. If you choose not to, then consider alternatives that might be acceptable to black tie, such as a dark blue two-piece suit (here is where your European "V" Wedge suit would look wonderful), a velvet blazer matched with dark-colored trousers and a pleated tuxedo shirt with a tie and matching pocket square, or a double-breasted suit in dark colors including navy blue, chalk-striped gray or winter-white dinner jacket.

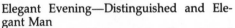

Elegant Evening—Distinguished and Elegant Man
Two-piece double-breasted silk-and-wool formal jacket with peaked lapels by Brioni, Daniel Schagen pleated white formal shirt, burgundy silk bow tie, black silk pocket handkerchief, gray-and-black-striped morning pants by Brioni, black lizard belt. Black silk-laced evening shoes. *Wilkes Bashford.* Shoes. *Walter Newberger for Wilkes Bashford.*

Elegant Evening—Casual and Down Home Man.
Single-breasted three-piece vested wool Brioni tuxedo with satin peaked lapels, white silk pocket handerchief, Daniel Schagen white cotton pleated shirt, black silk tie by Zegna. *Wilkes Bashford.* Shoes. *Walter Newberger for Wilkes Bashford.*

If a man does not own a tuxedo, then he has several viable options from which to choose:

1. Dash out to the nearest respectable clothing store and buy one.

2. You can rent a tuxedo. If you plan to rent a tuxedo, understand that you are going to be wearing a garment that has previously been worn by others. Also, it is a garment that has been altered many times to fit someone other than yourself.

3. You can borrow a tuxedo from a friend who is, obviously, the same height, weight, inseam and hem length as yourself—provided he will loan it to you.

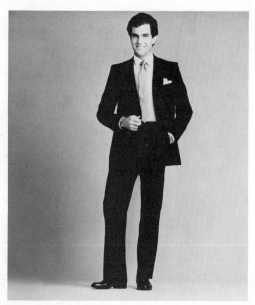

Elegant Evening—Sharp and Hunky Man. Double-breasted black velvet evening jacket by Brioni, black wool tuxedo pants by Brioni, black cap-toed leather laced shoes. Gray cotton shirt with white collar by Daniel Schagen. *Wilkes Bashford*. Shoes. *Walter Newberger for Wilkes Bashford*. Piaget gold watch. *Tiffany & Co.*

I would like to share with you men's fashion writer, Vincent Boucher's words on the power that formal attire gives you:

> Never is simplicity more telling, never is a man's personal signature more evident than when he's dressed for evening. Formal attire need not be confining; in the proper hands its rigorous elegance can enhance a man's individuality. Whether traditional and restrained or innovative and more exciting, formal clothes always look best when they take their inspiration from the classic.

Extremely sound advice! See yourself as Mr. Boucher goes on to describe:

> The rich contrast of midnight-black evening clothes and pristine white or ivory dress shirts that brings out the best in every man . . .

Elegant Evening "Distinguished and Elegant" man

Elegant Evening—"Casual and Down Home" man

Their personalities emerge anew against the stark and spare background of elegant evening clothes. And their individuality is further enhanced by a careful selection of evening accessories—classic bow ties in a width flattering to the face; superb but simply designed jeweled shirt studs and cuff links that add a trace of opulence to evening finery, and understated, gleaming evening watches. (*Esquire* magazine, December 1982, p. 110)

Can there be any doubt in your mind about which of the three choices (buy, rent, or borrow) is best? Be extravagant! Buy a tuxedo! Live sumptuously! Indulge yourself!

Elegant Evening—"Sharp and Hunky"
man

For women the words "formal" or "black tie" are an open invitation
to pull out all the stops: dress up! I don't know how many times I have
been queried as whether or not a floor-length gown is the only answer
to the dilemma of what to wear to a formal affair. For some unknown
reason, women have been under the illusion that it is not at all respectable
to wear cocktail-length dresses or pant-ensembles to lavish parties. So,
here and now, let's set the record straight.

There is absolutely no reason in the world why any woman cannot
wear something other than a floor-length dress to a formal affair (unless
the invitation specifies ball gowns), provided that the outfit is in the
best of taste, fits you to a T, and looks terrific. When the question of
pants comes into the picture, I am not referring to the kind you might

Elegant Evening—Chic Women. Left to right:

(A) Zoran three-piece black, red, and white silk outfit. *Saks Fifth Avenue*. Three-line diamond bracelet. *Tiffany & Co.*

(B) Vicki Tiel black silk faille strapless dress with a bodice tucked on the diagonal. *Wilkes Bashford*. Diamond clip pin, diamond and platinum earrings, pavé diamond and gray pearl ring set in platinum. *Tiffany & Co.*

Elegant Evening—Elegant Women. Left to right:

(A) Black V-neck, sleeved matte-jersey dinner gown with diamond-shaped appliqué encrusted with stones and beads by Felix Arbeo. *I. Magnin*. Platinum and diamond earrings. *Tiffany & Co.*

(B) Black-and-white-satin Valentino top and short black silk skirt. *Wilkes Bashford*. Angela Cummings' platinum-and-diamond swirled earrings, gold-and-diamond choker, diamond ring. *Tiffany & Co.*

be wearing to the office on a daily basis. Not at all. Instead, formal pants are usually classified as velvet slacks, tuxedo-striped pants, or dinner slacks. All of these can be matched with a white, red, or gray taffeta blouse, a silk charmeuse blouse, a silk-knot backless sweater or a knee-length sequin tunic.

Designer Zoran, noted for his simplified dressing techniques, recently introduced a new twist to formal dressing. Cashmere separates. He created red, white, and black cashmere separates, including tunics, pants, sweaters, and flowing capes, intended to be worn after the sun has gone down. Loose and easy to wear, Zoran's separates have paved the way for women to have lots more freedom when it comes time to dress for glamour and evening fun.

Elegant Evening—Glamorous Women. Left to right:

(A) Fabrice jade-green floor-length chiffon gown with silver bugle beads. *Wilkes Bashford.*

(B) Fabrice black silk multicolored beaded cardigan with black silk evening trousers and camisole. Amalfi black silk evening shoes. *Wilkes Bashford.* Shoes. *Walter Newberger for Wilkes Bashford.* 18K gold Schlumberger flame earrings, 18K gold and diamond triple-line bracelet. *Tiffany & Co.*

Elegant Evening—Spicy Women. Left to right:

(A) Whiting and Davis silver-black mesh halter. *Rafael's.* Black silk faille toreador pants. *Saks Fifth Avenue.* Black silk heel shoes. *Walter Newberger for Wilkes Bashford.* Interlocking hoop diamond earrings; ring of 17.97-carat tanzanite surrounded by pear-shaped diamonds. *Tiffany & Co.*

(B) YSL off-one-shoulder black wool crepe short evening dress trimmed with taffeta flounced skirt and taffeta ruffled neckline. *I. Magnin.* 5.55-carat canary-yellow diamond ring, triple-line diamond bracelet, and hoop earrings. *Tiffany & Co.*

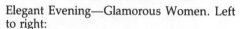

When it comes to wearing strapless dresses, ball gowns, and other sorts of seductive attire on formal occasions, a note on grooming: Powder your breasts, neck, and back with a pearlescent powder. There is a full moon outside, lots of romantic stars, and the jasmine is in bloom. Go ahead and reveal a bit of your fantastic cleavage, show a bit of bare back, and perhaps an inch or two of thigh.

You know how they frequently say that a particular actor or actress "made a great entrance." What is a great entrance, after all, except a human being who comes in the door looking terrific? And anyone who is secure in his or her knowledge that he or she does indeed look magnificent, will automatically acquire the presence necessary to make that great entrance.

That is *elegance*. You will probably find yourself dressing for business about 45 percent of the time, dressing for casually smart about 30 percent of the time, dressing for sport and leisure at home about 20 percent of the time, and dressing in your elegant outfits 5 percent of the time at most. But that 5 percent will be the times you remember the most! And I think you should search out more opportunities to dress elegantly because it is such a marvelous feeling to dress your very

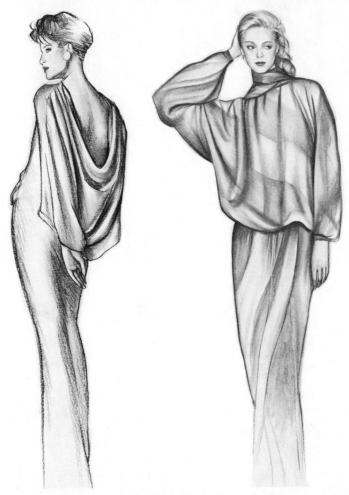

Elegant Evening—"Chic"
woman

Elegant Evening—"Elegant" woman

Elegant Evening—"Glamorous"
woman

Elegant Evening—"Spicy" woman

best. That's why I believe that the clothing you have for elegant affairs are just as important to you as the business and casual clothing, even though you may not wear them as often.

The important thing to remember is that these categories we have discussed so far, business, casually smart, and elegant evening attire, are, and should remain, separate and distinct. *Never* mix them up—never try to get away with wearing a business suit to an elegant affair, or wearing a casually smart outfit to a business meeting.

Truly well-dressed people have clothing that carries them appropriately through the spectrum of their day's experiences. They do what is called for in their behavior, and they do what is tasteful in their choices of clothing, too. If you do that, you will be giving yourself an edge over all the others who don't, who simply try to make do.

You'll never get in the fast lane by trying to make do. You will only get there if you know what to wear, when to wear it, and, most importantly, have the knowledge that you belong there.

Elegant Evening—dinner and theater suit for all four types of women

13

Dressing for Sport

THE ACTIVE YOU

"The end of labor is to gain leisure," said Aristotle a few hundred years before Christ was born.

"Increased means and increased leisure are the two civilizers of man," wrote Benjamin Disraeli, about a hundred years ago.

"You will enjoy your leisure hours more if you are dressed your best," says Robert Panté, right now.

Aristotle was right—with most of us, our working hours are spent in accumulation of enough money so we can enjoy our leisure hours more fully. The more money we have, the richer and pleasanter those leisure hours become. We can travel farther and in greater luxury if travel happens to be one of our passions. We can go to fancier and more exotic resort hotels if that is the way we enjoy spending our off-the-job hours. We can play more golf or tennis, buy larger and more powerful motorcycles, get boats or planes or surfboards, or we can simply sit in our back yards and lie in the sun and read books—we can, in other words, do whatever turns us on.

There are a few lucky ones among us who enjoy their work so much that it is also leisure. The real coup is when that happens; when our work and our play become one. And those who achieve that goal are, fortunately, increasing in numbers.

I think for most of us we work so we can afford to play. And there is nothing wrong with that—it has always been thus. Go for it! But always bear in mind one fact that Aristotle didn't say and Disraeli overlooked, but Robert Panté always remembers. That is that you *must always look appealing*, even in the midst of your leisure and recreation. You owe it to yourself to look vital no matter where you are, no matter what you are doing.

Some people—fewer and fewer all the time, fortunately, but there are still a lot of them around—feel that just because they are off on vacation, or away for the weekend, they deserve to look less than appealing. They wear the oldest, grubbiest, messiest clothing they can pull out from the depths of their closets, and they slouch around the house (or whatever) looking like last week's laundry.

They tell themselves they feel comfortable that way. But does their spirit soar?

Comfort is great. But remember that you might have to answer the front-door bell, and you never know who might be there. Unless you are a professional hermit off in the woods, you will be involved in social relationships, even when you are deep in your leisure time, so look inviting every time, all the time.

At *every moment of your life*, look good. If you feel like a winner five days a week, you owe it to yourself to keep it going on Saturday and Sunday.

The thing is that you can be comfortable in leisure clothing and, at the same time, manage to look like a knockout. More and more these days, American designers, as well as foreign designers, particularly the Italians and Japanese, are coming up with sports clothing and active or spectator sportswear that looks great and feels great, too. The cross over of active and spectator sportswear, also called street wear, is not always distinct. Designers of both are rapidly moving into each other's territory. The term "active sportswear" is an evolving category of clothing—sometimes best described as off-duty wear, weekend wear, or get-in-to-it sweat clothing. It can be "street active" or "game active" depending on whether you are a spectator or an actual participant. The main thing here is that it is definitely becoming a major area of clothing need to get concerned about. Basically it is "cut loose" clothing. It's a very comfortable, easy way of dressing and enjoying your free time. This is a time to make the most of your own active style. After all, how often do we see the hunky guys doing their shopping in their running suits or the Spicy lady coming from her exercise class in her Kamali jumpsuit with a lovely chiffon scarf or belt around her waist. The importance of these looks as fashion is being emphasized by international designers as the basis for their ready-to-wear sportswear collections. Take advantage of their creativity.

It began in the late '50s. A designer named Claire McCardell was among the first American creators to devote an entire collection to casual clothes. Although this sort of apparel had been in evidence before the '50s, McCardell was the first designer to dub the collection *sportswear*. Thereafter, sportswear became an all-important aspect of American fashion. At present, such illustrious designers as Calvin Klein, Geoffrey Beene, Ralph Lauren, Perry Ellis, and others dedicate more than 50 percent of their respective collections to strictly sportswear, otherwise noted in the fashion trade as casual separates.

Throughout the '60s and the '70s, sportswear branched out to include a varied group of silhouettes; some exceptionally trendy and short-lived, including Betsey Johnson's mini-skirts and Rudi Gernreich's hot pants. In the interim, other items like culottes, wrap-around skirts, Bermuda shorts, Capri pants, clamdiggers, pleated trousers, and strapless sundresses became history in the archives of American fashion.

As the '80s approached, more and more men and women took to perfecting the shapes of their bodies, and thus physical fitness became the pastime of the decade. As sportswear began to branch out to include clothes for active sports, such ensembles as jogging clothes, dance leotards, and the famed sweat wear became popular. Within no time at all, department stores and specialty shops have jumped on the bandwagon in this particular category and are presently offering their prospective clients an abundant array of active-wear fashions. Next time you are shopping at your favorite store, take a moment to look around. Chances are you will come across an entire section set aside strictly for this type of apparel. So overwhelming is the demand for informal, loose, and easy-to-wear sportswear, that numerous established designers have taken to licensing such ensembles.

But what does this have to do with you and your sportswear. *Lots!*

I am going to suggest some brand names in the hope that next time you go shopping, the suggestions will come in handy. The designers have taken "active" as a source of inspiration for their fashion thinking.

Notable in the area of men's sportswear and active wear are: Alexander Julian, Jeffery Banks, Bill Blass, New Man, Merona Sport, Perry Ellis, Jhane Barnes, Robert Stock, Ron Chereskin, Levi, Stanley Blacker, Lee Wright, High Gear, Saturday's of California, Gianni Ruffini, Ocean Pacific, and L.L. Bean (mail-order catalog). Basically the prices noted for the above-mentioned designers and manufacturers range between $25 to $300 for shirts, shorts, sweaters, trousers, sport jackets, and outer wear. When shopping, keep a keen eye out for good workmanship, superb fit, expert tailoring, tasteful styling, and fabric contents.

Among the notable designers and manufacturers in the women's area of exciting casual sportswear and active gear are: Calvin Klein, Ralph Lauren, Perry Ellis, Merona Sport, Hang Ten, Adrienne Vitaddini, Andrew Fezza, Norma Kamali, Oscar de la Renta, Geoffrey Beene, Halston, Bill Blass, Danskin, White Stag, Smart Pants, and last but hardly the least—Liz Claiborne. Claiborne's clothes are termed contemporary fashions, which means ensembles that are exclusively intended to be worn during the day, into the night with little or no extemporaneous changes. Her active wear accents style and comfort and is moderately priced.

Look around. The active influence is out on the streets!

Let's revisit our four women—Charlotte Chic, Emily Elegant, Gloria Glamorous, and Sparkee Spicy—and our three male types—David Distinguished, Shep Sharp, and Carl Casual—and see how they dress when they are out to play.

For the sake of comparison, let's first consider the four ladies as they are leaving for a vacation trip. They are traveling via plane, for a week of fun in the sun on the Hawaiian island of Maui, or perhaps it is in the Caribbean, or some other hot, summery place.

There they are, over by the check-in counter. You can easily tell which one is which simply by what the four are wearing.

Charlotte Chic will never let her Chic guard down, not while there's a chance someone might be noticing her. So even though she is going to be cooped up on a plane for five or six hours, she is still dressed in the height of fashion. That's her, in her oo-la-la traveling costume—a GI green jumpsuit worn with a smashing costume belt that has a large silver plate in the front. She has a handsome bag over her shoulder because all the ladies know their carry-on luggage has become an important accessory to the traveling lady. And, of course, flight bags are now considered tacky and are definitely out.

Right next to her, comparing itineraries, is Emily Elegant, always so proper, so smashing. She is her usual elegant self today, wearing an understated suit of peach cotton (it would, of course, be either light wool or silk, cotton or linen). The suit is simple, tailored, but comfortable, and with it she has a plain white blouse and a single strand of black pearls. She has a hat on, too, but she will stow that in the overhead rack as soon as she boards. Her carry-on luggage is more traditional, solid construction, roomy, practical.

I think Gloria Glamorous will have a much more exciting trip than

Sport—Chic Woman
Ungaro sport outfit in cotton, black jacket, turquoise blouse, yellow skirt with red wrap-around sash. *I. Magnin.*

Sport—Elegant Woman
Ralph Lauren white linen shirt and trousers, cotton cardigan in navy blue with white regatta stripes. *Saks Fifth Avenue.* Shoes: *Walter Newberger for Wilkes Bashford.* Patek Philippe tank watch. *Tiffany & Co.*

the others. She will probably make friends with the pilot, co-pilot, radio operator, and sixteen traveling salesmen in the first-class section, judging by how she's dressed. She has on clinging jersey slacks and matching jersey pullover, cut low to allow for a massive gold talisman to dangle from a heavy gold chain around her swanlike neck. In that outfit, she can curl up in her seat and make herself at home. Both the Chic lady and the Elegant lady will be able to curl up and be comfortable on the long flight, but the Glamorous lady isn't planning on doing any curling. She is dressed for action. Her carry-on luggage is as glamorous as she is—a large, gold-colored bag that really is simply an oversized handbag. Perfect for a flight.

And, finally, over there talking to the Hare Krishna solicitor is Sparkee Spicy. She'll be comfortable, too, because that huge, wrap-around skirt allows her to curl up inside it. She probably got it in Chicago in some little specialty shop on Michigan Avenue, and coupled with her peasant blouse, it lets her live up to her usual reputation as a daring, innovative dresser. It also gives her the freedom to travel in comfort. So does her carry-on bag, a huge item that can only be described as a carpetbag—because it is made from what looks like a hunk of rug, with a handle on top. She and the bag make a great-looking, spicy-looking team.

When you are traveling, dress for comfort. I suggest to my women friends and clients that they try a jumpsuit, like Charlotte Chic's. They can be Chic, Elegant, Glamorous, and Spicy, and they give a woman

Sporty "Chic" woman   *Sporty "Elegant" woman*

Sport—Glamorous Women. Left to right:

(A) Pinky & Diane silk skirt and top in white-pink-turquoise-and-gray striping. *Saks Fifth Avenue.* Shoes. *Shaw's Fashion Shoes.*

(B) Anne Klein fuchsia-black-and-white-striped silk top with black linen pants and shoes. *I. Magnin.*

Sport—Spicy Women. Left to right:

(A) Norma Kamali gray sweat jump sui[t] *Saks Fifth Avenue.* Black belt and boots. *Wilke[s] Bashford.* Boots. *Walter Newberger for Wilk[es] Bashford.*

(B) Ralph Lauren blue-and-red-stripe[d] polo shirt, red shorts. *Saks Fifth Avenue.* Blu[e] web belt. *Wilkes Bashford.* Slip-on flats. *Shaw['s] Fashion Shoes.*

the freedom to be relaxed while on that long and often uncomfortable plane trip. Or auto trip. Or train trip. Slacks and a blouse also make a very practical traveling outfit, as well, and can be Chic or Elegant or Glamorous or Spicy. In a plane, or other public conveyance these days, people don't dress to impress each other so much as they dress for sheer comfort. But I insist that it is possible to combine those two goals—to be attractive and comfortable at the same time—so you can manage to look great while feeling great. That's the goal to shoot for. But, remember that you will be wearing your traveling costume when you arrive at your destination, so you can't be just dressed to be comfortable. You must look important because you still have to convey clout when you register at a hotel front desk or meet your friends or business acquaintances at the airport. Wherever you go, it will be first-impression-time again.

And once you have checked in or settled in, the problem of what to wear becomes a little more complex. In nine out of ten cases, you will want to look your best throughout the whole day's span, morning to night. Even lolling on the beach can separate the men from the boys, and the women from the girls. With most of us, we want to look special always, and that's the way it will be.

Sporty "Glamorous" woman

Sporty "Spicy" woman

And it can be done. Playtime can still be good-appearance time. Let's see how our four fair female friends are faring.

Look at the Chic woman, over there under that palm tree. She is wearing a long, ankle-length beach coat, in terry cloth, with a bold pattern of four huge diamonds—one pink, one orange, one yellow, one pale green. She takes it off and—surprise—there is a dreamy, one-piece bathing suit, in just the right color to set off the color of her hair, fashioned in a unique design of straps and cutouts. Today's bathing suit designers are as boldly individual as dress designers. Don't settle for something plain and traditional, but shop in the better stores and treat yourself to a bathing suit that has some character to it.

Emily Elegant—there she is, over at the edge of the pool—has her hair wrapped in a black scarf, topped by a broad-brimmed straw hat with a black band. She is wearing a simple but eye-catching black bathing suit, slashed deeply in the front and rear. (Black is always a good color for bathing suits; it sets off the pale complexion of fair-skinned women and accentuates the skin of those ladies who have acquired a suntan or are naturally darker in complexion. White is good for the darker-skinned ladies, too.) The Elegant woman has on beach sandals that are remarkable—they have what appear to be ropes of pearls supporting the simple soles. (They are glass, not real pearls, but with her, everything comes off a little more special.)

Look around. There, on a bright scarlet beach towel, at the crest of the sand dunes reclines Gloria Glamorous. Is that a bikini she has on, or just a trio of postage stamps held together by rubber bands? Whatever it is, or isn't, it sure looks great on Gloria, but, of course, anything would. It's kind of hard to get a good look at her because of all the beach boys swarming around. They gambled the night away to see which one would get her suntan-oil-application rights.

Finally, sitting at the snack bar, sipping a Piña Colada, is Sparkee Spicy. Her beach coat looks like—by George, it is!—a warm-up jacket she somehow finagled from a member of the Detroit Tigers. Underneath, she is wearing a bikini whose components don't match—the bra is yellow, the bottom half is pumpkin-orange. Her beach sandals are something she got for $1.50 from a street peddler in Tijuana—the soles are made from old rubber tires, and a piece of orange plastic string holds them together. She looks positively zingy.

Between traveling on a plane and reclining on a beach there is a whole world of other things to do and places to go, and so there is a broad range of recreational clothing to wear. Obviously, the opportunities and choices are far too wide and diverse for me to give you specific recommendations of what you should wear where. But just let me suggest—no, let me *demand!*—that you live up to your potential at all times.

Be yourself! Act your type or types—Chic, Elegant, Glamorous, Spicy—because your audience expects it of you. When you go against type (a Chic woman dressing Spicily, for example) you will give those you meet a feeling that something is wrong or out of place. They may not be able to put their finger on precisely what it is, but they will come away from the encounter with a vague feeling that all is not complementing you. You have to be who you are; it gives you points. "Without distinction there is extinction!"

And remember, too, that wherever you are and whatever you may be doing, people will be watching you, judging you, assessing you. So never fall into the tragic trap of saying that, since you are on vacation, it doesn't really matter what you wear. *It always matters what you wear!* You won't feel complete fudging it for a moment because that moment might turn out to be the critical one when somebody comes along you want to impress—maybe a potential business opportunity, or a potential social contact, or a potential lover. If you have been less than who you are for that one crucial moment, and are dressed like a total glomp, then you start apologizing—and opportunity will have to revisit. Many people feel it is not worth it to handle lost expectations; get what you want from the start.

The same thing applies, of course, just as strongly to your grooming. Sure, on vacation it's a nuisance to have to go through all that with your hair, eyes, face, lips, fingernails. But elements of it must be done! Oh, perhaps you can cut a corner or two, maybe a compromise here or there will be O.K., but it's better not even to do that. You want to look at the peak of your potential always. Anyhow, once you have your grooming down to a routine, it's much easier to be consistent.

I said I wasn't going to get too specific, but I do want to bring you a few "snapshots" of our four ladies at various places, as they are seen relaxing by my roving, restless, prying, camera eye.

We are in the Hamptons, and there is Charlotte Chic in what she kiddingly refers to as "my street-walking outfit." She is wearing a pair of taupe cotton shorts with a purple-cotton T shirt under a cotton cardigan.

Now, the next snapshot. It is in the Napa Valley at a wine festival, and we find that renowned wine aficionado, Emily Elegant, looking her elegant self, in her white-linen eyelet tunic and short summer skirt. As she lifts the glass of Chardonnay and sniffs its bouquet, eyes turn to see what her reaction will be. Her approval may mean the beginning of a great wine.

Turn the page of the album and there is a snapshot of Gloria Glamorous. She is strolling down a boulevard in Mexico City's fashionable Zona Rosa, and the locals' eyes are popping out. She has on a big-shouldered, red-and-white-striped T shirt with white jogging pants, her sandals swinging loosely from her hand. With her bouncing hair the effect is devastatingly pleasing. (It's a good thing we had color film in our camera for that picture!)

Finally, we come to a picture of Sparkee Spicy, taken on a cruise ship, as it was edging into the harbor at Pireaus, after a great fourteen-day cruise through the Eastern Mediterranean. She is wearing her famous summer midriff suit—in green on white linen with a white-linen jacket and large, billowing, matching harem pants.

Sport—Distinguished and Elegant Man. Pleated white cotton trousers, white cotton bulky crew-neck sweater with single navy blue striped sleeve by Perry Ellis. *Wilkes Bashford*. White leather sneakers. *Walter Newberger for Wilkes Bashford*.

Sport—Casual and Down Home Man. Royal blue long-sleeve T shirt by Polo (Ralph Lauren), yellow cotton sport shorts, white leather sneakers, gym bag. *Wilkes Bashford*. Sneakers. *Walter Newberger for Wilkes Bashford*.

Now let's switch genders and see how our three men are faring as they embark on that same plane for that same vacation in Hawaii.

David Distinguished is, as you have every right to expect, a conservative fashion plate. He has on his oversized white-linen short-sleeved sport shirt, hemplike rustic linen baggy pants, and a pair of vanilla-colored fabric shoes complete the ensemble.

Next, we come to Shep Sharp. He's wearing jeans! The Sharp and Hunky man knows that good jeans set a man aside and somehow immediately label him as an "item." They're Levi 501s and they're quite tight, as is his yellow T shirt. Over his shoulder he's carrying a lightweight orange utility parka. His Adidas sneakers complete the attitude as he nonchalantly saunters up to the gate.

And there is Carl, the Casual and Down Home man. He could curl up in his seat and sleep his way to paradise because he's dressed for curling up—cotton slacks, a white button-down cotton shirt, and a

Sporty "Distinguished and Elegant"   *Sporty "Sharp and Hunky" man*
man

blue-and-white-cotton tennis sweater draped over his arm, and weejuns, of course.

I have some snapshots of these three worthy gentlemen in their recreational mode in my album, too, so let's catch a glimpse of them at play and see what they are wearing.

First, the Distinguished and Elegant man. He has rented a car and driver and is exploring the picturesque Cotswold country of England. He's dressed for it, too. Dressed in his striped shirting-weight blue-linen jacket, fine-line-striped cotton trousers, a linen tab-collar shirt, and white bucks he certainly cuts a distinguished figure.

Shep Sharp, as we see him in my picture, is evidently on somebody's yacht. Maybe it's his own, but I can't make out the name so it's impossible to tell. But we can see what he is wearing from bottom to top. He has on sneakers, a red-and-gray sweat shirt with navy cotton rugby shorts. You can't see them in the picture, but I remember him

mentioning that he has on his speedo black racing suit. No water clings
to him!

And, finally, let's take a look at our old buddy, Carl, the Casual
and Down Home man. He is being extremely casual on a camping trip
in the Smoky Mountains. I think it's autumn, because he's wearing a
coat—a mid-calf-length pea coat in a lush burgundy shade. Carl Casual
feels strongly about coats. The Casual and Down Home man feels that
his outer wear should last him from three to five years and that,
therefore, he must buy a coat that is a classic and won't go out of style
before it wears out. The pea coat is his idea of a good buy because men
have been wearing them since Horatio Nelson was a midshipman—
and they haven't gone out of style yet. He has his favorite baseball cap
on his head, a pair of blue jeans (nicely broken in), and a good-old-boy
blue-and-green plaid flannel shirt. On his feet, a pair of sturdy boots

Sport—Sharp and Hunky Man. Black cotton
split-seam draw-string sport pants by Claudia Reid, Ltd., black with red-stripe-trim
varsity jacket, white cotton mesh muscle
shirt by Claudia Reid. *Wilkes Bashford*. Sneakers. *Walter Newberger for Wilkes Bashford*.

Sporty "Casual and Down Home" man

for the great outdoors. Rugged wear and outdoor wear are major themes in his sportswear.

In their way, all seven of our friends are dressed for recreation, for comfort, for play, for making a good impression while they are enjoying their off-duty leisure hours.

And that is the key—the dual action of looking good while feeling good—and I stress it over and over and over again.

When you are thinking of buying clothing for your precious non-working hours, always remember that *what you put on on the outside can help determine your mood on the inside.* Buy garments that help fire your mood, help inspire you to greater emotional glory, keep you moving along the path you have chosen to travel.

I said earlier in this chapter that a person should clothe himself or herself in keeping with his or her personality type at all times. And that is certainly true. But I don't mean to inhibit your variety when I say that. Within the boundaries of those types there is ample room for experimentation, enough elbow, leg, and knee room so you can express your own precious individuality.

Think of your own personality or, if you prefer another word, your own nature. It is never constant. It varies. It has its moods, its ups, its downs, its highs, its lows. Your clothing type is the same sort of loose arrangement, and you have to give yourself plenty of room so you can express your various and varying moods.

Don't get stuck assuming that there's only one narrow way of expressing yourself. If you get set in a rigid style, if you see yourself only in one tight little way, then you will find that you get only the same types of reactions from only the same types of people you will be attracting with that act of yours. It's like my mother used to say, when I was a little boy and cried. She would say that if I didn't stop crying, my face would freeze like that, and I'd go through the rest of my life with a crying face. If you don't change your personality once in a while, it will freeze that way, and nobody likes a person who offers no surprises, no variety, only endless doses of predictability.

We have already established the fact that a man or a woman can best express his or her personality by the clothing he or she wears. And so it follows that if you want to have a free-form, varied personality, one that expands and contracts to meet various situations, then you have to have clothing to match. Be sure that you have clothing in your closet for all of your many moods—happy clothing, serious clothing, carefree clothing, careful clothing, fun clothing.

I believe this sort of freedom of choice is given the widest rein in this area of clothing for play, recreation, leisure, and travel. The other types of clothing—especially clothing for the working hours—are necessarily more restrictive in terms of tone and mood. But when you are at play, you can go all out as far as changing your clothing mood is concerned.

You want a closet that supports your intentions, whatever they may be. If you feel giddy and silly, rakish and frisky, you should be able to go to your closet and pull out something that totally matches and supports that mood. If, on the other hand, you feel like being conservative, very sober-sided, you want to be able to reach in and whip out clothing that helps you sustain that feeling.

Even the Elegant lady and the Distinguished and Elegant man have their irrepressible moments. I know that they have certain things in their closets—and the reason I know is that they have asked me to go shopping with them, so I have seen what they have bought—that are irrepressible and outrageous. And yet those garments are always within the limits of their type. You might call them classically adventuresome. It is possible to be elegant and zany at the same time, to be a distinguished clown. And, similarly, our Spicy lady can be very serious when she wants to be, and our Sharp and Hunky man can dress with the utmost propriety if the mood strikes him.

Dress for recreation as though you might have to confront an audience around the next tree, behind the next dune on the beach, following the next set of tennis. Today's leisure clothing permits that— lets you be comfortable and look great at the same time—so take advantage of it. Feel wonderful and look fantastic, too.

14

Dressing for Sensual Appeal

THE POTENT POWER OF PHYSICAL ATTRACTION

In writing about dressing for sensual appeal, I decided to have fun—to entertain, stimulate, and captivate you, the reader, with what can be one of the most enjoyable pursuits of being human.

Immediately a line from Nell Dunn's play *Steaming* came to mind—"Every day when I wake up you know what I pray for? I pray for courage. And a good sex life!" That expresses how many of us feel. Nell Dunn simply managed to state it candidly. The bottom line is that at certain times we are all dressing for sex appeal.

Sex appeal is a subjective thing. One person's turn-on is another's yawn. If you're one of those whose synapses start their electrical dance at the sight of a vibrant shape with "body language" that speaks out strongly, you'll agree with this: Hot-looking people are exciting. They come in all shapes and forms. It is that hidden message that comes to the surface in the form of attention-getting clothing that separates the alluring from the nice, the spunky from the wimpy—the word is "breathtaking." You've got each other's number.

First, let's get one thing clear: There is no such thing as a foolproof formula that will always work to tantalize admirers or those you hope to captivate. However, certain props, expertly chosen, can enhance your confidence and power. The right clothes are those props that will enhance your body language and play up those areas you want to accentuate.

The desire to charm, the fun of the chase, the pleasure of the game, are activities few would want to be without. Your pulse increases; your body responds; your mind envisions success, and you are hooked. So bait that hook. This is a time to get each other sizzling. What conveys your message most will be the choice of the clothing you select. You've decided upon your target, aimed your arrows, and don't want to miss. For some it will take being gutsy, nervy, and vitally alive. For others it is second nature.

Awakening the sensual responses in another person is something you were born with. Go all out and aim high. It is the prime catch you are shooting for. Hitting your mark takes all of you that is physically and emotionally stimulating. You know what is needed and wanted. I want to supply the finishing touches that will assure you leave the party with a new friend, cuddling close.

It is after six; the office is closed. Leave your seriousness behind. Nobody will be interested in your typing speed, how many deals you closed, or how well you run the Xerox machine. They will even care less about how many meetings you attended. It is your show now, there is no one to answer to. You are the chief executive officer now. Pull out all the stops and watch those meters register. Go for what you want; what you truly desire.

Sensual, sexy dressing can be described as: luxurious, tempting, radiant, revealing, provocative, teasing, accentuating, playful, wild, spicy, intriguing, and *inviting*. Its fabrics are: silk, leather, lace, cashmere, suede, angora, velvet—soft-to-the-touch fabrics, which are as good as bare skin. Sometimes your sexiness is your secret; like the feeling you get from these fabrics against your skin.

Non-sensual dressing can be described as: coarse, tailored, proper, prudish, nice, cute, bland, reserved, dull, stiff, ordinary, priggish, and *uninviting*.

There is certainly no doubt that sex is very important in our lives. After all, I started out this book determined to show you the way to more sex, money, and power. Because of its importance, I have always been amazed at the prudery of some people who consider as something distasteful the fact that we sometimes attract our partners through our physical savvy. Perhaps it is gone about too blatantly at times, but the individual and the social situation at hand determine the boundaries.

All creatures on the face of the earth have forms of premating ritual, and with us, it is often that our clothing plays a big part in how we attract each other. In truth, the importance of sex in enhancing the game of life doesn't need our vote—it has already won! And that is the natural order of things, so let's go.

My place in that order of things is to point out that how you dress is a major contributing factor in how successful—or unsuccessful—you are in attracting partners.

"Men always fall for flashy women," a famous comedienne once said, "because they put on the biggest show."

I don't totally agree that that assessment was correct, but I do know that men fall for the women who put on the best show—and, similarly, women fall for the men who put on the best show, too. And what makes a good show is a combination of many different elements—the inner person whose personality bursts forth; the magnetism of the body itself; and, perhaps equally contributing and inviting, the clothing that the person puts over his or her body. Clothing enhances the potent power of physical attraction; it's the *zapper!*

Your clothing must have wit, flair, romance, and style. Ever notice what a pair of fitted jeans can do for your social life? Take notice of what a tight shirt across a man's shoulders and chest can do to accent a muscular physique. Your fingers get the urge to touch. Or how a clinging silk Charmeuse skirt enhances long, shapely legs. Admiring is the rule of the game; wanting is the name of the game; having is the aim of the game.

A woman dressing for sensual appeal makes the subtle statement, "Let's play." She does it by astute selection of clothing—clothing that accentuates her finest physical features and attributes, diminishes, and conceals her least-attractive features, accents her entire aura of sensuality by her choices of color, fit, fabric, moods, and scents—topping it all off with her own brand of "body language" and "night makeup." You want to turn up the color intensity of makeup for night.

Here we go:

1. *A Dress* that plunges in the front or dips down the back. In this dress who wouldn't provoke! The opposite can also be true if the bust and entire body scream out "female pulchritude"—it can be high around the neck and conceal every piece of upper flesh, but its taut, clinging fabric of jersey or silk will set hearts pounding. Dress it up with smoky stockings and rhinestone-sparkled sandals.

2. *A Simple Leotard* is a second skin, enhanced with a playful, brilliantly colored wrap-around skirt that moves with the body—legs are free to prance and kick. Accented with a multicolored sash or wide cord belt and high slip-on sandals. It's a *pow!* of an outfit. An array of

Dressing Sexy—Distinguished and Elegant Man, Elegant Woman.

MAN Gianfranco Ferre fire-engine-red suede pullover, Giorgio Armani slate-gray leather pants. *Wilkes Bashford.*

WOMAN Pinky & Diane sapphire-blue strapless knit top, ivory silk trousers, black patent leather pumps. *Wilkes Bashford.* Shoes. *Walter Newberger for Wilkes Bashford.*.18K gold and black jade, hematite, and coral bracelet by Angela Cummings. *Tiffany & Co.*

Dressing Sexy—Casual and Down Home Man, Chic Woman.

MAN Tricolor suede jacket by Fodora Bemberg, black Polo shirt (Ralph Lauren), Rough Hewn brand blue jeans. *Wilkes Bashford.* Lizard boots by R. J. Foley. Brass, snake, and cowhide belt. *Wilkes Bashford.* Boots. *Walter Newberger for Wilkes Bashford.*

WOMAN Mink-lined-and-edged reversible suede vest, leather side-slit double-pleated skirt, turtleneck, boots. *Rafael's.*

multicolored, large-size beads with several bracelets clinking on the wrist completes the outfit.

3. *A Jumpsuit* that zips from the top to waist in bright red, blue, yellow, white, or shades of light blue, pale coral, or lavender rayon (parachute material), is enough to shift any man's motor into high gear. The jumpsuit legs can be worn stuffed into knee-high, soft, suede boots. Hair can be flouncy, long, and loose, or short, severely brushed, close to the sides—lending a chic, cool appearance of "aviation slickness"— a dazzler!

4. *Fitted Jeans* (you choose the brand) with a pair of very high,

open-toed, French or stiletto heels. Topped with a cotton, off-the-shoulder blouse or a slinky brightly colored silk blouse gathered around the neck, wrapped around the waist, or knotted over a hip. A lizard-skin or thin, braided roped belt in an accenting color to finish off the look of slimness. Hair possibly pulled up on one side and cascading down the other for dramatic impact. The idea here is soft, feminine curves, provocative from any angle—a seductive combination.

5. *A Loose-Fitting Jogging Suit* in soft, creamy, sweat-shirt fabric, tightly clinched at the waist, jogging shoes, bandana holding the hair

Sensual Appeal—"Elegant" woman

back and off the face. The suit is sky-blue, banana-yellow, or a pulsating purple cotton, breathing in all that cooling air circulating itself around your vitally alive body.

6. *Slit, Straight, Tightly Fitted Skirt* in black wool, side slits four inches above the knees, with a matching black jersey turtleneck top and a patent-leather belt, black or natural hose, and black patent-leather pumps—this evokes slinkiness.

7. *A Flouncy, Bouncy, Swirling, Cotton-and-Silk-Blend Skirt* that catches each breeze that passes its way, with an equally full-sleeved, open-neck, airy blouse, that dares to be worn braless—you choose the color combinations. High-heeled, ankle-strapped shoes and loose, flying hair completes the picture of "easy-does-it sensualness."

Sensual Appeal—"Chic" woman

Sensual Appeal—"Glamorous" woman

8. *Bare* arms, bare legs, bare neck, bare feet, bare shoulder or shoulders—bare midriffs, short leggy skirts, hip-teasing bathing suits, and all-out "second" skin garments do the trick. The appeal of twenty-one inches of deliciously curved bare back!

9. *Colors* can be rousing, stimulating, thrilling. Greens with orange, reds with violet, black and white, blue and yellow, magenta, hot reds, shimmering silvers and metallic golds, and black—you can add beads, sequins, and shiny threads weaving through silks, cottons, and linens.

10. *Jewelry* prominent and bold, or expensive and rich—on the flashy side—twisted or braided chokers, dramatic modern artsy pieces,

cascading playful glass beads of many strands and colors, Egyptian art objects wrapped around the neck, arms, or wrist. Dangling earrings of every shape, material, and size. Why not just one earring and long hair on the opposite side for balance, rings on three to five fingers, bangles that clang and announce your arrival, mysterious pieces of irregularly shaped jade, brass, semiprecious stones, and pendants! Each piece of jewelry is to call attention and accentuate. An onyx or crystal drop earring. Long ropes of pearls knotted below the breastline have a way of calling for attention. Or a long platinum lariat disappearing into the barest neckline. Why not add an ankle bracelet!

11. *Handbags* that hang and dangle, that are small and can be clutched tightly, that are shiny and glittering, that desire to be held closely by you—like pleated, soft leather—and that often swing at your hip and draw attention to your step and strut. This is the time to have many fun bags that will carry only the barest of necessities. Choose a material you can clean easily or just throw away when you soil or tire of it. Most of all, let your bag say you are on the run and have just enough time to have some fun.

12. *Belts* are to draw attention and accentuate the positive, the curvaceous, and add to the dramatic. Projecting out what you want prominent and tightening what you want smaller. The buckle is often silver, gold, or ivory and tastefully contrasts with the entire outfit. Shoe colors and materials don't have to match exactly, but pick up the feeling of the belt—the belt being definitely more prominent and eye-catching.

13. *Sunglasses* always do it! It is impossible to go astray here with oversized frames; full, rounded shapes, or narrow, wrap-around frames. There is often a frivolous woman behind those dark, mysterious eyes and bright luscious lips.

14. *Hats* that make you stand out in the crowd, that announce you as special, that recall times of movie heroines and underground women. Soft tammies, broad and very, very wide straw hats, an occasional mannish-style hat like a flirty fedora, and definitely an eye-catching feathered hat to tickle your suitor.

15. *Shoes* that are high-heeled, strapped, spiked French or Continental heels: Maud Frizon, Charles Jourdan.

16. *Meshed Halter Tops* in gold, silver, black, or several interwoven colors combined to create a sparkling and tempting top for evening suits, silk pants, wrap-around skirts, and simply whatever delights your man. The purity and innocence of an angora sweater.

Simply, each item of clothing you carefully select is to arouse, entice, and convey your message of "I'm interested." It must do just that! If your figure is easily overwhelmed by the wildest, boldest, barest, go for simple lines, inviting colors, seductive "come touch me" fabrics.

Let your choice of clothing captivate the aesthetics of onlookers. Romance will never be the same.

I just have to share the following with the readers of this book, especially you women who enjoy wearing fine lingerie. It is a series of vignettes written by Cynthia Robins for the San Francisco *Examiner*, "What Goes On Under the Surface."

Sensual Appeal—"Spicy" woman

Jessica Stein stood in front of the mirror adjusting her luxuriant, flame-red hair into a severe bun at the base of her neck. She had downplayed her makeup, sticking to a tiny bit of blusher, a soft mocha lipstick, mascara but no colored shadow. In an hour or so, she would be sitting down with the recruiting partner of a prestigious San Francisco law firm, interviewing for a job. She wanted to look just right, meaning no double messages. No sex. Just ability.

She had chosen a soft but conservatively styled silk blouse with a Peter Pan collar and a black grosgrain ribbon tie. It definitely camouflaged her prodigious bust and provided no view of the cleavage beneath. Her suit was Armani, black and cut severely. The skirt skimmed right below her knee. She had buffed her "sensible," four-year-old Gucci pumps to a burnished sheen. But before she placed her foot, clad in sheer, taupe real silk hose, into the shoe, she hoisted her skirt to check on her lingerie—a wispy silver-gray bikini drenched in lace with a matching garter belt and bra . . . [End of story.]

A young, mid-30ish couple walked into the elegant department store on Union Square. She was slender, petite and dark, wearing a feminine, three-piece silk suit. His hair was cut in a well-groomed, near Italian gigolo style and his immaculate gray suit was set off by a $75 Valentino tie. It was her birthday and he wanted her to pick out a very special present. They looked over the handbags and the perfume, the cashmere sweaters, the frilly Victorian blouses, they even took a sideways glance at the fine jewelry boutique. Eventually, they ended up in the lingerie department, where they found several saleswomen in their 60s standing behind the counter, tape measures draped around their necks. In a display case was an all-in-one combination corset, bra, girdle made of stretch-Lycra. With an impish grin, he leaned his head toward her and said in a stage whisper, 'Why don't we buy this and I'll fwap you around the bedroom in it?' The trained corsetier behind the counter turned away, blushing from her low-heeled shoes clear up to her neatly coiffed gray head. They asked to see a black-lace garter-belt and again, the gray haired woman blushed. They left, buying nothing . . . [End of this story.]

Jamie was a Berkeley senior when he fell in love with the woman who would eventually become his wife. They had met at the tail end of the Movement. He affected a bushy, full beard and plaid woodsman shirts; he smoked a lot . . . and was planning to go to dental school. She lived in grungy Levi's, war surplus khaki undershirts and fatigue jackets; she harbored a passion for law, hoping eventually to become a first-class civil rights lawyer. The first night they ever spent together, Jamie realized that this woman had a secret. On the outside, she was all business—a rabid feminist who would brook no possessiveness or sexist comments from her man. However, under all the olive-drab drag and the ubiquitous scent of patchouli oil, she wore black lace bikinis. It set the pace for future trysts and gifts, and now almost ten years later, Jamie spends more than $150 a month on his wife, giving her silk gowns and teddies, G-strings, French bras and black lace garter belts. They are gifts as much for him as they are for her . . . [End of story.]

Dressing Sexy—Sharp and Hunky Man, Glamorous Woman.

MAN Suede pants, black V-neck cashmere sweater. *Wilkes Bashford.* Shoes. *Walter Newberger for Wilkes Bashford.*

WOMAN Alaia cobalt-blue-and-black wool dress. *I. Magnin.* Shoes. *Walter Newberger for Wilkes Bashford.* 18K gold Elsa Peretti hoop earrings. *Tiffany & Co.*

Jamie, Jessica and the well-dressed young couple were all celebrating the same thing—the death of pantyhose and the rebirth of romance. Spice, sex, romance, quality and beauty, all wrapped up in fine lingerie and a new feminine consciousness. [End.]

(San Francisco *Examiner*, December 14, 1980)

How did you enjoy those three vignettes? There is a great deal to say about undergarments to make and enhance a woman's sense of her ultimate sensuality. And the man of her choice gets to play along with her secret. So what goes on under the surface is as important as what one can see on the top!

Dressing Sexy—Spicy Woman with Three Men.
  (Men's clothes previously described.)
    WOMAN Brown leather pants. *Rafael's.* Anne Klein fuchsia-black-and-white-silk tunic. *Saks Fifth Avenue.* 18K gold and oval rubellite ring by Paloma Picasso. *Tiffany & Co.*

Dressing sexy for men has its own unique characteristics. It all starts with feeling and believing that you are the best any woman could ask for. You appreciate feminine beauty and she gets that message from your stance, glance, stare, body positioning, and honest-to-goodness appreciation of her. When you're hot you're hot, and it comes through your clothing with your every motion, your gait, the way you stand— you're a buck, you're a dream, you're what the doctor has ordered. Maybe a stud, maybe a gigolo, possibly a hard catch.

It all boils down to knees buckling when gals catch sight of you. There is no mistaking, you unsettle the ladies with your presence. You are a woman's fantasies, her passions, her magic potion—a turn-on. A catalyst of turbulent emotions. The naked truth about American women is that they like to see their men in bikini underwear first, knit brief shorts second, and boxer shorts last.

For men, items of clothing must be put on the body before they give off a sexy message—selectivity is very important here. Have an arsenal of clothing that invites touches and caresses. Be a man with tons of courage: It's wise to combine raw masculinity with an air of romance, and smart to balance ruggedness with elegance.

1. Any pair of pants that make your buns appear to be firm and grabbable—instant turn-on!

2. Any shirt that either fits well to accentuate a solid "man-size chest" or that drapes comfortably to give a hint of the athletic, healthy body.

3. Low-slung pants that don't ride as high as the waist. They give the illusion of swagger and swivel to a man's pelvis, ridding yourself of tight restraint.

4. A shirt that has no sleeves, sleeves cut off at the shoulders— showing "women-holding arms"—is a sure win.

5. Jeans that fit just right, whether new or faded. (But please keep your oversized comb out of your back pocket.)

6. Sweaters of cashmere, soft cotton, or jersey that invite tantalizing touches.

7. That active sportswear look of a finely honed athlete: the jogger in slit nylon shorts, the tennis player in white fitted shorts, the surfer in a skin-tight black wet suit, the race-car driver in a shiny, satin jacket and baggy, loose comfortable jump suit with the neck of his white Nomex long johns showing. They give you the feeling of being "alive" and "active."

8. Those Speedo briefs of the Olympic swimmers.

9. The fitted cotton chinos and sweat shirts, sometimes worn inside out, that are so all-American looking.

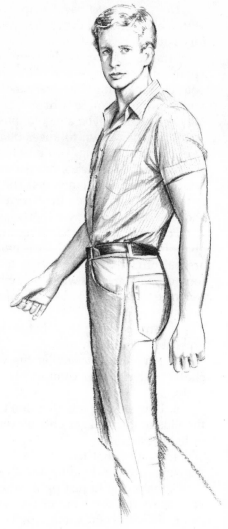

Sensual Appeal—"Distinguished and Elegant" man

Sensual Appeal—"Casual and Down Home" man

10. Sport jackets with large armholes and padded shoulders. Oftentimes a drop-notch lapel or a double-breasted jacket—fitted jackets convey shapely musculature and longer, leaner bodies.

11. Sweaters worn over a bare chest—no T shirt.

12. Leather or suede slacks, shirts, or jackets.

13. Shirts that unbutton low to reveal a hairy chest or a hairless one—both types of men score big. Some men try to out-plunge the women, opening their shirts down to the Mexican border. Save your belly button for some future moment of ecstatic discovery.

14. A hat that strikes a note of mystery—a fedora or panama.

15. Fitted, tight, leather gloves in the finest of leathers, constantly being knuckled and pulled.

Sensual Appeal—"Sharp and Hunky" man

16. A very loose-fitting outfit—baggy, comfortable shirt, and loose roomy trousers, pulled together with a tight fabric belt—nothing at all to restrict movement. Many times it is the implication of "vital health" that evokes a response. Less frequently it is that "helpless-vulnerable," "sloppily attired, country look" that provokes a response.

Sensual Appeal—Three types of men

Clothes for sensual attire for men must hint of what is underneath, plant a seed rather than being totally revealing.

Go about attracting women by exhibiting your marvelous taste in clothing, which demonstrates to them that you are demanding of excellence, are particular, expect to travel first class. At first glance women can tell an "almost-arrived" from one who has arrived: don't show them bulges, show them your taste and charm. Women generally know enough about clothing so that they can recognize the exquisiteness of our selections, and that alone is enough to excite them. They are attracted to "movers and shakers." *The best aphrodisiac for a woman is a man who has arrived and wants to share his good fortune and know-how with her.*

I want all of you to remember the following definition of sex: Sex is the sensual pleasure that is yours because others want to participate with you on a very personal, physical level. It is your appeal power that either magnetizes or repels another person. It is the game of bodies, minds, and spirits enjoying each other.

I like that definition, even if I made it up myself. I think it really tells, in precisely forty-five pithy words, exactly what we are all doing when we set out to captivate someone or to allow ourselves to be captivated.

And the important thing to bear in mind is that it boils down to two of those forty-five words: *appeal power*.

Those are the words that either make you or break you. How do you go about cultivating a well-functioning, successful *appeal power*? Mostly, by knowing you are hot. You are provocative, and that doesn't mean lewd. It means to dress in a way that will intrigue, stimulate, and captivate. It also leaves something to be discovered.

Always remain a high-quality find. The key is to invite a response to what you are wearing—push something close to the edge and create an interest point. That is what the sensual process is all about. The outfits need not always be covering up or daringly uncovering—as long as they catch the eye and hold another's attention. Grab the attention of your audience—stretch their imagination—give them the best illusion and emphasis of bodily appeal. By mixing color, fabric values, hues, and combining styles and fit, the onlookers have one person to focus in on—*you*. Playing safe is not what is called for here!

Be brave!

Have courage!

Be true to your inner yearning!

Be flexible and have fun! The only limit here is your imagination.

Release the need to be safe—be *desired!*

PART VI

Life in the Fast Lane

15

Fashion and Style

BLENDING: THE TIMELY AND TIMELESS

Be honest—does the man [or woman] in your life think that "Lacoste" is a small province in Spain and that "Saint Laurent" is the leader of a religious cult in France? Does "Valentino" bring a wistful smile to his [her] face as he [she] contemplates the romantic exploits of that celebrated screen lover? When he [she] hears the word "Polo" is the game all that ever comes to mind? Does "Lauren" suggest only "Bacall" and "Chanel" what the English swim?

Kerry Flug, *Vogue*, April 1978

If you find yourself answering "Yes" to these pointed questions, then you are ripe for this chapter. Take advantage of it. The rewards can be of great benefit to you.

How many times have you heard the word "fashion" and wondered about its meaning? How many times have you overheard the word "style" used in conversation and wondered? The truth is, many of us could not comprehensively define these two terms if asked.

To some, fashion is best defined as a fad, a momentary trend, filled with lively paradoxes. While to others fashion is dictated by the international contingent of fashion-name high-fashion designers who delight in altering their innovative designs once every six months. Yet to still others, those who understand and comprehend the meaning and have a sense of style, fashion is best described as the current custom in dress as established by the dominant social leaders of society— fashion's "custodians of perception." In reality it combines all three. Style, on the other hand, "is the elegant way of dressing, living and so forth; that distinguishes persons with money and taste" (dictionary definition). Style, I feel, is one of the most attractive qualities people can have, and at the same time it is one of the most elusive.

Oftentimes, the latest fashionable clothing is exciting to wear. They are fun clothes, and after all, it's always fun to have fun! The key here is to add those fashionable items that go along with what you want your image to say to others. Add these pieces to your collection of classic clothing that is so much a part of your on-going wardrobe. They add vitality and punch.

Remember the fads of the past; the so-called fashions of the last decade? Yes, in all probability, you certainly do. (Should we sneak a peek into your closet?) Don't despair and shrink with embarrassment. Everyone is entitled to buy one, two, or even three fashionable fads, as long as these types of ensembles don't dominate your "carefully planned" wardrobe and inasmuch as you fully understand the difference between a fad and fashion. You want to purchase what looks best on you, and not your neighbor or best friend and what fits in with your life-style. If you are an executive and your accounts include some of the more conservative establishments in town, then, obviously, the faddish, high-fashion items of the moment are not what is best for you at this time. Eventually they may assimilate their way into the more conservative realms of business attire. This often happens when a fashionable item has the capacity to become classic.

The abuse of fashion is worldwide. A woman I know used to spend thousands upon thousands of dollars on what she thought was fashion. Yes, the ensembles were the supposedly "latest" and the designer labels were supposedly the "chicest," but something was missing. As the woman graduated from one position in her accounting firm to another, she noticed that she was feeling uncomfortable and uneasy about her wardrobe. She said, "Whenever I go to a luncheon meeting or a client presentation, I keep expecting someone to tell me how fabulous I look or how much they like my fashion-debuting suit and my shoes of the latest design. But, no one ever does, and I am beginning to think I don't know how to put my clothes together."

How right she was! We all know the feeling of going too far when the environment is not safe or wise for experimentation. When clients looked at her, chances were they were beside themselves with bewilderment. So what's the answer for this woman? Simple. Although she might have been wearing a thousand-dollar suit, the color and attitude were totally wrong, the proportions too dramatic, the accessories piercing, and the outfit would have gone over better in the evening, not during daylight hours. Of course no one around her had the guts to comment on the ludicrousness of the outfit because it obviously was her statement—one that was overdone and tasteless, and it is sometimes difficult to tell someone the truth about her / his clothing when she / he has so much invested in it. Be attuned to others' reactions to your physical presence. Their obvious discomfort is a signal to you to tone it down next time.

To be able to spend lots of hard-earned dollars on clothes is not the issue or the criterion for looking fashionable and stylish. If you have a great deal of money, great. If not, then you want to be very select and buy fewer items, with greater insight and foresight in selecting your wardrobe so that it will evolve into exactly what you want. Its workability and adaptability gives you greater range of expression of yourself. You can always count upon it to come through when you need to look fantastic. And why else buy an item of clothing unless it thrills and supports you in making things happen.

Fashion and style can walk hand in hand. The man or woman who knows himself inside and out is the one who ultimately gets noticed in the crowd. Fashion can be bought; a sense of style must be developed and nurtured. Just because clothes hang on racks in department stores or boutiques is not to be misunderstood as the best in fashion. No, my friends, style is a weeding-out process in which you clearly and precisely choose the fashion statements that will support your individual style. Fashion becomes style when the personal dimension is absolutely the main criterion at hand.

For instance, let's take Betty. She's thirty-five years old and owns an art gallery in a chic part of town. She's five feet three, weighs 115 pounds, and thinks she wears a size eight. She's attractive and earns a hefty income and has an active social life. When Betty dresses for work she tends to lean toward the *au courant* styles ranging from the architecturally inspired silhouettes, which are far too overpowering for her short stature, to the little girl, "Orphan Annie" styles, which make her look like Laura on the television show "Little House on the Prairie." Even though Betty spent about ten thousand dollars annually on her wardrobe, and is proud as a peacock that if you were to open her closet you would catch a glimpse of the best and the most well-known designers in all of France and Italy, there's something noticeably lacking. *Style.* I repeat, *style.* Whatever Betty wears tends to make her look like an actress straight out of a period play, past or future. Since she has allowed herself to be dictated to by these so-called "last-word designers," she has accomplished the miraculous feat of emulating someone else's style. Not hers! Unfortunately, she does not know what style is all about and what sort of stylish fashions are best suited for her and only her. When I asked Betty if she ever took the time to look in the mirror and see what she really looked like, her reply was, "Sometimes I do, but if I am in a hurry, I don't bother." Perhaps Betty's career and life would drastically improve if she only took a few minutes to check out how ridiculous she looks in her broad-shouldered leather ensembles or her full-pleated silk polka-dot dresses, which look absurd on her.

Thus, fashion and style are not yet working for Betty. Sure, she has examples of fashion in her closet, but she sure doesn't have style hanging there too. Instead, fashionable style is about men and women who have their own mannerisms, their own savvy, their own definition of what's best for them. It's all about knowing what's right for you and only you. It's all about people and real clothes. More than anything else, fashionable style is about taste and elegance.

> Style is impossible without a thorough understanding of yourself— who you are and who you wish to become. Cary Grant, who's a cynosure of style, was recently asked whether he had always been "Cary Grant"— if his real self had always coincided so neatly with his movie and off-screen persona. His interesting reply serves as a key to the notion of style in relation to an individual. To paraphrase: "At a certain point in my early life, I decided what sort of person I wanted to be, and over the years I've become that person. Now I no longer remember what part of me is original, and what part of me is the person I've invented. The two have merged." That's a fascinating and probably truthful piece of self-analysis.
>
> Peter Carlsen, "The Pursuit of Style," *Gentlemen's Quarterly*, May 1982. (Courtesy *Gentlemen's Quarterly*. Copyright © 1982 by The Condé Nast Publications Inc.)

An individual look, a feel, a flair for doing what's right at the right moment, is to incorporate style into fashion for your everyday life. *Style comes about as your personality comes into its full fruition*, while fashion knows no endings and no beginnings since it is mobile and continues to move on and on. Fashion means change: Style is best interpreted as everlasting presence.

For Hubert de Givenchy, one of the world's most prestigious designers, the importance of style is never downplayed. He said, "I consider it very important for someone to have a feeling of his own personal style. When I dress some of the most beautiful women in the world, I make sure that she knows what she wants, not what I want. Fashions may change, but one has to be able to adapt them to one's own personal fashion."

He added, "One thing that I find very disappointing is that many people follow the momentary fashions and submerge their personal style. It is important for young and old people to keep a hold of their personal style. For me, to be stylish means to have a feeling for what's currently fashionable and still to simultaneously remain true to oneself."

"A woman must have her own style," says the famous Parisian Hubert de Givenchy. In another interview, this one with Marylou Luther, the Fashion Editor of the Los Angeles *Times*, he stated that women should be very careful that they are not swept away by momentary fads.

"The most difficult thing," De Givenchy said, "is to be with the moment—to be with the time. Another thing is to avoid the temptation to be vulgar—never to touch the eccentric just to get attention. As my great friend, Cristobal Balenciaga, told me before he died, 'You must be honest to your work and to your customer. The best compliment is when someone wears your dress for years and years.'"

Among others who have great style and epitomize the meaning of the word *style* is fashion doyenne Diana Vreeland, who at one time in her fancy-free life was fashion editor of *Vogue* magazine. Undoubtedly, Mrs. Vreeland's notable style is due primarily to her perfected public image as the empress of fashion—a woman whose style is as personalized as her wardrobe. Never does Mrs. Vreeland venture out in public without her fingernails painted in ruby-red nail polish and her cheeks covered with ruby-red rouge.

And still others with style might include Parisian society maven, Jacqueline de Ribes, a majestic-looking woman whose style includes a closet filled to the brim with Yves Saint Laurent suits and Dior ball gowns, yet still she manages to wear those famous-name labels with distinctive style all of her own and with personalized touches of class. For this woman, there are no trendy jewels, no faddish makeup, no impulsive buys evident anywhere in her wardrobe. Rather, a mixture of elegance and an attitude of style.

Designer Yves Saint Laurent, often acknowledged as one of the greatest fashion designers in the twentieth century, a living legend in his own time, defines style as clothes that are classic. He said, "For men, the word classic does not say ancient or dated. On the contrary. It is the summit of art. In art, classic stands for purity, simplicity, and modernism. It is the same in fashion. A suit, no matter if it be for men or women, does not suddenly go out of style if it is a well-proportioned silhouette and the line of the garment is simple, not adorned. Style is something that is intrinsic to most people, since it is in his spirit, his movements, his way of living."

And certainly if God is in the details, His residence is surely in Galanos!

Take a look, a hard, close look, at most of the famous models currently active in the fashion business. There's Iman, a glorious-looking creature who works the fashion collections all over the world. Her fee is usually a thousand dollars a show, and since she does about ten shows a day her pay is around ten thousand dollars a day. A black woman, Iman was born in Africa and stands at about six feet tall. Not only is she magnificent to look at, but she is perhaps one of the most stylish people I have ever met. When she moves, she's elegant. When she talks, she's intelligent. And when she dresses, she radiates style at its best. When once asked if there were any particular type of clothes she preferred to wear, Iman answered, "I try not to wear too many designer clothes, because they are simply status symbols and not always representative of my personality. I like to improvise and create a look all my own. I try to be stylish but not trendy."

Ted Dawson. This distinguished gentleman you've likely seen in hundreds of ads over the years is always impeccably dressed. What this famous model brings to the clothes he advertises is a special feeling of "rightness"—something men want to attain. You will always see him bringing class, savvy, and a certain panache. He's a manufacturer's delight, bringing "attitude" to whatever he wears.

Next, there's the model named Karen Graham, whose face graces the advertisements for Estée Lauder's cosmetics. Her style is strictly a no-frills one, since she confesses that she wears only the most classic and understated clothes she can find. She said, "I am happiest in fashions that don't try to overpower my personality."

Let's take a quick glance at movie stars and television personalities. What does the late David Niven's name bring to mind? Always impeccably dressed! Bon vivant of style! Surely a gentleman at all times. What about Katharine Hepburn, the grande dame of film and theater? She has succeeded so well in establishing her own style—those turtle-neck sweaters, pleated trousers, and checkered necktie scarves. Her presence is overwhelming, so much so that designers Perry Ellis and Willi Smith have occasionally dedicated entire fashion collections to clothes worn by Katharine Hepburn.

> Men like Mailer and Buckley and a few hundred others I can think of belong because they have a personal style that's constructed of years, talent, intelligence and intuition. Such men know when to say "no." And they work at their crafts. I know very few idlers who truly possess style.

They may own some good clothes. But that doesn't mean they have style. They merely have fashionable closets.

James Brady, "The Expression of Style," *Gentlemen's Quarterly*, January 1983

The primary pillar of style is quality. Quality implies a degree of perfection. It separates the magnificent from the mediocre. Before you can even attempt to distinguish fashionable style from fashionable gimmicks, you must realize that quality is the key to good taste. Value, superb fabric, expert tailoring, and classic silhouettes are the outline to style. Without quality in style, your quest for achieving the most out of life is thwarted. Without quality, it is almost impossible to dress with style. Americans today are having a love affair with quality. Style and quality go hand in hand. You'll soon understand that one without the other is like marriage without love.

Now you know what style is and who is stylish; let's talk about how you develop style. We each have our own personal style. It is up to each of us to discover his / her own. Here are some insights, clues, and personal notes as to how you can unlock your personal style:

Style is your imprint on the world.

A person with style (you) never makes any comparison at all between himself / herself and others.

The projection of style can be effected by three principal means: our speech, our mannerisms, and our appearance.

Wit is the voice of style. *It is knowing the rules well enough to know when you can break them.*

A basic rule of style: Something that cannot be wholly cancelled should be deliberately displayed. (Jimmy Durante's nose; Martha Raye's mouth.)

Style is impeccable, natural, sophisticated, vivid, easy—it is the little things that count.

"Style is the dress of thoughts"—Lord Chesterfield.

It is the spirit and faculty of the artistic you.

Strain your potential until it cries for mercy. Practice, improve, and polish your technical style skills. Great style can create great wealth.

Say, "I will place my uniqueness on display."

Style exceeds knowing what to wear; it is beyond this. It is the audacity to be unique.

Once you know that style exists you know its power.

Style is highly personal and the mark of people who are supremely confident of their own taste.

Style is your mood of expressing yourself.

You can convert your style into riches and enjoy them, or you can enjoy your style just the way it is.

A modest sufficiency cramps your style; extreme passion enriches it. It drives you to heighten your experience of yourself.

Style is unlike mathematics where there is only one right answer.

Do people stare at you in a way that they are looking into a world of dreams? If they do, then you have style.

People with style go beyond their fear of not getting agreement. They consider themselves important.

Style is the way in which men and women can, by confidently expressing their individuality, add to their stature.

The key is to find, in a designer's collection of sixty to eighty items, one to three that have the capacity to become classic.

"True style," says the noted designer Bill Blass, "is a kind of natural elegance of the senses."

Here is a list of people, places, things, and even some companies that I feel epitomize style. Notice what pictures they conjure up in your mind. (Not for you to imitate but to be daring enough to aspire to that level of uniqueness.)

Tallulah Bankhead	Tiffany & Co.
Cannes	Estée Lauder
Loretta Young	IBM
Sutton Place	Diana Ross
Eleanor Roosevelt	Bulgari
Rodeo Drive	Bloomingdale's
Diana Vreeland	Gump's Specialty Store
Bianca Jagger	Baccarat Crystal
Golden Gate Bridge	French Quarter, New Orleans
Ella Fitzgerald	Polo
London Bridge	Backgammon
Charlie Chaplin	Judy Garland
Tennis	Salvador Dali
Steuben	San Francisco
The Concorde	The Mansion, Dallas
Warren Beatty	Rod Stewart
The Savoy	Harry S. Truman
Frank Sinatra	*Architectural Digest*
The New York *Times*	Walter Cronkite
Hugh Downs	Texas
Napa Valley	The Plaza
O. J. Simpson	Rita Moreno
Gandhi	Carol Burnett
Jane Fonda	Yehudi Menuhin
Picasso	Pope John Paul II
Hewlett-Packard	Wilkes Bashford

Fabergé	"W" magazine
Montreal	Kyoto
Beekman Place	Orchids
The New York City Ballet	Cleopatra
Frank Lloyd Wright	Lacrosse
"M*A*S*H"	Bijan

Since the beginning of time, never has there been another like you. None that came before, none that live today, and none that come tomorrow can walk, talk, move, and think exactly like you. All men and women are different. *You are a unique creature.* None can duplicate your brush stroke, none can make your statement, none has the ability to present himself / herself with your special presence. You can capitalize on your richness of expression and promote it to the fullest. *You are nature's greatest miracle.* In truth, no one can present your individual style, nor can you truly present someone else's. Instead, you must place your uniqueness on display in the marketplace. You must proclaim it. You are rare, and there is value in all rarity; therefore, *you* are valuable. *You are nature's greatest miracle.*

I would like to end with a quote from Yves Saint Laurent about the uniqueness of people and how in the end it is you who makes fashion and style come alive:

> Fashion is an incomplete art because, however inspired and creative the work of the designer, a garment can never stand on its own as a painting or sculpture can. These works of art are an entity unto themselves, but clothes are nothing without the human body to give them form. Fashion is a mixture of design, technique, line, material, and color. Each one of these elements is essential to the artistry, but none of it can come to life until worn and seen in human movement.

Knowing the nuances of fine dressing, like appreciating fine art, confers a certain cachet among the well-dressed.

16

Having It All

HAVING MORE MONEY: IT INCREASES YOUR CHOICES!

Let's talk about money. The game is still heavily stacked toward those who have it or those whose inclination is to have it. Having more money increases your choices: where you live, how you vacation, the automobile you drive, the school you or your children attend, the restaurants you frequent, the stores you patronize, the charities you support—a life-style of plenty.

You have to give yourself permission to have more money by letting go of your old fears, beliefs, and conditioning about money. Start developing a money mind-set, frame of reference, context. Money wants you as much as you want it—it has no intention of leaving the planet! And one thing is sure about money, it represents "delivered production" on quality services and quality products from quality people. It is a basic law that when you have something special that another person wants—a product, skill, service, or expertise—that person will be most willing to pay a price for it. Money wants you as much as you want it—it is the life-blood of our economy and commercial structure. A frame of reference in which you see yourself as wealthy is a definite context to assure your financial success. *You must make a stand and decide not to live with meager finances.*

Money is impersonal and equally available to all. You must use the money you have, combined with your joy at having money to "circulate," and encourage its increase in your life and the lives of others. When thinking about how much money you would like to have at your disposal, ask yourself this question: "Am I willing to be independently wealthy?" If your response is a positive "Yes," then ask yourself this next question: "How much money do I need to have to give me the feeling of independent wealth?" Be sure that when you choose how much money you want in your life you include a "surplus amount" that is tagged on to what you need to purchase those things you desire. This way you will always have more than you need and you will never feel pressured with money-survival. So many people want just enough and find that "just enough" still causes money crazies! So make room for more than you actually need. Remember the cave people and how their entire existence was one of searching for more food. Each day they got up from a night's sleep and were again in the pursuit for more food and nourishment. Had they had a reserve, they could have filled much of their time with other enjoyable pursuits. If you have money confusion, then begin to clear away your uncertainties one by one. (Money is earned, spent, invested, saved, and contributed.)

A wonderful truth about money is that it is always somewhere and in some places—learn to be where it is. It makes a lot more sense than looking for it where it isn't! Surround yourself with environments of "lavish abundance": attend concerts and grand opera, tour majestic cathedrals and new architectural wonders on the main streets in our big cities, visit beautiful and lush gardens, frequent exquisite restaurants, stroll through acclaimed art galleries and museums, visit beautiful jewelry stores and wonderful department stores—and your flame of richness will reignite itself deep within you, so your desire will be intensified. Desire is God, the Universe, Knowing—calling to you to claim many of the goodies for yourself.

When you get into a state of lack or want, it is so real to you that you cannot think of anything else. Your static and undisciplined thought prolongs the lack. Begin to think and act rich, and you will be rich. *Make your ways prosperous* no matter how small of a breakthrough it is in the beginning. Really enjoy spending and "circulating" the monies you have; look forward to each of those times you must pay for something. Get very comfortable with letting your money give you pleasure. Remember how easy it was for you as a child to use your money for things you liked! The more willing you are to increase others' wealth, the more willing they are to increase yours. Give your money the opportunity to exercise itself and develop money muscles. That is called smart investment—spending money on what will produce fun and happiness for yourself and others. I remember reading that accumulating money "by the inch it's a cinch, by the yard it's hard," in *Open Your Mind to Prosperity*, by Catherine Ponder. So wherever you stand on your ladder to financial success, take it step by step until your courage expands and you are ready to take massive steps that will assure your getting the money you demand for your life-style. A pure money motivation alone is not enough. You must couple it with a purpose—a cause and personal gain to keep your motivation and passion churning.

Getting rich is like learning to eat with chopsticks; at first your main concern is getting the food into your mouth by using whatever skills you have at hand—eventually you become more dexterous and adept. Be willing to start over and over again.

Next time you want to show someone your love and appreciation, instead of sending them one bouquet of flowers, send him or her a bouquet for each room in the house with a note attached saying, "I am with you wherever you go in this house." Imagine the impact you will make on those you love. Imagine the impact you will make on your sense of abundance!

Notice: It isn't the other way around—that until you are successful, you cannot act prosperously. It starts in small ways. Wealth is a thought and action before it becomes things. It takes courage to start the ball rolling. Dressing well and circulating the money you have are vehicles for increasing your wealth.

I believe that being wealthy is your inheritance, everyone's right and privilege, something every one of us can achieve. These guideposts will point out to you the road to greater wealth, and there is certainly much to say for that ambition. Many of the richest people in the world today did not have it dumped in their laps. Not all of them were born to wealth. Today's successful people have had to "claim" their inheritance. *The amount of money that you could be making but aren't is your biggest expense.*

You must magnetize your brain cells to respond with moneymaking actions and ideas. You must begin to think and look like the richest person you can imagine. (Follow all the earlier tips in the book about looking good.) Get the right stuff, the right attitudes, that support those great pieces of clothing in your wardrobe. You can carry off any piece of clothing if you dare to wear it with the attitude of richness. Give yourself permission to claim what is awaiting you in the world of richness, affluence, and abundance. Remember—more can be better.

Have a brilliantly clear picture in your mind about how you want life to be for you. Do what you say you're going to do.

> "Most real wealth originates in individual minds in unpredictable and uncontrollable ways. A successful economy depends on the proliferation of the rich, on creating a large class of risk-taking men [women] who are willing to shun the easy channels of a comfortable life in order to create new enterprise, win huge profits, and invest them again. It will be said that their earnings are 'unearned' and 'undeserved.' But, in fact, most successful entrepreneurs contribute far more to society than they ever recover, and most of them win no riches at all. They are the heros of economic life, and those who begrudge them their reward demonstrate a failure to understand their role and their promise."
>
> *Wealth and Poverty*, by George Gilder

Over the years, I have spoken to thousands of people in my Presentation Salon / Seminars and in lecture halls, and I know I have aligned them with their intention to have it all. And these are the guideposts that have shown them the way and helped to clear up their uncertainty regarding where to begin and how to excel:

1. The key is that money and substance—the cars, the homes, the art works, the jewelry—are all *passive* things. They never move to you, you must be *active* and bring them into your life. In your mind, you must begin to think, feel, and know that you are going to have enough money in your life to live in the fast lane. Ideas that spring into your mind—those mental images—always happen before you initiate physical action. So, the very first thing you must build is a wealthy consciousness. Many people demonstrate this consciousness by tithing and / or donating to people, organizations, and institutions that support their aliveness. Even the IRS takes care of you with these tax-deductible contributions.

2. Never compromise when it comes to presenting yourself. Your kingdom is not so great that you don't have time enough to groom yourself completely. You must fine hone everything about you that is physical, and in turn, your mind will be fine honed and together with your body you will be fine honed for greater wealth. And you will produce products and services that represent the finest output you are capable of. You will radiate excellence! Get focused and stay uncluttered.

3. Get the best for yourself. I applaud what Stanley Marcus said: "There is something about having the best that equates with getting more out of life." Treat yourself to the finest. Ask the price for your services and products—whatever the traffic will bear; don't sell yourself short. Be certain you are filling a need and want.

4. Dressing is one facet, and a very important one, of what I call living well. If you do not support the fine restaurants, ballet companies, the great clothing stores, the fantastic artists, they will all die out for both you and the entire human race. Keep them alive in your life, and you will always have the finest for yourself. Take a millionaire to lunch monthly.

5. Your clothing can support a *concrete plan for success,* a new approach, an investment. Always broadcast your success through your physical presence. Enjoy the sense of being in control as to how it will turn out, and make it O.K. to turn out better than you can imagine. Do what you tell yourself you're going to do.

6. The way your clothes treat people—people will react! The name of the game is to treat yourself big and make it all right for others to win big. It must be a win/win situation, where everyone gets to look great and wear what he or she has always wanted to be seen in.

7. When you are out playing in the world of well-dressed and well-groomed people, you should ask yourself this question: "Do you want to play in the Sandbox League, the Playground League, the Small-Town League, or the Major League?" You have to realize that you have the choice to choose the scope of how you want to appear to others. Drop your fears of being "too much." Extravagant living is not what you may have believed—it's optimum expression.

8. Beauty attracts beauty. Wear one beautiful piece of jewelry and one great piece of clothing, and the law of attraction takes over. You must be willing to accept the fame and the fortune that accompany high appeal. Be accountable and responsible for each dollar you spend, and you will be given greater insight and drive to accumulate more.

9. To break the bondage of lack, in the area of clothing, begin to think and act rich each day. Instead of keeping your great outfits for a special day, use them for most occasions. Instead of looking for the price of an article, look for what you want. Knowing you can have what you desire makes one feel important and powerful. There is a time to "let go" of your intense pursuit for money—so that you have it and it doesn't have you.

10. Remember, when you shop, that your power to tune into quality clothing is in direct ratio to your power to tune out inferior merchandise. Eliminate those things that you definitely know don't and won't work for you. And what is left will be those clothing pieces that give you the look you definitely know will work for you. Most people don't succeed because they don't look as though they want to succeed.

11. You can look more successful, better educated, more worldly and sophisticated—and feel all of those good things. Remember, all reality comes from agreement. Associate with people who choose to

make life an experience of richness and plenty and whose way of life is to search for and find the best in everything.

12. Try to have a statistical edge over your yesterdays. Every day do one additional thing that puts you into the world more brilliantly, more attractively, and more triumphantly than you ever were before. You will win more quickly—if you dress richly.

13. Get one piece of beautiful clothing or jewelry because beauty multiplies. Pay twice as much and get half as many articles of clothing. Develop your instinct for quality, and I believe we all have a gut knowledge of what true quality is.

14. Remember that a fabulously rich mind produces fabulously rich environments, clothes, objects of pleasure and joy. Associate with people and visit places for the beautiful contribution they are making to others. Initiate a strong desire—then decree—then control—then attract those things you want to enjoy in your life. Make it O.K. to have plenty of what you want. Acknowledge those who have arrived.

15. Remember you don't serve until you serve the rich in yourself. Speak to the rich in others, see the fantastic in yourself and in others. This gives less time to the cheap, the tacky, and the tasteless in yourself and in others. People who surround themselves with beauty and abundance tend to stay young and grow wealthier. The quality of your clothes should be equal to the quality of your life.

16. Enlarge your consciousness. If your consciousness is small, you will experience smallness in every department of your life. St. Paul said, "Be not confined to this world, the world of the human mind, the world of small thought, but be ye transformed by the renewing of your mind." Think in terms of abundance and you will experience abundance in every department of your life. Pray, affirm, and decree your wealth to yourself.

17. Don't be discouraged if you do not get everything you want immediately. It often takes a willingness to keep going, keep working and pursuing those things you truly want before the results are clearly evident. Look at the farmer who must prune his trees year after year, but eventually he is rewarded by larger and more plentiful crops of fruit.

18. As I said earlier, money is a form of energy that constitutes the lifeblood of our economy and commercial structure. Money is impersonal and equally available to all. To get it, you must have determination, persistence, a strong desire to accelerate your money-producing activities, and the constant refocusing so that it comes to you. You need not be so fixed that you are unable to change your direction if need be. Your willingness to "circulate" money with a sense of abundance creates more affluence.

19. Go into your closets today and give thanks for what you already have. Much of it you will be throwing away or giving away to make room for what will be characteristic of your new life. But be careful, what you give away—what we put out in life we frequently get back! And so if your old things would make somebody look poor or like a beggar, then don't give them away. Simply throw them away. The giving and spending of money is a natural expression of the self. Glow with gratitude.

20. Show your prosperity awareness by removing all your old beliefs, fears, considerations, and false information about the idea of richness. In their place, develop a deep and continuous desire for affluence. Become aware of more of everything in you, in your thoughts and in your actions. Of course, use all those beautiful things you already have—clothes, china, silverware, crystal, fine jewelry.

21. Your every act, tone, and look should express a quiet, rich assurance of success. At times, however, you have not wanted to be so quiet about your success. There is a time for openness about your success and wealth, and a time for quietness; don't be stuck with either. Look at the difference among Boston wealth, Los Angeles wealth, San Francisco wealth, Philadelphia wealth, Chicago wealth, Palm Springs wealth, Texas wealth, New York wealth, Miami wealth—each place has its own way of expressing its wealth, and none is wrong. Why not incorporate all of the wealthy manners and styles?

22. This one is important: If you don't listen to your heart, you will be less happy than if you do. Your heart may tell you to spend money on something that inspires you, or give it to a worthy cause, and you may ignore that urging and, instead, have to spend the same amount of money in uninteresting ways—broken windows, stolen lawn chairs, missing hub caps, etc. Money, you must understand, likes to keep flowing and moving on. If you don't spend it on something you really want, then that same money will find its own way of spreading itself around. My feeling is that none of us would have come to this playground we call earth if we thought that the other kids were going to beat us up. So we are required to learn the money game and the laws of affluence and rich living as soon as we realize the joyful results that can be ours—mentally, physically, and spiritually.

23. You must have a consciousness large enough to appropriate the supply that is already established by the universe for you! You don't have to go out and develop your inheritance. You have to claim it and take it and use what has been earmarked for you as it presents itself every day to you in many forms and situations. Are you receiving and accepting your good at your greatest level of intake? Or do you refuse so many opportunities because you are uncomfortable about accepting

and taking what is meant for you? Also, the question of giving your all and "your best" has to be looked at. At times what seems as though you are giving "your best" doesn't always get you the results you want. It may be that you have to develop further toward the more potent and comprehensive you. If "your best" falls short of what is required—then go beyond your present best and do what is required to bring about what you want to achieve. At the moment we do our best our next best action is ready to emerge. Our best has a way of enlarging itself as we do!

24. Money in action is God, the Universe, Knowing in action. Money is not the same as Mammon. Mammon represents hoarded money, that which is removed from circulation. Money that is in "circulation," however, is God in action. Hoarded money is useless, for money is only a medium of exchange. As the Bible says in Ecclesiastes: "A feast is made for laughter, and wine maketh merry, but money answers all things."

25. And, finally, keep this thought always present in your mind: "Man was born to be rich, or inevitably to grow rich through the use of his facilities." Those words were written by Ralph Waldo Emerson. And, of course, when he said "man" he wasn't referring to only the masculine sex, he was referring to mankind, and definitely meant females as well as males. To become wealthy you have to give up your poverty ways. One thing about the rich and very rich—down deep they love the choices and opportunities money provides and they do what they can to attract it to them more quickly.

In essence, then, the way to wealth is to project a money magnetism through the way you think and act: your appearance and air must invite wealthy situations to you; your frame of reference and context for life must include financial, physical, and spiritual soundness; the quality of your output of services, skills, and products must represent excellence and buyability; and you must relish the joy, fun, and cheerfulness that accompanies a truly wealthy person who is greater than the sum of his / her money and who is living all out. If you do these things, and do them well, you will continue to influence people—especially those with wealth. And never forget that all things multiply when you pass them on to others. We always win big when others get to share in our joys and our good fortunes. Continue to develop a keen sense of what it means and feels like to be living in the fast lane, and continue to operate with a high level of dynamic passion coupled with definite action and achievement. Go from ordinary dressing to extraordinary dressing, and your life will go from the ordinary to the extraordinary.

Make your money destiny a reality.

17

It Works!

It works! It really does!

I don't mean to sound overbubbly and overenthusiastic, but that's my normal posture. I do tend to get enthusiastic when I see good things happening to the people I work with, and since it happens regularly, I often am bursting with happiness and enthusiasm.

Dress well and good things will start to come your way. Automatically, inevitably, like falling dominoes. Perhaps you won't make it all the way to the fastest of the fast lanes in one jump, but you will be well on your way. I want you to listen to the experiences of some of the people I have personally worked with. These are people who have either attended my Presentation Salon / Seminars or lectures or else had me help them with their shopping and dressing, or both. And they have all experienced, as you will read, almost miraculous changes in their lives, relationships, and careers, changes that have been *the direct result of dressing qualitatively*.

It is so simple, so logical. Dressing better produces looking better. Looking better, in turn, makes you feel better about yourself. And when you feel better about yourself, you project more self-assurance. And the self-assured are the ones who triumph in this world; they attract success like a magnet attracts steel shavings.

"I had to write to you," starts a young man in his letter from Phoenix, Arizona, "and share a tremendous win for me. This past weekend I flew to Los Angeles to attend my ex-flame's wedding, so naturally I wanted to be in top form. In the preceding weeks, I got a wonderful tan, a classic hairstyle, and purchased the most fabulous two-piece suit of my life. The jacket is European cut, non-vented design, with straight slashed pockets and medium-width notched lapels. So elegant! With it, I wore an outrageous white, satin-striped, cotton shirt by Daniel Schagen, a gorgeous deep burgundy silk tie with a small repetitive square print, a gold collar bar, black belt and shoes, and, Robert, at the wedding I looked smashing—even better than that!

"People I knew didn't recognize me, and when they did they were blown away. What a hit I was! I received great compliments all day long. Friends said that I looked like a man of the world, like after the wedding I would be photographed for *Gentlemen's Quarterly*. Can you imagine how I felt? Donna's family was extremely impressed, they still remembered me with long hair and overalls. I looked *so* rich. I *was* rich. I have never felt so comfortable and appropriate with myself and everyone else. I was clearly the best-dressed person there. My mother would have been so proud. At the reception people wanted to know what I did for a living, what I thought about things, one discussed his investments with me. I'm still overwhelmed. Donna was very proud of me, also."

Reading between those lines, you can tell what happened to this young man. Obviously, he used to be pretty colorless, someone you would have deliberately passed by. Now he's a new man. And you can see what a difference outer appearances can mean to anyone—he changed his hairstyle and bought himself one terrific outfit. And this young man now has supreme confidence in himself because he has seen what a difference appearance makes. They even discussed investments with him! He's halfway to the fast lane already.

And now let's hear from a woman I helped.

"Last night, I went to a dinner party in an outrageous dress and an outrageous mood to match. Harold told me how beautiful I was and how my sparkle was making such a contribution to the room. I never went to a party where people stopped to tell me how beautiful I was, and the most amazing part was that I *knew it!!*

"Robert, I want you to know what an enormous contribution you made to the breakthrough that night, and to my life. I sat in your seminar last December and a part of me said, 'June, you're every bit as outrageous as he is, and as he says you are; why don't you stop lying about it?'"

She wore a new outfit—a provocative new outfit—and that immediately affected her mood, which became playful, to match what she was wearing. And the people who met her sensed the change. They told her how beautiful she was, but their words were unnecessary. She already knew it! And believing it made her project it. It was great to get the corroboration of the others, but she already knew it. You can understand what that would do to any woman's ego and self-esteem. And it was all because of her new clothes.

Here's another letter from another lady:

"As I think about the changes in my life, I am amazed. I have had two raises and am now financially secure enough to give some of it away.

"There are wonderful changes in my sex life with my husband, and two men have asked me to join them on their business trips, and I have been followed home twice by two others who saw me stopped at a red light. It was a little disconcerting, but pleasing nonetheless.

"I'm not always sure how to handle my personal power, but it is a lot more fun to be playing from strength than it was from insecurity.

"And last Sunday, I played in a softball game. We won by the slaughter rule, 15 to 3, in the fifth inning. A little power goes far in the world."

I really can't take credit for that softball score. I do feel that the rest of her story is due to the soundness of my principles. If you dress up to your potential, then that personal power she refers to can be yours!

A businessman I consulted with writes:

"Since I have been 'Pantéd,' I stand taller, feel and act with greater confidence, and have never felt better in my life. It's as though my inside and outside are now matching—hooray! An interesting and unexpected benefit is that my productivity level has zoomed—as though I'm saying, 'Hello, world—watch out,' and the world is saying to me, 'It's about time.'"

He brings up an interesting point—his productivity level "zoomed." When you think about it, that is inevitable, because when you are happy with yourself, you will naturally work better. People don't work up to their ability when they are low, depressed, worried. But when you feel good about yourself, those negative feelings evaporate, leaving only the positive—and positive is productive. So anything that makes you feel good about yourself leads to increased productivity, which, in turn, makes you noticed by your employer and brings you one step closer to your mark. Dress better and you'll feel good about yourself. It cannot fail to happen!

I love this short note from a woman, who, evidently, had been on the receiving end of a direct talk from me during the Presentation Salon / Seminar she attended. At those seminars, I sometimes do talk very directly to people, cutting through the platitudes in order to awaken them and make them see themselves as I, and the rest of the world, see them. Only then can they realize the impression they are making on everybody, and then set about to change themselves so they can make a better impression in the future.

"I hated you all day Monday," she wrote to me. "I hated myself all day Tuesday. Today, I bought a luscious cranberry silk shirt—me, the one you called 'the sexless filing cabinet!' I've never owned anything cranberry-colored in my life, let alone *silk!* Thank you so much for empowering me. You are magnificent. I love you."

I love it when she writes that I "empowered" her. That's such a good word, and exactly what I want to do for you, my reader, and the entire world. We can all be full of power—power fueled by a cranberry-colored silk shirt!—if we learn the simple truth, which is that power comes from within, and it is a product of our feeling pride in ourselves. Our appearance is a fundamental part of ourselves, and the better we look, the prouder we are of ourselves. And so, the better we look, the more power we have.

The benefits of looking good are clearly expressed in this letter from a man who attended one of my Presentation Salon / Seminars:

"I did your presentation salon in May," he writes. "And I want to acknowledge you for the many miracles that your workshop has sourced for me these last weeks.

"My life has been an incredible professional and financial expansion. Prior to the salon, my pattern for spending money on clothes was to spend at most $200–$300 every other year. Since the salon, I hired a service and have spent about $3,500 on a simple yet impressive wardrobe. I am very clear that this is only the beginning. I invested another $2,500 beautifying my apartment, and just recently purchased the building. I also purchased the first car I've owned in many years—a beautiful prestigious Audi 5000. But perhaps the most important miracle has been professional. Before the salon, my earnings were $200–$300 a week; I now make $500–$600 a week.

"Clearly, your salon gave me an experience that I had sold out for less than I could be, and rekindled a natural desire and ability to have the best in life."

Right at the very beginning of this book, I told you that if you stuck with me, and followed my instructions, I would show you the way to get more money, romance, and power. You can see that these people who have written these letters did follow my instructions and, as a result, they are getting all of that. Listen to this next letter, from another satisfied client, whose experiences demonstrate what happens when you decide not to settle for being less than you can be.

"Well, you conceited braggart, it didn't work. The Salon had only the slightest effect on me.

"The only changes were:

"I bought Sherman's instead of Merits, Au Natural instead of Diet Pepsi.

"A handsome co-worker gave me three white roses.

"A rich Lebanese man stopped me on the street, took me out for a coffee break, and asked me out.

"I bought two fabrics—one bright red, the other a lemon-yellow.

"I bought three pairs of Charles Jourdan shoes.

"I hardly ate at all and what I did eat was an absolute delight.

"I got gloriously laid."

And then there was this thrilling postscript to her letter:

"P.S. I'm not boring anymore."

Here is a note from a Chicago photographer who attended one of my Presentation Salon / Seminars in that city:

"When I took your salon, I never imagined the world that awaited me. Stories I could tell *for days!* I just want to thank you for giving me the chance to double my photography business, work with Chicago's top models, have everything I could want, including a gold chain I found the Monday morning following the salon. Most of all, I want you to know that the inspiration you gave me has been turned loose in Chicago with so much zest that there is no end in sight.

"My mode of dress has improved and with it my business, my friends' dress habits, my apartment is cleaner, my relationships are more intensive and more in number. The best is that my love life actually has reached a fever pitch."

Now there is one man who got it all—sex, money, and power—from just one Presentation Salon / Seminar! (I don't take credit for the gold chain.)

After I spoke at a Winner's Circle Breakfast Club in Honolulu, Hawaii, I received this incredible letter from one of the young businessmen who had been in the audience that day.

"I want to thank you for all the love and support and courage you have given me to have my life elegant and rich and loved and prosperous and dynamic. Since you have departed this state, there have been so many miracles in my life, and I have you to immediately thank for them.

"I have been coming through one of the hardest financial times of my life since September of last year, although I did maintain a prosperous life-style. Still the worry and pain I have been hanging onto has been excessive. Then I listened to you at the Winner's Circle Breakfast Club . . . and it was the push I needed, and your instincts were accurate.

"One miracle I want to share with you. I had been hanging out with cleaning up my closet since Sunday when I left the Salon. I did nothing on Sunday or Monday or Tuesday." (He then talks about going out to various places with various friends and drinking and partying.) "I had now spent my last dollar, and I said to myself, 'Give us this day our daily bread.' I felt so secure in my heart that all would work out. I fell asleep at one A.M. and awoke with my body tingling, horny, excited, crotch on fire, at three in the morning. No one was there to help me relieve my excitement. I just could not calm down. All of a sudden, I got up and went to my closet and started throwing things away like a madman. All kinds of thoughts and voices started coming up. The main voice was that of my mother telling me how much more wear I could get out of this piece or that piece and how poor we were and how we should conserve what we had. I simply held up each item and asked myself, 'Do I feel elegant or magnificent in this piece?' Needless to say, my closet is almost empty. You should have heard the racket from 3 to 6 A.M. with all the stuff going down the trash chute. I was sure security would come by and arrest me. I then put on my running shoes and ran to Waikiki Beach and stretched out doing your facial exercises and body stretching. It was beautiful among the large, elegant hotels and having the famous beach all to myself.

"The rest of the week was great and money kept appearing as I needed it. All of a sudden, I got a phone call from a realtor, and she said she had been trying to reach me for months. She had a check to return to me for $1,573 that I had left as a deposit a year ago. That was last Friday, five days after your salon. I want to tell you that—it works!"

He calls that experience "a miracle" but really there is nothing miraculous or supernatural about it. It is simply the natural order of things when you—as this man did—get rid of the old to make room for the new in your life. You thus open yourself up to new successes and to new adventures in your life, and when you are open to them, then the "miracles" automatically follow.

One last letter. This is from a young lady in my home town, San Francisco. She wrote this letter to me after attending one of my Presentation Salon / Seminars:

"I finally bought a terrific suit from Kristina's on Union Street. I just walked in, tried it on, and I knew that was it.

"It will take me a couple of months to pay for it, and it is worth it!

I feel like a million bucks in it and people treat me like a million bucks. I've already had miracles out of it. I just have to tell you about one of those miracles:

"I started volunteering at an international office here. The first day that I wore my new suit, the Swedish ambassador was coming over. And they chose me to greet him and escort him on a tour. It was wonderful."

You can just sense that, for that particular lady, that first honor is only the beginning. In her powerful suit, she attracts success. Escorting the Swedish ambassador will be only the first of many successes that will come her way. She had the courage to spend more than she was used to spending on one outfit, and she *began to reap success immediately!* It happens just like that.

It works! And I have files bulging with hundreds more letters that give case after case of great things happening to people when they begin to look as good as they can look.

It works! And there is no reason why it shouldn't work, is there? It isn't metaphysical or supernatural or mysterious in any way. It is all very simple and logical and sensible. It is an orderly progression, a step-by-step affair:

STEP ONE: Buy yourself clothing that makes you look better, makes you look like the *Living Human Treasure* you really are.

STEP TWO: You look better, and you know it. And when you know you look better, you begin to feel better about yourself. Your asking price, salary, and fee all go up.

STEP THREE: If you feel better about yourself, you will begin to radiate confidence.

STEP FOUR: The people you meet will sense that new confidence of yours and, moreover, appreciate your new and more attractive appearance.

STEP FIVE: The "miracles" begin to come your way—more money, more and better sex, more power—but they aren't miraculous at all. They are simply the result of your looking and feeling wonderful. Good things always happen to people who look appealing and who know that they look tops.

If you take the first step—buying yourself clothing that really makes you look more dashing, alluring, and appealing—then Steps Two, Three, Four, and Five happen automatically. You couldn't stop them from happening even if you tried.

This success of my training methods has not gone unnoticed by the press. Here is how one reporter in the Seattle *Times* expressed it:

"Panté's focus is fine-tuning all that is physical about a person to

Business Makeover—Before.

Business Makeover—After.

Casually Smart Makeover—Before.

Casually Smart Makeover—After.

Elegant Evening Makeover—Before.   Elegant Evening Makeover—After.

assist in promoting a dynamic physical image that creates a statistical edge in social and business settings."

Every person is born with the potential for utilizing his power, for enhancing his capacity to allure, and for accumulating and attracting greater reserves of money. Some people manifest these traits naturally. Some never recognize that they possess these gifts in abundance— *money, sex, and power.* When the opportunities to cultivate these three basic life forces appear they don't take full advantage of them. Money, sex, and power don't run you anymore—you are calling the punches and controlling the shots. You have taken charge of these three powerful forces, and they are now working for you. People now see you as living all out. You are now *being* the totally powerful person you are meant to be.

Picture for yourself what it would be like if you were invited and taken to "the mountain of great beauty and high finance" for ten days and ten nights. All of the world's leading body specialists, hair specialists, and grooming experts worked with you and performed their magic on you; all the world's noted financial wizards and advisers educated you in the knowledge needed to amass large financial fortunes. At the end of these ten informative and revealing days you are asked this one searching question: "What is the one opinion you have been holding on to, the one belief you have been living by, the one compulsion that has dominated your actions throughout your adult life, the one way you have consistently persisted on governing your life so that if you left it on 'the mountain of beauty and high finance' and came back down to where you have been living your life, you would immediately begin to experience yourself becoming more attractive and appealing and more successful and financially wealthy?"

I repeat: "What is that *one* opinion, practice, belief, compulsion, or habit that stops *you* from propelling your life forward?"

This is the perfect time and place to start. By removing outdated ideas, beliefs, fears, and considerations you are now free to propel

Stepping Out!

forward. I have chosen your physical presentation as the place to begin because it is the closest and nearest to you. Have you ever tried going to the doctor without your body! What you do with any aspect of your physical presentation will have a catalytic effect on your entire life.

Look your best. You are a *Living Human Treasure*. Grasp and hang on to the golden ring. Get a strong footing in the fast lane and dress and groom yourself as if your life depends upon it—that's the totally satisfying life you have always wanted. It is yours now. This is it. You have the know-how to turn a situation like dressing and grooming into a parlay for all of your life's situations. You will have all of those wonderful things because you are *you*, and you are a *Living Human Treasure*. Nature has created a gem in you, and the artisans of the world are waiting to polish it. So take on a first-class, world-class look. Make the world your oyster, with you the pearl.

Give yourself permission to have it all the way you want it!

Only know in advance and instead
     that ordinary words will not be
     vessels or stores for some kinds
     of knowing.

Lawrence Kushner
Honey from the Rock

ROBERT PANTÉ ENTERPRISES, INC.

If you would like to receive information about Panté Presentation Salon / Seminars, corporate and individual programs and services provided, please write to:

Robert Panté Enterprises
Opera Plaza
106 Van Ness Ave.
Suite 67
San Francisco, CA 94102
Business Phone (415) 776-3466

BLACK AND WHITE PHOTO CREDITS

Suzanne Estel: The photographer.
Barbara Gerard: The clothing stylist.
James Avila: The hair stylist.
Robyn Kaufman: The makeup artist.
The Model Agencies: Grimmé, Sabina, Model Management, Brebner, Top Models, Bianca.
The Stores: Whose generosity and outstanding merchandise truly conveys the message of quality. I would like to thank the following San Francisco stores:
Firuze / Farnoosh—women's business fashions and accessories.
I. Magnin—women's elegant evening, sport, sensual day dressing, and casually smart fashions and accessories.
Rafael's—women's business, sensual day dressing and casual smart fashions and accessories.
Rims & Goggles—fashion eyeglass frames.
Saks Fifth Avenue—women's business, elegant evening, sport, sensual day dressing, and casually smart fashions.
Shaw Shoes—shoes shown with clothing and also "still" photography.
Tiffany & Co.—fine jewelry, earrings, necklaces, watches, bracelets, tuxedo studs, and cuff links.
Walter Newberger for Wilkes Bashford—shoes shown with clothing and also "still" photography.
Wilkes Bashford—men's and women's business, elegant evening, sport, sensual day dressing, and casually smart fashions and accessories.
In addition I would like to thank the following people who contributed their talents and time in the selection and assembling of the clothes: Sonja Caproni, Elizabeth Glass, Ken Nakamura, Cass Shaler, David Rafael, Ricca Kindler, Alexandra Kindler, Ellen Barbier, Firuze, Shaw, Farnoosh.

INDEX